THE QUEEN'S ATLAS

THE QUEEN'S ATLAS

SAXTON'S ELIZABETHAN
MASTERPIECE

David Fletcher

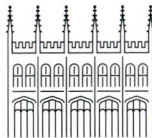

BODLEIAN
LIBRARY
PUBLISHING

With love, to my mother, Pauline Fletcher

First published in 2025 by Bodleian Library Publishing
Broad Street, Oxford OX1 3BG
www.bodleianshop.co.uk

ISBN 978 1 85124 620 5

Text © David Fletcher, 2025
Images © Bodleian Libraries, University of Oxford,
2025, unless specified on p. 221.

This edition © Bodleian Library Publishing, University of Oxford, 2025

David Fletcher has asserted his right to be identified as the author of this Work.

PUBLISHER Samuel Fanous
MANAGING EDITOR Susie Foster
EDITOR Janet Phillips
PICTURE EDITOR Leanda Shrimpton
COVER DESIGN by Dot Little at the Bodleian Library
DESIGNED & TYPESET by Lucy Morton of illuminati in 11 on 16 Dante
PRINTED & BOUND in China by 1010 Printing International Ltd.
on 157 gsm Top Kote matt art paper

FSC
www.fsc.org
MIX
Paper | Supporting
responsible forestry
FSC® C016973

British Library Catalogue in Publishing Data
A CIP record of this publication is available from the British Library

CONTENTS

Llangytho · dayn · Tregaron

Nantguille
Henuenyu · Kilkennyn · Capel bettus lekye
Capel Chryst · Llanachayryn · Treulan
Llanynay · Capel Garthelye · Llanthewy breuye
Llanarche · Killyaron · Talaserne · Llangyhye
Llanllohayrne · Istrad · Llanlleir · Llanuaiercledogye
Llantisiho · Debewid · Bettus bletherus · Pescotter flu:
G   A   N · Sylan · Kellan
Bidder flu: · theforest · Mathern flu: · Cothy flu:
Capel kenon · Llanbeder · Llanacroys
Dettor flu: · Llanunnen · Capel Ilanpymsent
Capel Llantisilued · Turghe flu:
Kery flu: · Llanwenok · Pencarok · Conwelgaio
Capel Llanfra · Tryuy flu: · Llanumberher
Tredraier · Llandyssil
Llanuaier treligon · Llangynllo · Llanlloynye · Llansawel · Cothye flu: · Taltlughay
Llanuaierotlloyne · Llanyhangle yorothe · Dulas flu: · Lansadurn
Kilgwyn · Llandeureog · Abarmarlas
Newcast memlyn · Henllandynye · Banger · Abergorlech · Cothye flu:
orth · Capel pencader · Llany hangle · Deneuer cast
Llangeler · Penbayre · roscorne
Pengwernolye
Capeleuan · Gwilye flu: · Llanllanthog · Llanunyethe · Dulasse · Llandilouawre
Cowen flu: · Llanypimsent · Breghuaygothy · M · Newton
C   A   R · A
bettus · Treleghy bettus · Llanyhangle kiluargen · Llandouyson
Canweleluet · Llangathan · Deneuer cast
Talacouth · Eglosnewith · Drus · one cast
anwenyo · Comgwilye · Istradworell · Llangwood · Goldengroue · Cape
Kilsant · Sct Nicholas · Glanranelthe · Llanhangl ugwely · Llanihangle aber buhigh
Ebbernant · Llanarthney · Cast Carreg
Merther · Capel dewye
Mydrim · Abergwelye · Cast Carreg · E · N · lladebea
Carmarden · Llangunnor · Llantharog · Parkreame
Caradh kery flu: · D · Capel llanlloch · Capel llanthithgayne
Llaginnin Cardyth forest · Llanginog · Llangendayrne · Bettus
Cleare · Llanyhangle abercowen · Capel llangellithon

ACKNOWLEDGEMENTS

IT HAS BEEN A PLEASURE reconstructing the story of Christopher Saxton's life and work. I have had help along the way from many people: I can mention only a selection here; my thanks, though, extend to everyone. Samuel Fanous, head of Bodleian Library Publishing, was invaluable in setting up the project. Janet Phillips, my editor, and Leanda Shrimpton, my picture editor, have given vital guidance and encouragement along the way. I would also like to thank Lucy Morton and Robin Gable for their skilful and elegant production of the book. Nick Millea and his staff at the Bodleian Map Room have been a great source of help and advice in tracking down maps.

I have also had useful correspondence and discussions with many experts. These include Peter Barber, Stephen Bowd, David Bower, Stephen Gadd, Tom Harper, Roger Kain, Mary Pedley and Alexandra Plane. My sister, historian Anne Fletcher, helped me with aspects of Tudor history. Guidance, especially about the provenance of surviving Saxton maps and atlases, has come from staff at a wide range of college, university, local and national libraries and specialist archives and museums in the UK, Ireland and the USA. Any errors or misinterpretations, which I hope are minor, are mine.

I should like to conclude by giving my greatest thanks to my mother, Pauline Fletcher, for her help with proof-reading and for her support and encouragement throughout.

Knaresburgh forest

Wharfedale

Ribston hall — Colthorp — Tockwithe — ANSTY — Wilsthor

Plumpton toure — Washford — Ingmanthorp — Bikerto — Bilton — Hute

Pannell — Follyfote — N: Dighton — Spoford — Spoforth — S: Dighton — Synnynthwate

Stainber — Walton head pk — Stokell — Walton Thorp arche — Wigill — Hea

Lyndley — Almoselyffe Kirkby — Sicklinghall — WETHERBY

Denton hall — Weston — Farnley chap: — Letheley — Weton — Keerbye — Lynton

Stubhm — New hall — Casley — Wharfe flu: — Collingho — Clyfford — Newton — Smauis

Ilkley — Burley — Poole — Wodhall — Rigton — Wotersim — Ogglethorp — Tadca

OTLEY — Cayley — Arthingto — Harwood — Bramhm

Morton — Riddlesden — Addle — Gauthorp hall — Badsey — Hedley — Leadha

Rushforth — Gyseley — Alwoodley — Shadwell — Thorner — Haselwood

Byngley — Hawkesworth — Bayldon — Horsforthe — Kidhall — Aberforth — Sax

worthe — Harden — Shipley — Ave flu: — Moretowne — Barwick in elmet — Ludderton — Huda

Hallowes — Idle — Caluerley — Chappeltowne — Barmbow — Mickelfeld

olme pk — Ollerton — BRADFORTHE — Bramley — Crystall — Whidkirk — Ansthorp — Garforthe — Newt

Thorton — Leuenthorp — Hortons — Bowling hall — Pudsey — Armley — LEDES — Newbiggin — Kipax — Le

Clayton — Rodeshall — Tong — Farnley hall — Hunslet — Rodwell — Olton — Swillington — Ledston

Wibsey — Beston — Ollerton

N: Owrum — Okenshaw — Morley — Middleton — Medley — Castleforth

laworthe — Colay chap: — Wike — Heaton chap: — Adwalton — Thorp — Houghton

Quenden — Shibden hall — Estfeld — Burstall — Topclyff — Dunnyngley — The owt wood

HALYFAX — Howley hall — Tynglaw — Westerro — Altoftes — Fetherston

brig — Harteshead — Batley — W: Ardeslay — Stanley — Newland — Aketon

skircotes — Clyfton — Leuersage hall — Suthill hall — E: Ardeslay — Warmfeld — Normanton — Snydall

S: Owrum — Crumwell — Kirklesse — Deweſbury — Chidsall — Wrenthorp — Acwor

d Copley — hall — Elandhall — Mirfeld — Offet — Heathe — WAKEFELDE — Sherſton — Foulbye

land — Eland — Raſtrik — Thornhill — Harbury — Sandall — Foulbye

aneland — Bradle — Bradley — Caulder flu: — Denbye grange — Crofton — Watterton hall — Wragby

land — Fixbye hall — Kirkheaton — ashe — Netherton — Sandall east — Chete hall — Nostall — Bad

Wharmbye hall — Hutherffeld — Whitley hall — Bretton hall — Kinsley

laughwethe — Lockwod — Almondbury — Emley — Wolley — Hemsworth — Kir

Crosland — Woodsom hall — Huland — Royston — Felkirk — Brearley pk — Hought

hdenchap: — Honley chap: — Kirkhurton — Shelley — Darton — Burton grange — Houghta puat

Methm — Farnleytyes — Shepley — Denby-hall — Barmbye hall — Newhall — Billi

Thurſteland — Cumberworth — Cauthorne — Gunthwate hall — Derfel

Holmeforth — Ouer Denby — BARNESLEY — Drax

Ingbirchworth — Silkeston — Dodworth — Wombell

Howle — Oxpringe

ONE

WHO WAS CHRISTOPHER SAXTON?

CHRISTOPHER SAXTON is often referred to as the 'Father of English Cartography'. Though he was helped by important cartographic ancestors, siblings and descendants, this strong claim made by many earlier scholars of cartography still stands. His mapping of the country was to provide an enduring template for English maps for nearly two hundred years until the advent of the Ordnance Survey. In less than a decade during the 1570s he produced a map of England and Wales and its constituent counties, unprecedented in its detail and completeness.[1] How did this happen, why did it happen and who was involved? The man at the centre of the enterprise was a hitherto obscure map-maker. Who was he; who inspired, encouraged and sponsored this endeavour; who used the maps and what was their contemporary significance and influence?

In this book I examine these questions by telling Christopher Saxton's life story through his work, influence and legacy. The answers come from shining a light into mid-Tudor England. We see a link between the developing technology of scientific map-making and a government and society keen for its benefits. The Tudor era was a time of great social, economic, cultural and administrative change, and Saxton's extensive mapping project was part of these transformations. In studying Saxton, a striking contrast emerges between an otherwise obscure individual and his tremendous and enduring impact in mapping a nation. The very idea of having a detailed map of the whole nation is taken for granted in the modern day. Saxton was the first to make this a reality.

CHRISTOPHER SAXTON'S EARLY LIFE

It is understood that Christopher Saxton was born circa 1542 to 1544.[2] The reason for this uncertainty is plain when his background is considered. As he was not of gentry or noble

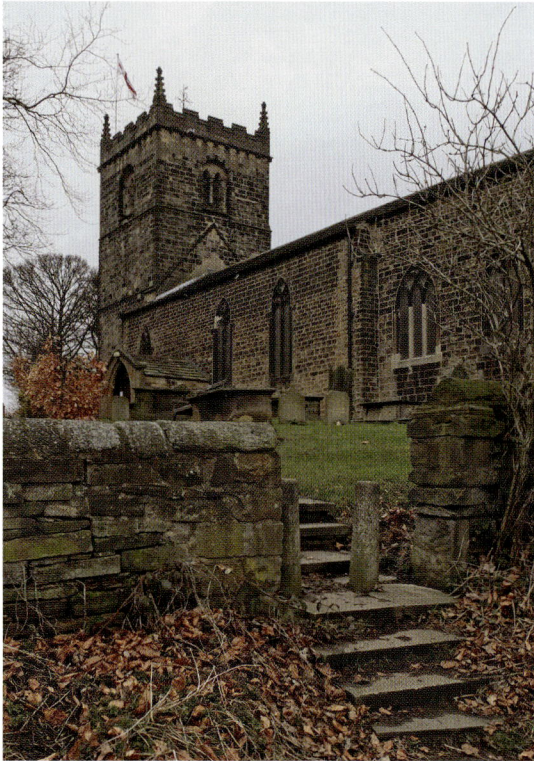

FIG. 1 St Mary's Church Woodkirk, or West Ardsley, in the West Riding of Yorkshire, a surviving remnant of Woodkirk Priory, photographed in 2013. Christopher Saxton's home at Dunningley was in this parish, and he probably attended this church with his family.

years 'or thereabouts'.[3] Tracking Saxton down requires some detective work.[4]

Saxton's place of birth is equally uncertain. He was long associated with the hamlet of Dunningley, as we will see, but it seems that he was born in Sowood, also in the West Riding of Yorkshire, where he spent his youth. While the sources for his birthplace are scant and inconclusive, his later home in Dunningley is well documented and certain. One problem is that there are two villages named Sowood in the West Riding. One of these is Sowood together with nearby Sowood Green in the vast ancient moorland-edge parish of Halifax. It seems much more likely though to have been the Sowood near Ossett, an outlying chapelry of the parish of Dewsbury. This location is more probable, being closer to Dunningley and the parish where his later patron Rudd was vicar from 1554 to 1570. Furthermore, Bower notes that Saxton's grandmother Alice was recorded as being from Ossett and there are references to the family name here in the Wakefield court rolls.[5]

Christopher Saxton probably spent the first twenty years or so of his life in Sowood before moving on to Dunningley, about 5 miles to the north in the neighbouring parish of West Ardsley (alias Woodkirk), also in the West Riding of Yorkshire (FIG. 1). Evans and Lawrence cite evidence that the Saxtons lived at Dunningley, at least by 1567, as Thomas Saxton, father of Christopher, was wealthy enough to be assessed there for tax and paid £4 3s 4d: an indicator of a certain level of wealth.[6] An

stock, pedigree was not of crucial importance. Whilst it was vital for the more elevated strata of society to maintain and document their bloodline to secure the transmission of property through the generations, for those of more common origins registration of vital events had yet to become commonplace. Indeed, it was only slightly before Saxton's likely birth year that parish registers had been first called for. Hence it should come as no surprise to find that Christopher Saxton himself was unclear about his age and was given to indicating it in

FIG. 2 Map of *The County of York* engraved by Thomas Jefferys, 1771–72, showing towards the eastern edge Ossett and Dunningley, where Saxton was probably born and the locality where he lived later, respectively. This depicts Saxton's home region probably little changed from his time at the dawn of industrialization.

assessment for 1606 gives Christopher as the only Saxton living at West Ardsley, proving his long connection with the place.[7] Like Sowood, the area is now part of the West Yorkshire conurbation, with a high density of population and urbanization, crossed first by turnpike roads and canals, then railways and now motorways. Nevertheless, there are considerable agricultural areas, and the Dunningley and Sowood areas are both still farmed. The terrain is undulating and relatively low-lying, compared with the Pennines to the west.

West Ardsley has a long history, being mentioned as Ardsley in the Domesday Book. Like neighbouring Dewsbury parish, this was a land of mainly small hamlets rather than nucleated villages. This must have struck Saxton as a distinguishing feature when he mapped other areas of the country with very different patterns of village and rural settlement: a challenge for any map-maker. West Ardsley was part of one of many monastic estates which had only recently ceased to own nearly a quarter of England. Woodkirk had been a priory of Austin

Friars founded in the reign of King Henry II as a subordinate cell to Nostell Priory, 9 miles to the south-east. The story goes that this cell was endowed by a member of the local Soothill family to atone for his sins.[8] It is possible that early in Saxton's life some monks remained in the area; he would have been aware of the tremendous social changes around him. After the dissolution the estate came into the hands of the Savile family, who were squires in the time of Saxton. Sir John Savile was to build Howley Hall nearby. This mansion, now lost, was considered a fine exemplar of an Elizabethan country house.

West Ardsley lay within a wider administrative hierarchy, being part of the Wapentake of Agbrigg, Lower Division, within the West Riding of Yorkshire. The parish was subordinate to the huge ancient manor of Wakefield, annexed to the Duchy of Lancaster in the reign of Mary I. This extensive ancient estate, extending way outside the county of Lancaster itself, was, and still is, Crown property, administered as an entity distinct from the Crown Estate. Perhaps this explains Saxton's employment by the Duchy to map some of its estates, as will be seen in a later chapter. The parish was later to be characterized by coal mining, brick making and the manufacture of woollen goods and stuffs. In Tudor times the parish was likely to have been predominantly agricultural, the land being fertile, though as part of a dual economy with the flourishing woollen manufacturing trade.

Dunningley was a hamlet in West Ardsley parish. In Tudor times the place name was written as either Dunninglawe or Dunynglawe and seems to have consisted of only a few houses on the crown of a hill, rising over 120 metres above sea level and surrounded by valleys and becks. This was typical of the scattered, non-nucleated settlement patterns of this locality. Living on higher ground above undulating terrain may have accustomed Christopher Saxton to viewing the landscape from an elevated vantage point: an asset to the later map-maker. He lived at Dunningley Hall, which was probably more modest than its grand name implies. It was demolished in the mid-nineteenth century and no remains are left. Today at Dunningley there stands a collection of farm buildings, none of ancient origin.

Saxton's West Riding of Yorkshire was still a rather remote part of the kingdom as seen from the centre of political power. It was part of what is often generically termed 'the North'; not always a helpful and sometimes a rather prejudiced generalization. Nevertheless, the way it was perceived from London mattered. Religious non-conformity and adherence to the old Catholic faith remained stronger in such distant parts in the decades after the Reformation and continued to be a focus for dissent or rebellion. After all, the uprising called the Pilgrimage of Grace was of recent memory and had spread from Lincolnshire to Yorkshire in reaction to the closure of the smaller monasteries in 1536. One element driving Saxton's mapping project was the need to monitor religious difference and its spillover into political dissent. At the same time, in rendering England in a series of corresponding county maps, the appearance of uniformity across the land might be suggested.

SAXTON'S SOCIAL BACKGROUND

Christopher Saxton belonged to the class of yeomen, one of the many social gradations which characterized early modern England. A yeoman was imprecisely defined as a freeholder of a small estate, or a tenant farmer, below the rank of a gentlemen but above other denizens of the countryside. The contemporary chronicler William Harrison in his 1577 *A Description of England* defines yeomen as freemen with an annual land rental income of 40 shillings or more and usually living affluently in good houses.[9] Forty shillings was also the voting qualification outside the towns. The Saxtons and their like had their toes on the first rung of the political ladder.

The Saxton family were probably clothiers as well as farmers and probably frequented nearby Wakefield, the principal local market for woollens. A great increase in upland population in Yorkshire, noted in legislation of Mary I's reign, was driven by a significant expansion of the wool trade, by means of which previously barren lands now

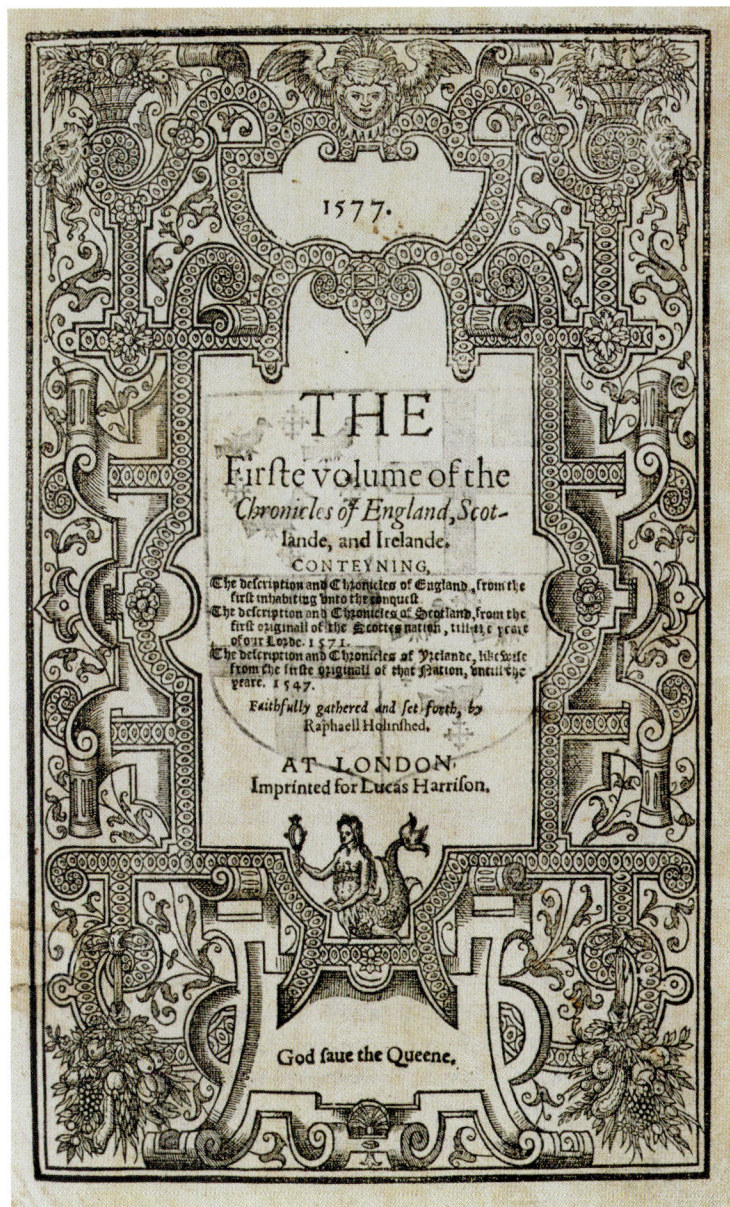

1577.

THE Firste volume of the Chronicles of England, Scotlande, and Irelande.

CONTEYNING,
The description and Chronicles of England, from the first inhabiting unto the conquest
The description and Chronicles of Scotland, from the first originall of the Scottes nation, till the yeare of our Lorde. 1571.
The description and Chronicles of Yrelande, likewise from the firste originall of that Nation, untill the yeare. 1547.

Faithfully gathered and set forth, by Raphaell Holinshed.

AT LONDON Imprinted for Lucas Harrison.

God saue the Queene.

FIG. 3 Title page of *The Firste volume of the Chronicles of England, Scotlande, and Irelande*, 1577, by Raphael Holinshed. This incorporates William Harrison's *A Description of England*, an important contemporary source on the topography of the country and one that Saxton is likely to have drawn upon.

thronged with people. Christopher Saxton would have witnessed such demographic changes and their accompanying impacts on the landscape. We may conjecture that this planted in his mind the importance of recording the changing topography of his country.

It is a characteristic of the English class system, in contrast with its Continental equivalents, that it was fixed and fluid at the same time: fixed in conception, but fluid in practice, especially when the accumulation of money was involved. Saxton was able to take advantage of this fluidity and through his initiative permeate the barriers to enter the heraldic arms-bearing gentry class later in life. Having started with relatively modest financial means, Saxton increased considerably in wealth through his mapping and the material recognition it brought. Just how much, we cannot be sure as no will of his has ever been traced, though we can infer some of the facts from the grants of land and privileges that, as we will see, came his way. By 1596 Christopher Saxton described himself as 'Gent.' of Dunningley in the parish of 'Westardesleye'.[10] He had clearly 'arrived' in his own estimation, and probably that of others.

Saxton's immediate social connections are not known, but it is intriguing to find that a mansion in the locality had been the seat of Sir John Topcliffe, Lord Chief Justice and Master of the Mint in the reigns of Henry VII and Henry VIII. Topcliffe's monument survives in West Ardsley church today. It seems, then, that the area had important court connections and was unlikely to have been a backwater. Furthermore, since the reign of King Stephen, who reputedly established it by royal charter in 1139, Tingley in the same parish of West Ardsley has been home to the Lee Gap Fair, perhaps England's oldest horse fair. This fair used to last three weeks and still occurs for a couple of days annually. It is thought to be named after local vicar Dr Lee, who kept the fair going in Tudor times when there was Puritan resistance to such festivities. The fair was visited then, as now, by travellers from far afield: the area was far from cut off.

SAXTON'S FAMILY

Christopher Saxton was one of at least four children, including sisters Alice and Margaret and an older brother Thomas, who corroborates our notion of the family's social standing by describing himself as a yeoman in his will of 1608. This older brother was probably named after their father Thomas, and their mother Margery probably gave the variant of her name to her daughter. By 1581 Thomas Senior owned at least two messuages (dwelling houses, outbuildings and immediately associated land) and considerable landholdings in various hamlets in West Ardsley parish. We know this because in that year he conveyed some of this property to his sons. Though by 1581 Christopher Saxton had probably started to profit from his own labours, this gain in assets would have further enhanced his economic security and social standing. We can only speculate how Christopher and his brother managed their landed properties; they may have simply drawn the rents, or they may have taken an active role in management. The latter is quite likely as many surveyors and map-makers had other roles, and land management would not have been an alien concept to one such as Christopher Saxton so familiar with traversing and recording it. The family were certainly not immune to the obligations facing the property owner. Local court rolls of 1608/09 indicate an obligation to scour ditches alongside the highway from Tingley to Wakefield to avoid flooding: a requirement enforced on pain of statutory penalty.[11]

From Christopher's brother Thomas's and his son Robert's wills we have some genealogical information. Even then, we do not know the name of Christopher Saxton's wife, though given when their children were born it seems likely she was rather younger than he was. Five children of the union are known: sons Robert, Christopher and Thomas; and daughters Grace and Elizabeth. Only Robert followed in his father's cartographic footsteps, and we have evidence of them working together as map-makers at least by 1601, as well as later on their own. Like his father, Robert uses the term yeoman of himself.

EDUCATION AND EARLY INFLUENCES

Just as with his vital details, Saxton's education is also a matter of some conjecture. He may well have attended the forerunner of Queen Elizabeth Grammar School in Wakefield. The school in his day was based in the parish church and was run by the clergy. This claim that Saxton was a former pupil is made in a history of the town, and as Wakefield is only a few miles from Sowood and Dunningley, and probably the nearest school of appropriate standing, the suggestion is plausible.[12]

The same history asserts that Christopher Saxton went on to Cambridge. Whilst none of the college records extant in the mid-sixteenth century has a record of him, by no means all students were registered in this era of religious turmoil and alternation between Catholicism and Protestantism. Registration required taking an oath, a possible danger should the religious regime change, as it was wont to do. Given Saxton's later connections and employment, a university education at one of the only two such seats of learning in England at the time does seem likely.

Whilst our picture of his education is sketchy, we know more about Saxton's mentor, John Rudd, also educated at Cambridge, decades earlier.[13] Rudd went on to become a fellow of St John's College there, and was a crucial influence upon, and enabler of, Saxton. John Rudd was a colourful and accomplished figure. He had changing fortunes during the upheaval of the Reformation, but was eventually to be a senior clergyman, though an often absentee one, as well as a cartographer. Rudd's absences are not explained only by his plurality (holding of several remunerative scattered church livings), common enough at the time, but also because of his recognition as

The South Prospect of the Ruins of SANDAL CASTLE; and TOWN of WAKEFIELD. 1722.

This Castle near WAKEFIELD in y.e West Riding of YORKSHIRE, was built by John Plantagenet Earl of Warren &c Surrey, in the Reign of King Edw.d the 4.th near which was a Battel fought; between the Families of York & Lancaster; on the 31 Day of Decem. A.D: 1460 in the Reign of King Henry the 6.th; where Richard

To JOHN SMYTH of Grays Inn Esq.r this Prospect is humbly Inscribed by his most Obliged humble Serv.t S Buck

Duke of York (then the Owner) & his Son Edmund Earl of Rutland, were slain: In Memory of which, King Edw.d the 4.th (Son of the s.d Duke of York) built a Beautifull Chappel, now standing on WAKEFIELD Bridge but much defaced. The Castle was Demolished after the Grand Rebellion in the Year 1648.

FIG. 4 Prospect of the ruins of Sandal Castle and Wakefield. All Soul's Church, Wakefield, can be seen from a distance: this probably housed Saxton's school in his day. From an eighteenth-century print by Samuel Buck in *A Collection of Engraved Plans, Views, etc., of Parts of Great Britain and Ireland.*

an important map-maker, a useful asset to the Tudor state. It has been suggested that Rudd's many promotions and ecclesiastical offices, sources of great profit as well as status, were means of recognizing his value to the realm more as a cartographer than his merit as a churchman. This pattern of payment through patronage carried on with Saxton. As long ago as 1534, Rudd declared himself a student and teacher of the map-makers' art, placing him at the forefront of the Tudor revolution in cartography as some have termed it. His profitable ecclesiastical appointments included prebends

(stipendiary canonries) in the cathedrals of Durham in 1550 and Winchester the year after, and livings including the vicarage of Dewsbury from 1554, a parish next to Dunningley, perhaps explaining his encounter with Christopher Saxton.

The story goes that while briefly imprisoned for opposing reform in 1534, Rudd cleverly arranged for his map of the Holy Land to be sent via an intermediary to Thomas Cromwell, his ultimate jailer and a keen advocate of the value of maps, especially in statecraft. Rudd claimed that his map surpassed all previous ones in accuracy, and, in perhaps a unique case of a map-maker's skill being used successfully in mitigation, he was released. Rudd clearly went on to regain royal favour in a big way, for in the 1540s he had become royal chaplain and clerk of the closet. This responsibility for the royal privy chapel brought him into close personal contact with Henry VIII. As we will see, royal patronage was important for Saxton as well and it seems likely that Rudd's connections were useful to him.

Saxton seems to have been apprenticed to Rudd by the 1560s, the decade before his county mapping of England. Rudd had travelled the country making surveys and checking information locally, in keeping with Renaissance scientific ideals, which he professed, stressing the importance of original survey rather than compilation of the labours of others. To this end he said he must 'travel by his own sight to view and consider divers parts of our said realm'.[14] Acknowledging this, the queen herself ordered Durham Cathedral to pay his stipend for two years while he went to view different parts of England at first hand and complete a map of the country 'both fairer and more perfect and truer than it hath been hitherto'.[15]

But in spite of decades of map-making, royal patronage, and access to many maps as clerk of the closet to Henry VIII, Rudd's survey seems never to have been finished. The completed work was though quite possibly incorporated in the map of the British Isles by Gerard Mercator published in Duisburg in 1564. Some of Rudd's manuscript maps, such as his 1569 map of County Durham, were incorporated alongside Saxton's map proofs in the Burghley Atlas, discussed later in this book. Rudd's young assistant on these expeditions was none other than Christopher Saxton. We know he was apprenticed to Rudd at least by 1570, and probably for some time before. In April that year Saxton signed a receipt at Durham to collect £8 6s 8d for his master, Rudd's quarterly stipend.[16] We can assume that by then the master had passed on many surveying skills to his pupil; for Saxton's later achievements, we must afford Rudd considerable credit.

THE ENGLAND OF ELIZABETH

Well beyond the confines of Dunningley, Christopher Saxton was a product of Elizabethan England, as well as ultimately furnishing it with its finest cartographic image. The England Saxton knew was unrecognizable from the country we know today, both in physical appearance and in how it was perceived. Most noticeably, the population of Elizabethan England was far lower. In 1550 it was just under 3 million, though by 1600 it had grown to just over 4 million, still tiny compared with today. Taking the midpoint of these estimates, the population and its average density were less than 6 per cent of that of today, though with rather different distribution. A modern visitor would find much of it an empty, wild or sparsely settled land, apart from the small and densely packed towns.

The overwhelmingly agrarian nature of this pre-industrial land and society stands in stark

reproche of them, that be diftruftfull, is a peece of Theognis verfe, intending, that vvho doth moft miftruft is moft falfe. For fuch experience in falfehood bree-deth miftruft in the mynd, thinking noleffe guile to lurke in others, then in hym-felfe. But Piers thereto ftrongly replyeth vvith another peece of the fame verfe, faying as in his former fable, vvhat fayth then is there in the faythleffe. For if fayth be the ground of religion, vvhich fayth they dayly falfe, what hold then is there of theyr religion. And thys is all that they faye.

June.

Ægloga fexta.
ARGVMENT.

THis Æglogue is vvholly vovved to the complayning of Colins ill fcceffe in his loue. For being (as is aforefaid) enamoured of a Country laffe Rofolind, and bauing (as feemeth) founde place in her beart, be lamenteth to his deare frend Hobbinoll, that he is novve forfaken vnfaithfully, and in his fteede Menalcas, another fhepheard receiued difloyally. And this is the vvhole Argument of this Æglogue.

Hobbinoll

FIG. 5 The month of *June* from Edmund Spenser's *The Shepheardes Calender Conteyning Twelue Æglogues*, 1579. There is an eclogue, an old term for a poem, especially a pastoral one, together with a picture for each month. Spenser's poems and illustrations convey an Elizabethan perception of landscape and its emotive force.

contrast to today. About a third of the country was waste: heaths and moors and land unable to be farmed. Another third was grazed, and this reflected the importance of the woollen industry. A further third was arable, still much as open fields held in common and divided into furlongs, though more predominantly in the midlands than other parts. Only a tiny fraction could be said to be urban and the nature of towns was remarkably different, being far smaller – save London – and more compact, often confined by defensive walls.[17] This was the country Saxton was going to map in detail for the first time.

Furthermore, Elizabethan England was a fundamentally unequal society. The fabulously rich existed alongside the starving poor, with many gradations in-between. At the apex was the queen. England was not a democracy: the personal rule of the queen, quite literally monarchy, defined the sovereignty of the land. Queen Elizabeth had advisers, but all decisions in the end were hers. That was at least the image. In reality, the queen had to heed advice and make concessions to powerful interests in the land. Her precarious finances made it vital for her to do so; as Hammer observes, 'given the hefty debt inherited from Mary, Elizabeth's government had always tended to frugality.'[18] It is just as well, then, that she was also a clever, resourceful and tactful politician, and this made promotion of a strong image still more important. Elizabeth embodied England, the last sovereign to do so before the union of crowns with Scotland. Elizabeth's reign was celebrated as the peak of Tudor monarchy: *Gloriana* in Edmund Spenser's contemporary poem *The Faerie Queene*. Some have argued that Elizabeth herself was the focus of patriotic devotion rather than any abstract notion of England. It was politic, therefore, to paint a favourable impression of a charismatic and distinctive absolute ruler, and Saxton did so

magnificently in the frontispiece to his county atlas.

The queen was surrounded by what was loosely termed 'court': her councillors and retinue. The court moved with the sovereign and was to some degree peripatetic in Elizabeth's reign since the queen would make progresses around the country to see and be seen. She would stay with favoured local notables, a great honour but a mixed blessing as the expense would often be ruinous. The queen would take advice from anyone she chose to, but usually her right-hand man was the Secretary of State, for nearly all her reign William Cecil, later ennobled as Lord Burghley, a keen advocate and patron of cartography, including Saxton, as we will see. Saxton's county maps may well have come in handy in planning these excursions.

The country at large was managed through local officials. Each county had a Lord Lieutenant, the sovereign's representative there. Then there were Justices of the Peace: the queen's peace. In Tudor times JPs had administrative as well as the judicial functions we know today; effectively running the localities for the queen. These officials were her eyes and ears across the land. All these county appointees were drawn from the gentry class and thus had a vested interest in protecting the status quo. Hence, the landed gentry and noble classes had virtually all the power under the queen at a local level. They were collectively few in number; most estimates suggest little more than 15,000, rather fewer than one in two

FIG. 6 *The Royal Procession of Queen Elizabeth*, by George Vertue, 1742, probably based on a drawing by Robert Peake the Elder dated 1601. The court became more familiar with the geography of the country from these travels and this may have fostered an interest in maps among them.

hundred of the population. This arrangement bears almost no relation to modern elected local government: Elizabethan government at central and local levels was about national and local security and rather less social welfare, except regarding the management of the poor. In keeping with this, we will see that the main rationale for commissioning Saxton's maps was protection against threats to the security of the state, from without and within.

Given the county's importance as the highest tier of local administration, it is no accident that Saxton's maps were county maps and that this unit formed the basis for regional scale mapping until, and including, the Ordnance Survey in the mid-twentieth century. In fact, not until National Grid mapping was introduced after World War II was the county

series of large-scale maps phased out. Arguably Saxton created a precedent which was to shape cartography for centuries to come.

CULTURAL AND INTELLECTUAL INFLUENCES

Culture flourished in Saxton's England. Literature, architecture, the theatre, poetry, music and many other facets of artistic expression took on a new prominence and were favoured by wealthy patrons. Elizabeth's reign was a propitious time both materially and in terms of the spirit of the age for bold creative achievements. Her England was a land of growing prosperity, at least for the upper classes, who had increasingly deep pockets to sponsor their cultural interests. The wealthy were growing in number. William

Shakespeare, Ben Jonson and Christopher Marlowe were among those who enriched England with their writing. Attending their plays would be a social highlight affordable to all classes. Cultural expression was gaining more support: only from the 1570s were permanent groups of theatrical players established by the patronage of the rich. Before then theatres had been tightly controlled and censored. Queen Elizabeth herself patronized musicians, actors and artists, probably reflecting personal interest, but also so she could be seen as having a sophisticated and civilized court. William Harrison claimed that England's court was one of the most magnificent in Europe and unsurpassed in visible decorum. In spite of the apparent opening up of theatre, Elizabethan plays often had a subtle or obvious political message. Much propaganda favourable to the Tudor regime was conveyed in Shakespeare's works. In the same vein, map-makers including Saxton would portray a glorious England, in its neat array of well-governed counties.

New and bold architectural styles also developed in late Tudor England, which again drew upon the pride and resources of the wealthy, new and old, and promoted national as well as individual confidence. In a less war-torn era, decoration and elegance took the place of defensive priorities. All was about appearance or 'show'. A new professional and landed elite, enriched by the dissolution of the monasteries, spent their riches competing with each other, often at ruinous expense, in displays of wealth,

taste and loyalty to the monarch. To this end, extensive state apartments in mansions were created should the queen ever visit. Saxton's age was one of conspicuous consumption and visual appearance: in modern terms 'optics', all of great importance as influences shaping a budding cartographer in an England eager to capture its glory in maps.

Many aspects of Elizabethan cultural and social development were home-grown and reflected the queen's own intellectual bent and achievements and those of her court. Yet, we have to remember wider influences from beyond the kingdom, especially the intellectual new dawn known as the Renaissance. A widespread European phenomenon, it originated in late-fourteenth-century Italy, promoted by humanist scholars, most notably Erasmus. It revived interest in the writings of classical scholars and notably the flourishing of art in Florence under Medici family patronage. The term 'Renaissance' in this context was coined in the nineteenth century, the word 'rebirth' being used in sixteenth-century Italy. Classical culture did not completely vanish in the Middle Ages; nor did medieval attitudes completely die out in the Renaissance. Though there were some earlier classical revivals, the Renaissance was perhaps the most significant one, ushering in, and coinciding with, important developments in philosophy and the applied arts which often consciously drew on classical models. The Renaissance had implications for the arts and sciences, and developments dependent on them such

as exploration, astronomy and architecture. Humanism involved a degree of liberation from the mental constraints of orthodox religion – though again, as with all ideas, there were continuities with the past. To an extent humanism created a climate in which existing knowledge could be questioned; the learning of the ancients was rediscovered and reappraised. Science as practised by the likes of Galileo and Francis Bacon would be based on real-world observation and experiment. Important inventions were stimulated in this cauldron of new ideas and learning, such as printing, vital to the spread of ideas, and advances in navigational compasses, crucial to exploration and overseas colonization. Cartography was a notable fusion of the arts and sciences and it matured dramatically in this era. Maps developed from being mainly illustrations of theological ideas to practical tools for recording spatial relationships, as well as symbols of wealth and status. The Renaissance took perhaps a century or so to permeate the English mindset, and the Elizabethan era is usually seen as its high point.

The intellectual developments of the Renaissance were accompanied by other, perhaps more discernible, changes in England wrought by the Reformation. Though the Renaissance had originated in Italy before

FIG. 7 Eighteenth-century printed view of an Elizabethan great house: Hardwick Hall, Derbyshire, then known as Hardwick House. These mansions, often expanded from older manor houses, were much in fashion among the elite in Saxton's day. From *A Collection of Engraved Plans, Views, etc., of Parts of Great Britain and Ireland*.

spreading to much of Europe, Italy had mainly remained loyal to the Pope and the Catholic faith. Religion was to be a perennial problem throughout later Tudor times and not least in Elizabeth's reign. Her father Henry VIII had initiated a break with Rome. There were various changes and reversals by his successors Edward VI and Mary, but their half-sibling strove to make what has become known as the Elizabethan Settlement. This was intended to resolve the Catholic 'problem', as it was conceived, with a compromise position between Catholicism and Puritanism, though often pleasing neither.

Elizabeth's policy on religion had to be pragmatic. She may have been at the apex of political power in England, but that power was highly vulnerable. She reigned by the grace of God, but her reign was characterized by chronic insecurity. She would not marry lest it gave a man a political advantage over her, nor name a successor lest it gave another a vested interest in her demise. In fact, her beautifully decorated, embroidered and jewel-encrusted clothes were continually refurbished and repaired; an allegory perhaps of semblance concealing substance. Above all, there was religious turmoil in an era when political and religious authority could not be separated. Catholicism was not replaced in England at a stroke and, as we have seen, significant areas, especially the North, retained the old faith. Beyond the shores of England, the threat from Catholic Europe was significant and perennial. It shaped foreign policy and internal security.

Mary, the deposed queen of Scots, was not the only Catholic claimant to the English throne who might be proffered by hostile powers. We have no evidence of Saxton's religious affiliation, but he must have been very aware of the sensitivities and the climate of insecurity.

The queen's actions reflected these dangers. She maintained her precarious power by managing to avoid calling Parliament more often than ten times in her forty-five year reign. She prevented any adviser from monopolizing influence over her, and so for instance played off William Cecil against Robert Dudley. Moreover, after the Duke of Norfolk's execution in 1572 England had no dukes or other overmighty subjects who might challenge her. The bishops were now partly emasculated, no longer having adherence to the Pope across the water. By good fortune, Elizabeth had no surviving legitimate siblings and few close relatives who might make a play for the throne, save Mary, the deposed queen of Scots. Nevertheless, the queen still felt, and probably was, at great risk. Policy would reflect this; and, as we will see, state security was a key motive for commissioning Christopher Saxton's county maps.

A significant legacy of the Reformation in England was the dissolution of the monasteries from 1536. Perhaps more than anything else, this meant the end of medieval society in the kingdom. In his 1509 essay *In Praise of Folly*, Erasmus articulated and encapsulated the long-developing feeling of anti-clericalism; a movement against the theologically irrelevant self-serving and corrupt practices of clerics that

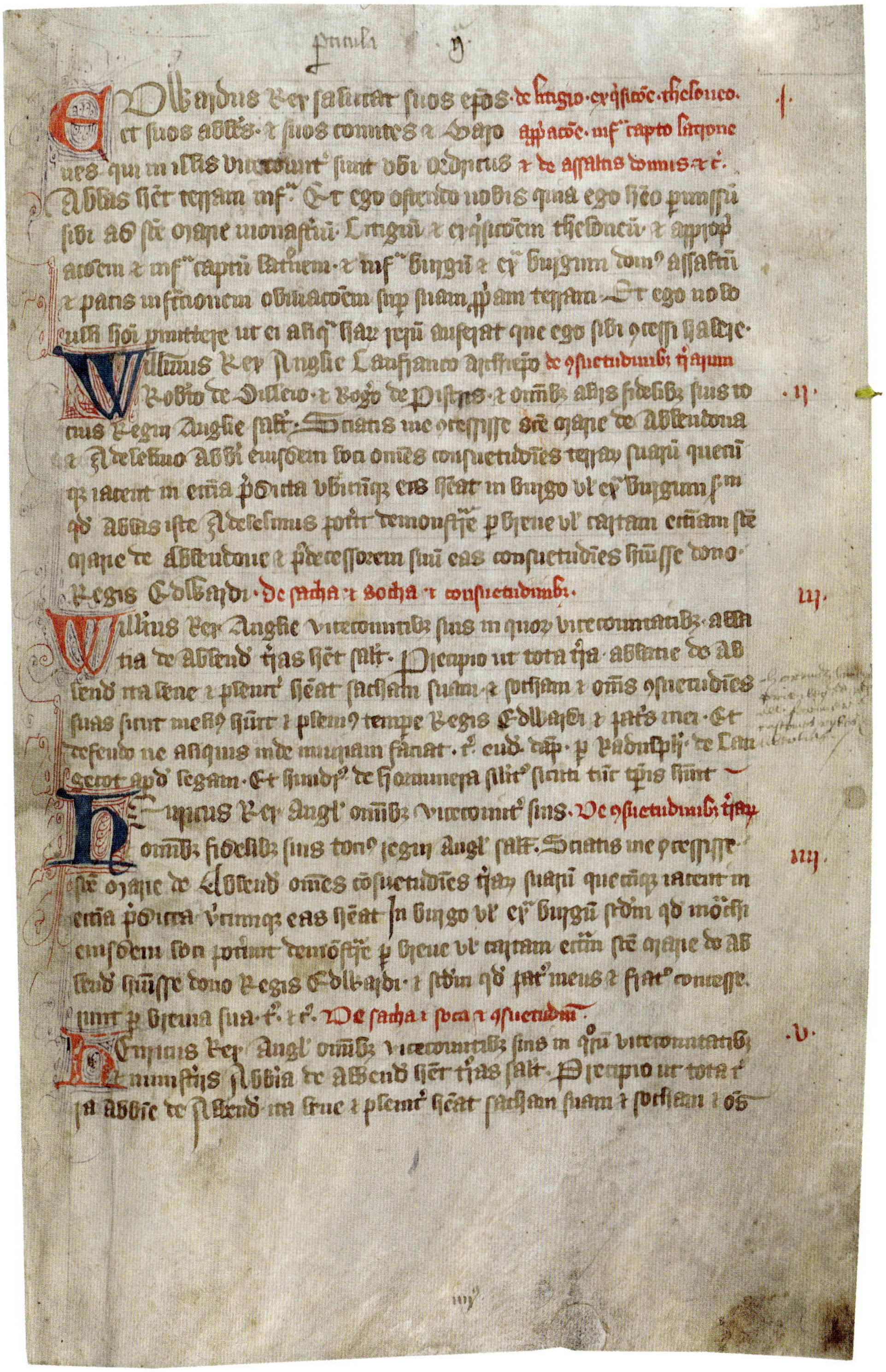

FIG. 8 Cartulary of Abingdon Abbey, circa 1345–56, and additions of the fourteenth and fifteenth centuries. These could be viewed as the title deeds of the Abbey: this page shows royal grants of land, later to be confiscated by the Crown in the Reformation. Property was usually recorded in longhand rather than cartographic form in this era.

had kept them in luxury. Such abuses were probably exaggerated: useful propaganda to lay the ground for the wholesale confiscation of monastic property. Before the dissolution, the religious houses owned about a quarter of the country's landed wealth, as well as controlling about two-fifths of remunerative benefice nominations. The resulting redistribution of this property and lucrative ecclesiastical patronage had effects far more profound than the most visible sign, the destruction of monastic architectural heritage. There was a tightening of central control over the localities under Tudor rulers, with demands for increasing amounts of information from them. One signifier of this was the 1535 *Valor Ecclesiasticus*: a nationwide written survey of ecclesiastical wealth and perhaps a precedent for a national cartographic survey by Saxton a few decades later.

The dissolution of the monasteries precipitated an active market in land. The main beneficiaries were the rising gentry class, who bought considerable ex-monastic property from the cash-strapped Henry VIII. These new estates generally appreciated greatly in value, having often been sold in haste and too cheaply. These increasingly affluent and socially climbing subjects often had an interest, both aesthetic and practical, in having their estates mapped. The significant uptake in estate mapping, however, only happened in the 1570s. Why, then, was there a delay of a few decades after the dissolution of the monasteries? It would seem that new technology and

methods like estate mapping take a while to be adopted. It took time for the gentry and nobility to become familiar with the idea of maps as useful estate management tools and for them to become familiar with the new writings on maps and mapping techniques. Furthermore, the necessary scientific surveying techniques were, as we have seen, still developing in this period. The boom in estate mapping of the 1570s occurred at the same time as Saxton was making his county maps. This may have been another encouraging factor as interest in one kind of mapping is likely to stimulate another. A map symbolizes ownership, belonging and sense of place. Saxton's county maps would allow newly prosperous and powerful gentry literally to see their position in county society at a glance.

The end of the monasteries was part of broader social and economic change and shifts in mindset with far-reaching ramifications. An active market in land was enabled not only by supply of ex-monastic property, but also by a broader move from feudalism to capitalism, which had been some time in the making. The growth of Protestantism has often been linked to that of individualism. Property was now being transferred from the institutional ownership of religious houses to the private individual, who may have had more incentive to improve property rather than passively draw rents. Such individualism was perhaps a key to the spirit of innovation and improvement of which cartography was one manifestation practised by the self-improved grammar-school boy from Dunningley; a case of sixteenth-century social mobility.

Christopher Saxton recorded England's geography at a time of vast change alongside many continuities with the past. His picture is of a land at once strong and flourishing, and at the same time vulnerable and threatened. This atmosphere must have rubbed off on Saxton, and his maps should be seen in this light: reflecting the splendour of Elizabeth's England, whilst quietly safeguarding that glory from all manner of foes.

The South View of the Ruins of FOUNTAINS ABBEY, in Skeldale; three Miles from RIPPON.

This Famous **Monaſtry** *was founded A.D.MCXXXII, by Arch Biſhop THURSTINUS for the Reception of thirteen Monks, who retired from St Marys at YORK, for the exercise of greater Auſterity, and at firſt, had no other—*

To the most Reverend Lord, Arch-Biſhop of and Primate of all England, inſcribed, by may it pleaſe Yr Graces most dutifull and Obedt humble Servt, Samuel Buck.

Father in GOD: William, Canterbury Metropolitan This Proſpect, is Humbly Yr Grace,

Shelter than an Elm Tree; But were ſoon after incorporated by St BERNARD, into the Ciſtercian Order, and therein acquired great Riches, which when they ſurrendred to K. Hen. VIII were valued at 3072 Pounds P. Annum.

FIG. 9 A ruined monastery: *The South View of the Ruins of Fountains Abbey* in Yorkshire, an eighteenth-century print from *A Collection of Engraved Plans, Views, etc., of Parts of Great Britain and Ireland*. The dissolution of the monasteries took place just before Saxton's lifetime, well within living memory in his era.

Dunkeske
Glacaurno
Twamay
Lughninagh
Skateryk
ARGLAS
Dundrome
HIBER-
Grene cast.
Carlingford
DUNDALK

NIÆ
Drodagh

PARS
Lambay
DVBLYN
Brey
Wikelo
Arkeloue
Glafcarig
Wexford

S. Maria Insula
Wirkinton
Blenrake
Cokermouth
S. Andrew S. Michael
Balacuri
Douglas
MAN
Bala
Set: Michael Insul:
Millum caf.
S. pole of foosdrae
Egremond
Ulferston
Fotheby Insul:
Glasson caf.
The pyle
Ruffin caste
The calfe of man
Kirk

MARE

HIBERNI-

Holy-head
Innys lligod
46
Aberfraw
Newburgh
Preftholm Insul:
Bewmaris
Ormeshead
Hilbre Insul:
BANGOR
Abercomny
S. ASAPH
Caernarvan
Cast. Dolbaden
DENBIGH
42
FLYNT
41

Caer Ievionvhod
cast: Dolachlan
cast: Dolwran

CVM.
Nevin
Pullhely
Brachipull poynt
Sidwall Insul:
Bardsey Insul:
Barwouth
Harlech
Delgelle
Bala
44
43
Llanuilling
Wulshpole
cast
MERI

Aberdovy
Machenllet
Caartufe cast
Abereiftyth
Rossfaur
Llandwrowo
Llanidlos
cast: Dindod
52
Treadeon
Llanvheuevy
59
Knothon
RADNOR
Llangadok
Beale
BRECKNOK
48
CARDIGAN
Kilgarvn cast
Newport
Nerton
Piscara
Abermarlas
Llandfilouaurn
Deneuey cast:
S. DAVIDES
noch cast:
Wifton
Narbarth
CARMARTHIN
HERE

The bishop and his clarks
Ramfey Insul:
Brde bay
Mauerverd caft
Pixton cast
Kiduefly
Llanethy
Gresholme Insul:
Scalme Insul:
Harolditon
Cavern
Tenbye
Leohor
Swanfey
Aberawon
Milfword hauen
PENBROK
Caldie Insul:
Set Gouens point
Wormeshead point
Pennarth caft:
Bridgend
LLANDE
Cowbridge
Set Donits
Barry F Holmes
BRIS

Lundye Insul:

Combemarten
Minhead
Watchet
Axbrdge
29 WELL
Ilfracome
Barneftable
Bideford
Dunfter
Southmoulton
Torrinton
Wheelecome
Stratton
Holsworthy
Crodimo
Launton
Tavnton
Willington
Tintagel cast
Bow
Crediton
Boscastel
CamelfordLaunfton
EXCESTER
30
Padftow
Lyston
Theofordr
Set mavnn
31
Lydford cast

Scala Miliarium.
10   15   20   25   30   35   40

Saxton
Christophorus descripsit.

Augustinus Ryther Anglus
Sculpsit. An.º Dñi 1579.

duertendum, nos
r locorū angustias
tantū oppida mer-
a castella et loca
m celebriora hac
ula incluisse

TWO

THE ORIGINS OF SAXTON'S MAPPING SCHEME

MAPS WERE FAR FROM UNKNOWN when Christopher Saxton was born in the mid-sixteenth century. Map-making in some form had probably developed over about four thousand years before he entered the field, and mapping appears likely to be as ancient as any other form of literacy. As representations of all or parts of the Earth's surface, maps take an enormous variety of forms. Although they occur over millennia, they were for a long time a great rarity.

In the present day most of us take maps entirely for granted. They are everywhere; on our phones and laptops, and for the more traditional of us in our atlases and folded maps. We refer to maps to navigate, but many of us also read them just for pleasure, especially when we can visit somewhere exotic in our minds or can be transported back in time by looking at old maps. Our tendency to resort to a map for a variety of practical and aesthetic purposes was

not the norm in Saxton's era. Often, it was not possible because of the scarcity of maps, and it was not likely as the habit of mind was yet to be formed; two developments which go hand in hand. In Saxton's day maps were far from commonplace objects; they were compiled here and there, often for ad hoc purposes. The idea of an off-the-shelf map ready for all occasions was a prospect for the future. In the mid-sixteenth century if you were inclined to have a map of England, then you would probably need to be wealthy and lucky. Should you want a detailed map of a particular area of the country, then you would need to be much more fortunate still.

MAPPING OF ENGLAND BEFORE SAXTON

Saxton's achievement and the foundations on which he had to work are evident from a brief examination of earlier mapping endeavours. On the earliest maps of Europe, Britain was typically represented less accurately than

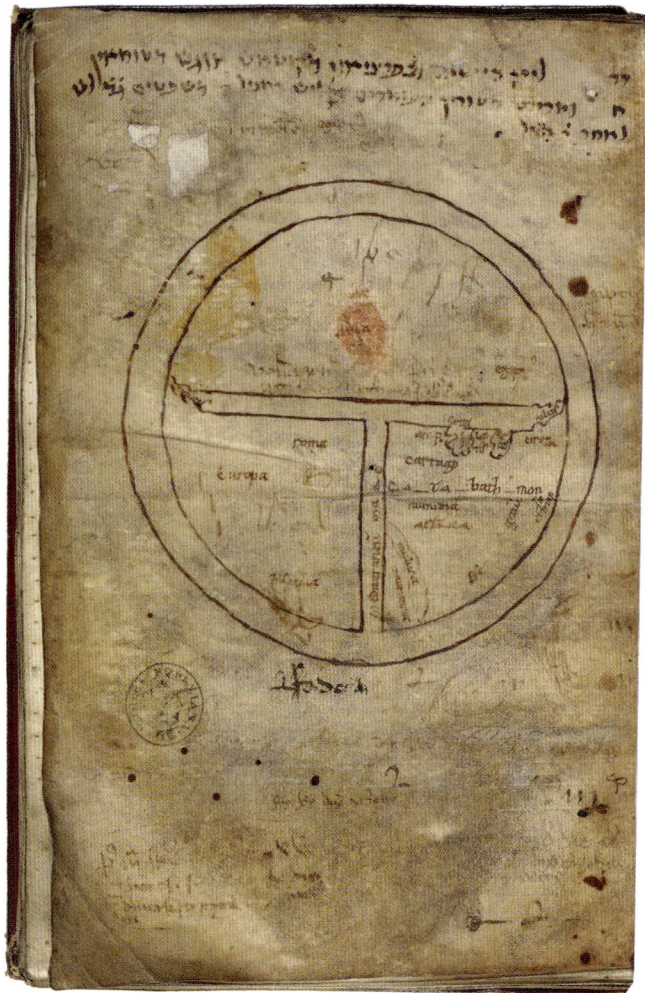

FIG.10 A *mappa mundi* in the form of a T–O Map included in an early-twelfth-century codex from southern France reproducing works by Sallust. A T–O map was an early simple diagrammatic cartographic form showing the three continents of the Old World: Europe, Asia and Africa.

map.[1] The Psalter Map of circa 1262 also depicts the British Isles in an identifiable way.[2] This cruder portrayal is not surprising as most of this mapping of the known world centred on the Mediterranean Sea. Britain was far away from the centre of this Old World civilization; out of sight and out of mind. Most such early maps were *mappae mundi*: maps of the world, which may have prioritized communication of a theological message, usually an interpretation of the Bible, over geographical exactitude. Such maps are essentially diagrams, structures within which much theological and anthropological information was annexed to the geographical in order to be encyclopaedic in scope.

Mappae mundi were idealized representations of the world, sharply contrasting with the accurate maps at consistent scale which dominated in Saxton's time. Many medieval maps were called T–O maps: drawn with east at the top and depicting Africa, Asia and Europe as three sections in a circle divided by a *T* (FIG. 10). Accuracy, geographical completeness and consistency were not necessarily the priority in these maps; nor did the technology exist to deliver them.

Although the story of mapping is not one of straightforward progress, there are some discernible stages which we can recognize as preparing the way for Saxton. A key step forward from diagrams like the *mappae mundi* is the medieval map of Great Britain made circa 1400, one of the greatest treasures of the Bodleian Library. Known as the Gough Map

much of the European mainland, though the geographical outlines of the island were still recognizable on early maps, such as the circa eleventh-century Cottonian World Map or Anglo-Saxon map contained in a scientific miscellany and probably copied from a Roman

after its former owner Richard Gough, because the map-maker is unknown (FIG. 11), it was bequeathed to the Library in 1809 as part of his enormous collection. We owe many of the topographic survivals of the time to him, though these were not always valued by his contemporaries: he was able to acquire this map for a mere 2 shillings and sixpence! As an accurate geographical representation, this map is a major improvement on any of its predecessors. The Gough Map was long thought to be the first comprehensive road map of Great Britain. Recent scholarship suggests, however, that the red lines once thought to be roads are rather distance lines between places.[3] The map also shows over 600 place names and around 200 rivers. Though probably rare, there were once copies of the Gough Map. Hiatt finds one of these made between 1422 and circa 1450 in the British Library.[4] Likewise, Thomson notes that Leland mentions in his *Itineraries* finding a twin copy of the Gough Map at Merton College, Oxford.[5]

Surviving maps showing England or the British Isles are few before Saxton's century and, as noted, often showed Britain alone or at the edge of a larger map. Most depended considerably on older sources, thus presenting little new geographical information. One word of caution: we cannot be sure whether surviving maps are representative of the rather greater number probably once produced.

Evidence suggests that detailed maps of local areas were even rarer. The greatest ever national survey of its time, the Domesday Book, completed in 1086, was made without use of, or inclusion of, any maps at all. Until beyond Saxton's time, the written rather than mapped survey of property was the norm. Skelton and Harvey's major study of local maps in England found a total of only thirty such maps surviving from before circa 1500, most made late in the period.[6] In contrast, we should bear in mind that England was rich in written topographical information, including details of legal circuits, itineraries, tax records, written surveys of manors and, from the thirteenth century, increasing amount of data on latitudes. All these might foster mapping of topographic information once the utility of the graphic record had become widely recognized.[7]

MAPPING IN SAXTON'S CENTURY

In contrast, the sixteenth century marked a fundamental transformation, what some regard as a Tudor revolution in map-making and awareness of maps, just as the historian Geoffrey Elton proposed a Tudor revolution in government.[8] Saxton's commission was an important fulfilment of this revolution. Maps tended gradually to become more practical with continuing improvements in geographical fidelity. Concern with scale was vital for maps used for navigation such as portolan charts, and essential too in maps meant for terrestrial

FIG. 11 OVERLEAF The Gough Map, arguably the crowning glory of early British mapping and of the Bodleian's map collection, circa 1400. This anonymous map was an important source for map-makers for many years afterwards and is a treasure trove of early-fifteenth-century geographical information for us today.

Insula de Orbeney

mare orientale

Norfolk

Suffolk

mare occidental

administration or distance indication at a national scale, as with the Gough Map, and at a local level as with the emergent genre of estate maps.

The needs of commerce were an early spur to more practically useful mapping. An important genre was the portolan chart, maps used for navigation which came to supersede their written predecessors. The oldest surviving portolan charts date from the late thirteenth century. A further spur to map-making and map awareness was the upsurge in global exploration and subsequent colonization by European countries. In the lead-up to the sixteenth century this had seen Christopher Columbus's 1492 journey to the Caribbean, a precursor to colonization. In the other direction Vasco da Gama had sailed round Africa to India in 1498 and Jorge Álvares had reached as far as China by 1513. The mental concept of the Old World was rapidly being superseded. Appropriately, there survives from 1492 the world's oldest extant globe, made by Martin Behaim. By 1507 the German map-maker Martin Waldseemüller had published his woodcut world map, which combined the traditional geographical knowledge of Ptolemy with information gleaned from the voyages of Amerigo Vespucci and used the revolutionary technique of printing. Indeed, the cartographer named the New World after Vespucci. Maps were indispensable tools for the explorer and lucrative commercial assets to be safeguarded for the colonizing powers. Maps, discovery and empire were inextricably linked. The growing familiarity with maps would spill over from global discovery into other areas, including the mapping of a nation.

Recent maps of England would have been instructive examples and sources for Saxton's work, illustrating important technical and stylistic advances. As we will see, they would also alert Saxton to the political sensitivities of the time. Maps were becoming less solely reliant on their medieval or ancient ancestors and were enhanced using material from portolan charts and the revival of Ptolemy's maps, along with altogether new information to improve the picture of the country.

There were several key cartographic milestones. In circa 1537 a map appeared with the description 'Anglia Figura...', often known as the Cotton Map after its collector (FIG. 12).[9] This map of Great Britain, also anonymous, is seemingly a revised version of the Gough Map. Its depiction of Scotland is an improvement on other derivatives, though Wales and Ireland are still drawn as fairly crude rectangles. It is the best depiction of England itself so far. The map is pioneering in having latitude and longitude scales along the margins and having north at the top, rather than east as had been customary with most earlier maps.

Sebastian Münster's woodcut *Anglia II Nova Tabula* map of 1540 in his *Geographia Universalis*

FIG. 12 The *Anglia Figura*, or Cotton Map, named after its collector, circa 1537, one of the earliest accurate maps of the British Isles. It is anonymous, like the Gough Map from which it is derived, and has cartographic refinements such as latitude and longitude scales in the margin and north at the top.

Hirtha.

North.

9.

Lewissa.

ORCHA
INSVLÆ

Pomona
Verbal

Orchec loquitur ʒ ʒ ʒ in
sub ipecio sestos.

Droax.

Donesbe
prior

61

61

Skia.

Hobrene
prior

Catha
nesia.

Cana.

60

60

Ros
sia.

HEBIDES
SEV

Consim licet
a regia si
Pictenis existit

Jona.

MEVANI
AE INSVLÆ

Salutis post.

Eminis.

Maria.

SCO

Morauia
olim Vierans
dicta.

Mene.

Onst.

Dunbaphana
olim Euonia
Loquu Rognauallis
haberia.

Lorna.

TI

Atho
lia.

Fisa.

S. Andreas

Mare Germanicū

Anglia figura triquetra e
Ciu Longissimū lat̃.Ine ōua
hii et septentrione a s Burien
ad bentū castellū experien
hii circat 4.00 m̃. p̃ sibi
vendicat Lat̃ vero quod ad
austrū conatitur a s buriē ad
douentū. 300 m̃. p̃ occupat Ciu
par e reliquū lat ad oritē expasu
Scotia vero longitudine pace sibi ve
dicat ʒ ed latitudiae longe isecios est

58

58

57

57

West

Est

56

56

Aran

HYBER

Hebanu

Media.

S. Iannis mos.

Drothea.

Lambar.

Aquil

Horte

Aran

Gladn'nios.

Achha.

MARE
HYBER
NICVM

Ma
ma

A

N

N

A

G

L

I

A

NIA.

Comatia.

Lagenia.

Aberfrow.

Desi
mon
ia.

Momonia.

Mare Hyber
nicum

Trule

Bleseu

Kerry

Cocke

Dorsey.

Inissa
S. Michaelis.

MARE BRITANICVM,

Normaoie.

piccatie

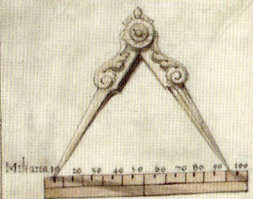

Miliaria 10   20   30   40   50   60   70   80   90   100

was very influential and circulated widely. This also derived from the Gough Map. It has an interesting back story. On a 1522 visit to London, Ferdinand Columbus, the son of Christopher and a significant map collector, bought a map of England dated about 1520 in eight sheets, which is sadly no longer with us. Barber suggests that this may have been the basis for the *Anglia II* map.[10]

George Lily's 1546 map of the British Isles broke new ground as the first printed map of the country from a copperplate engraving and was produced as an illustration of a book about Britain: *Descriptio Britanniae, Scotiae, Hyberniae,...* by Roman bishop Paolo Giovo.[11] As one of the first post-medieval printed maps of the islands not derived from Ptolemy, Lily's *Britanniae Insulae* makes further improvements to the depiction of Scotland, perhaps using work by the Scot John Elder, who had presented a map of Scotland to Henry VIII in 1543, about whom more later (FIG. 13). George Lily was the son of William Lily, who was close to Thomas More and was chaplain to Cardinal Pole, who though a cousin of the king effectively led the Catholic opposition in exile. The prominent Catholic Lily drew this map from his exile in Rome. It is therefore likely that he depended on the work of others, perhaps falling back on the medieval

FIG. 13 *Britanniae Insulae*, a 1558 printing of a 1546 map of the British Isles attributed to George Lily. This makes further improvements in geographical fidelity compared with its predecessors, especially in the depiction of Scotland. This map was produced to illustrate a 1548 book on Britain by Paolo Giovo, a bishop in southern Italy.

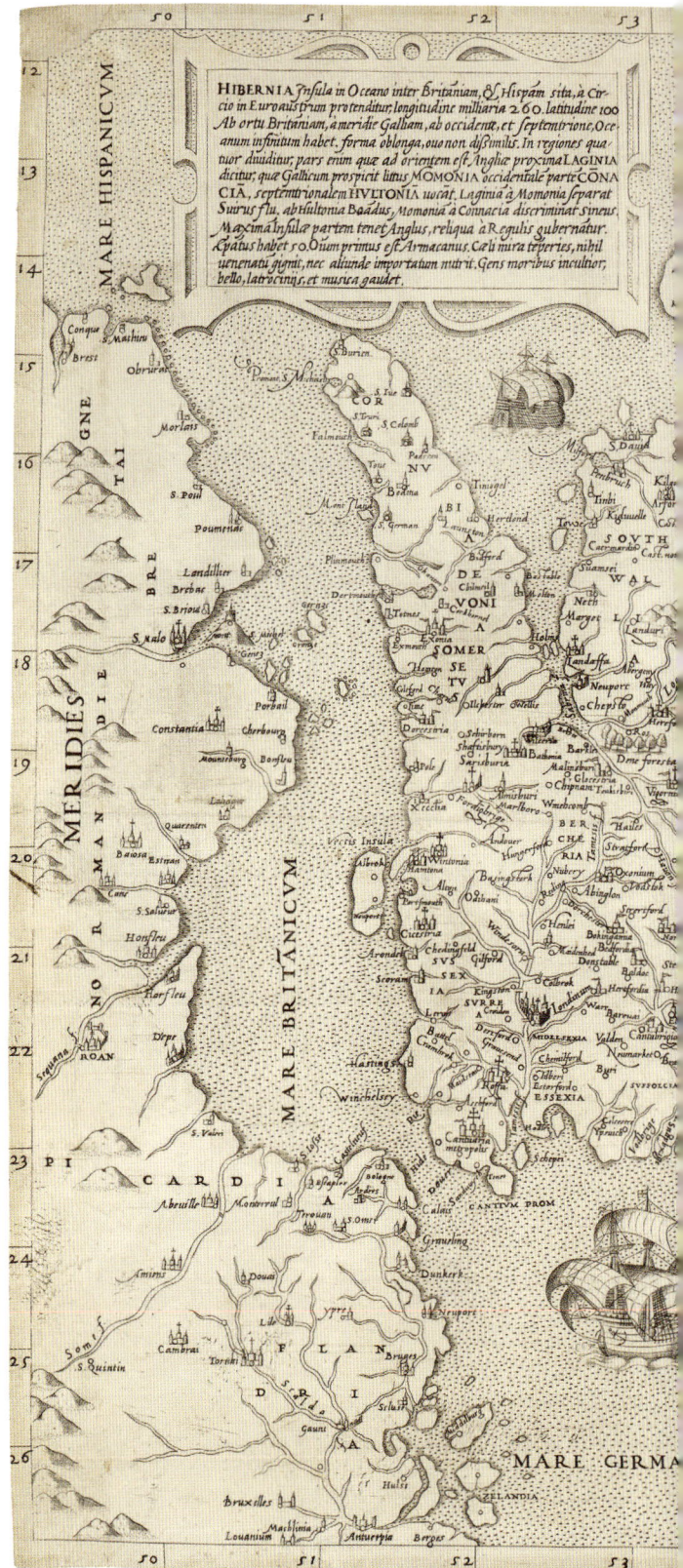

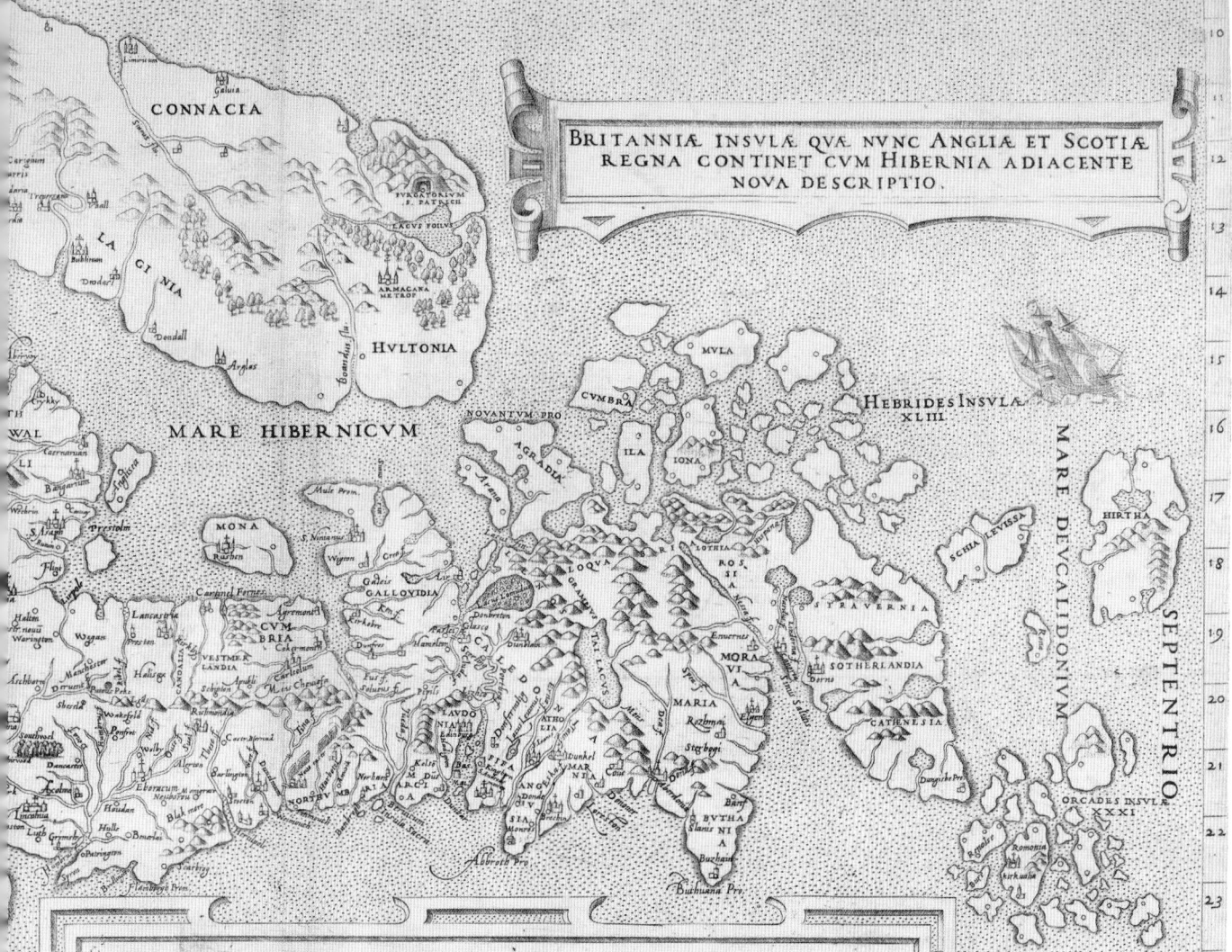

OCEANVS VERGIVIVS

HON SOIT QVI MAL Y PENSE

Sorlinges

OCEA

IRLCONNACHT ANDIA.

Vlster.

Leynster

Mydie

Momonia

Conel

S. Patrici

Quulst:

terter.

OCEANVS BRITANNICVS

MARE HIBERNICVM

Corn.

Devon

Soud Walis

Nort Walis

Herford

Salo pia

Chester

Vigornia

Wallis

Montes

Peke

E. bor.

Notin gam

Nor thum bria

Lauo donia

Merchia

Edenbor.

Lincolne

Norfolk

Suffolk

Ely

London

Middle ton

OXO nium

Barckshire

Hamp ton

Sussex

Kent

Dorset

Somerset

Wiltshire

BRETAIGNE

NORMANDIE

PICAR DIE

OCEANVS GERMA

Milliaria Anglica

Map detail text (within illustration): Hebrides infulę. · DEVCALIDO · NIVS · CVS · Orcades infule · and various place names.

IAE, SCOTIAE, ET HIBERNIAE, SIVE
NNICAR: INSVLARVM DESCRIPTIO.

Britannia omñ infularum Occidentis & Septentrionis maxima & potentiſſ. eſt: cuius potiorem hodie partem Angliam vocamus, ab Anglis videlicet Saxonum gente, quę ſub Valentiniano eam ingreſſa, tenuit. Hęc veteribus Albion dicebatur, ad differentiam, quum reliquę oěs eo tractu Britannicę dicebantur. Ab Occaſu viciniam habet Hiberniam, hodie Irlandiam appellatam; & reginis Anglię ſubditam.

Cum privilegio.

Gough Map as a source where new information was lacking. This reminds us that geographical information gathering and mapping were a collaborative exercise and a cumulative process: a lesson for appraising Saxton's project too. Lily's map recalls the fable of the curate's egg: his map was fresh in parts but rather stale elsewhere.

The accurate picture of Britain took sharper definition with the publication in 1564 of a wall map of the British Isles by Gerard Mercator of map projection fame. The map is huge, measuring about 129 by 89 centimetres, or over a square metre, and is engraved in eight component plates by Mercator himself at Duisburg in Germany. Again, it reveals a mixed picture of progress; there are improvements in the depiction of Wales but the south coast of England is 15 per cent longer than its true length. The great size of the 1564 map allowed inclusion of unprecedented amounts of geographical information, over 2,500 names in all. It was also unsurpassed in accuracy. The Flemish Mercator, by then working in Germany, never visited the British Isles; therefore his survey information was indirect. He claims to have engraved the map under some duress as a favour to a friend, a claim probably reflecting

FIG. 14 Map of England, Scotland and Ireland, circa 1580, from Abraham Ortelius's *Theatrum Orbis Terrarum*. This Bodleian Library exemplar is bound with a copy of *Saxton's Atlas of England and Wales*. Based upon Mercator's 1564 British Isles map, it represents a further advance in the accuracy and detail of depiction of the islands.

political sensitivities across Europe at the time.[12] Mercator tried to distance himself from the project, thinking the map would be perceived as a security risk by the English and an asset to her enemies. It might be handy in planning invasions, for example, by indicating landing places. The actual survey work for Mercator's map was undertaken at royal instigation after 1554 in Mary's reign, probably by John Elder. Mercator tried to appease the then Catholic regime by omitting the new Church of England bishoprics, such as Oxford and Gloucester, created by Henry VIII two decades before, even though they had been reinstated by 1564 when the map was published.[13] Mercator may have thought this omission would appease Catholics. He also depicted obscure royal seats like Copped Hall in Essex, of importance personally to Mary. Saxton may well have learned something from Mercator's politic approach.

THE PERCEIVED NEED FOR MAPS IN ELIZABETHAN ENGLAND

Although they were important cartographic milestones, none of these recent maps showed the component counties of England in separate detail as did Saxton's in the 1570s. The genesis of Saxton's project lay in a combination of long-term trends in technology and taste, and specific circumstances of the mid-sixteenth century. There had been a growing interest in the use of maps by government since Henry VIII's reign, partly attributable to the king's own enthusiasm for maps; he created a climate where mapping was in vogue. We have seen that there was a step change in the quantity and quality of maps of England and its localities in the sixteenth century. This was due partly to technical developments, examined in the next chapter. These advances were part of a virtuous circle with demand for, and interest in, maps promoted by Henry VIII and his ministers and sustained by their Tudor successors. The king had been influenced by Renaissance thinkers like Machiavelli who were keen on maps as a tool of government. English writers like Sir Thomas Elyot, secretary to the Privy Council under Cardinal Wolsey, in his 1531 *The Boke named the Governour* likewise advocated map use to ministers for practical purposes and enjoyment (FIG. 15).

This interest in maps took practical form in the 1530s with Henry's fortification-building programme, necessitated by the threat of invasion. This concern is specifically reflected in the command of February 1539 by Henry VIII, prompted by Cromwell, that expert men from every coastal county view the shores and recommend fortifications where there is a danger of invasion.[14] This led to what Barber calls 'the most extensive government-sponsored cartographic survey to be undertaken before the nineteenth century'.[15] A large number of maps, mainly of coastal areas, were made after 1539 as a result. Many can be found in the Cotton Manuscripts in the British Library, and it is thought that many more once existed than have survived. The new wealth from the dissolution of the monasteries was to

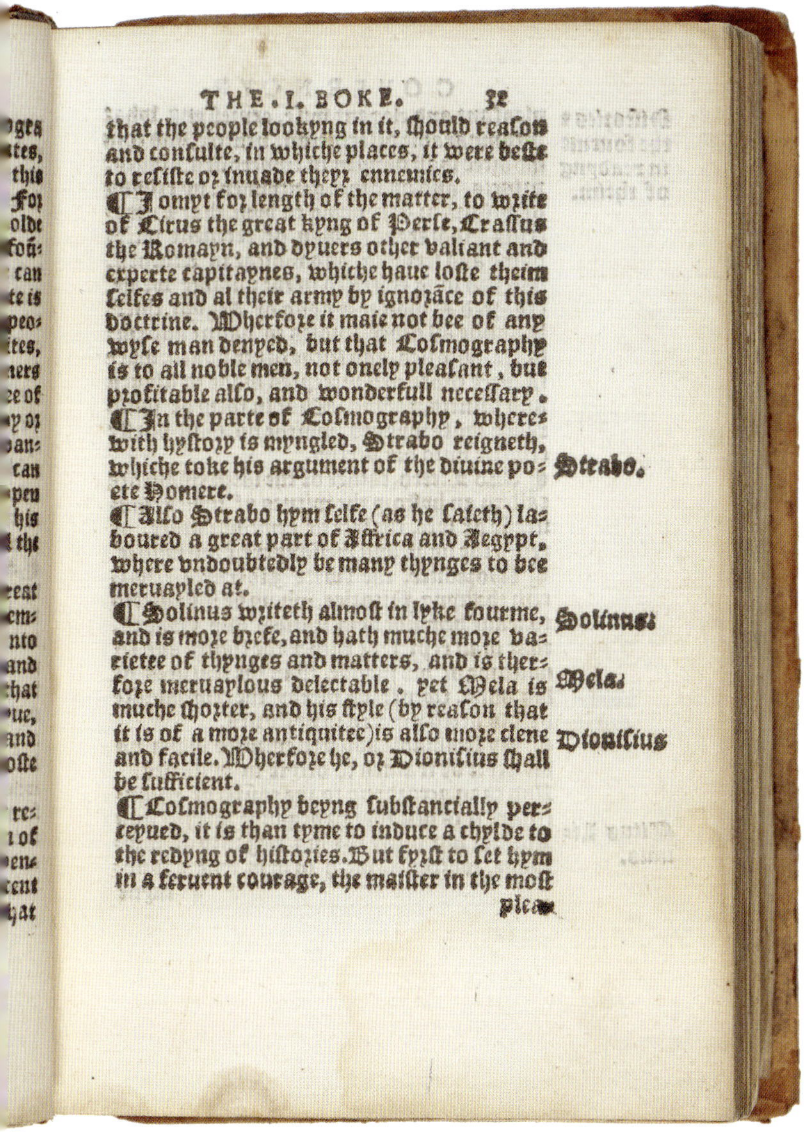

THE. I. BOKE.   32

that the people lookyng in it, fould reafon
and confulte, in whiche places, it were beft
to refifte or inuade theyr ennemies.
¶ I omyt for length of the matter, to wryte
of Cirus the great kyng of Perfe, Craffus
the Romayn, and dyuers other valiant and
experte capitaynes, whiche haue lofte theim
felfes and al their army by ignorāce of this
doctrine. Wherfore it maie not bee of any
wyfe man denyed, but that Cofmography
is to all noble men, not onely pleafant, but
profitable alfo, and wonderfull neceffary.
¶ In the parte of Cofmography, where=
with hyftory is myngled, Strabo reigneth,   Strabo.
whiche toke his argument of the diuine po=
ete Homere.
¶ Alfo Strabo hym felfe (as he faieth) la=
boured a great part of Affrica and Aegypt,
where vndoubtedly be many thynges to bee
meruayled at.
¶ Solinus wryteth almoft in lyke fourme,   Solinus.
and is more briefe, and hath muche more va=
rietee of thynges and matters, and is ther=
fore meruaylous delectable. yet Mela is   Mela.
muche fhorter, and his ftyle (by reafon that
it is of a more antiquitee)is alfo more clene Dionifius
and facile. Wherfore he, or Dionifius fhall
be fufficient.
¶ Cofmography beyng fubftancially per=
ceyued, it is than tyme to induce a chylde to
the redyng of hiftories. But fyrft to fet hym
in a feruent courage, the maifter in the moft
                                         plea=

FIG. 15 Sir Thomas Elyot's 1531 *Boke named the Governour.* Elyot advocated that ministers use maps for government work but also for enjoyment, including vicarious travelling pleasure. This reflected a growing climate of map-consciousness, recognizing the utility of maps for a variety of purposes.

fund these maps, and half of Henry's vast military spending from 1539 to 1547 was on fortifying the coasts of England.

Maps were being called for, or their use may have suggested itself, in other contexts. The 1541 Act in Restraint of Sanctuaries aimed at the curtailment of these places which offered immunity from arrest.[16] Mayors and other trusted persons were to perambulate, or record the bounds of, such places in their environs. Though the Act does not specifically require maps, the town authorities in question must have thought them useful for the task. Such maps had to be sent to the King's Chancery and survive for Norwich and York in the National Archives. Government edicts like this would further spread experience of map use beyond court circles. As a result, Barber concludes that by 1550 maps had become fully embedded as an aid in policy formation and administration.[17]

Many of the educated had also become familiar with maps and their usefulness. By the 1550s many young men had grown up with globes and maps as everyday objects, especially those whose families had court connections. The mental habit was rapidly forming of resorting to a map as an analytical tool for handling any issue with a spatial element. A map could be used to plan, summarize, display and persuade, and people became aware of this potential of maps as a powerful means of argument and influence.

This wave of interest in maps was sustained and amplified after Henry's reign and into the reign of Elizabeth – Saxton's era. Though she was the ultimate patron of Saxton's project, it is not clear whether the queen was herself a particular proponent of maps. Still, the enthusiasm of many around her made mapping likely to flourish.[18] Evidently Roger Ascham used Ptolemy's maps to instruct his royal tutee as a princess. Many of those close to Elizabeth were map enthusiasts. Robert Dudley's house inventories reveal his possession of many maps for display and information. William Cecil had his first appointment as surveyor of lands to the then Princess Elizabeth in 1550, a task calling to mind the map as a tool for this advocate of cartography. Another senior courtier, Sir Francis Walsingham, the queen's spymaster, festooned the galleries of his mansions with maps. The queen's wider circle included men such as John Dee, who gave her advice on navigation and exploration. He was a student of Gemma Frisius, a friend of Mercator and a keen advocate of maps for statecraft, and had contacts with Christopher Saxton later in life. Perhaps surprising to the modern observer is that Dee as an advocate of the progressive science of map-making was also a revered exponent of the seemingly regressive art of astrology, from whom Dudley was to seek advice on the most propitious day for Elizabeth's coronation. Different times indeed!

A FAVOURABLE CLIMATE FOR A MAPPING PROJECT

Alongside this increased interest in maps, a number of favourable circumstances coincided in the sixteenth century to make a detailed large-scale government-sponsored mapping project happen and give Saxton his opportunity. Perhaps of first importance, the administrative needs of the kingdom were an important stimulus to mapping. Many processes of government were modernized under the Tudors. Henry VII, the founder of the dynasty, had done much to place his regime on a sound financial footing. Further administrative reforms came then and in later reigns, of which Thomas Cromwell, from 1534 chief minister to the king, was the driving force. Indeed, the Reformation was a major spur to other reforms. The break with Rome removed an alternative source of sovereignty; power was now concentrated in the hands of one sovereign, the king. Cromwell set up many central government agencies to administer ex-monastic finances, such as the Court of Augmentations in 1536, together with a permanent administrative bureaucracy in Westminster. Such expansion and centralization of government might well have been thought to require maps for local and wider administration. A set of county maps, such as Saxton was to produce, might also serve as a visual tool to promote the idea of a unified realm bringing together all the disparate corners of the country in one atlas.

The state took on new functions or directed that they be provided at a local level. Previously, the monasteries had provided ad hoc poor relief by distributing alms and the like. The dissolution created a hiatus in the amelioration of poverty. In 1536 Thomas Cromwell ordered that poor relief should become the responsibility of the parish. Two years later he further required that all baptisms, marriages and burials be recorded in a book dedicated to the purpose by the parish parson. This was to be the basis of vital registration for the next three centuries. Record-keeping was clearly to be important for the administrators of the Tudor state. Maps duly took their place among the tools with which the state's servants in Westminster recorded and understood the localities under their ultimate jurisdiction.

Beyond civil administration were the imperatives of defence. We have seen that fortification maps were important earlier in the Tudor era. Elizabeth's reign had a constant and heightened air of insecurity, mainly focused on a general sense of a threat from Catholics at home and abroad. There were particular acute episodes around the time of Saxton's mapping commission which gave it more salience. Of course, the break with Rome in 1534 was the most evident starting point for the schism. In 1569 there was a failed Catholic rising in northern England which aimed to replace Elizabeth by Mary, Queen of Scots. The following year, 1570, saw the *Regnans in Excelsis*, Pope Pius V's excommunication

and deposition of Elizabeth. This injunction created a crisis of loyalty for Elizabeth's Catholic subjects, who were urged thereby to kill her. Closely following was the 1571 Ridolfi Plot. Roberto di Ridolfi, a Florentine banker, had also planned to replace Elizabeth with Mary. The plots did not cease. To fend off such a concerted onslaught, good intelligence was vital. A national series of accurate maps was to be an important part of the security toolkit. However, mapping had to be paid for. Although Elizabeth was perennially short of funds and was necessarily highly conscious of how she spent them, the ongoing and intense threat of invasion and internal unrest in the 1560s and the 1570s in the lead-up to Saxton's survey was evidently seen to justify the expenditure needed for a national survey of the country, and especially its coasts.

Indeed, maps became central to intelligence-gathering by the Tudor state. The key triumvirate in these cloaked matters were Cecil, Leicester and Walsingham. They employed spies and agents, such as William Herle, who often accompanied his letters with maps illustrating the point at hand.[19] Though often just sketches, these maps could play a pivotal role in intelligence dissemination as well as raising the profile of a budding agent seeking patronage from the powerful. Herle sent hundreds of letters to his paymasters in the first three decades of Elizabeth's reign, many accompanied by maps showing fortifications, strategic locations and a range of other subjects. Seen alongside the letters, the maps

Ptolomeus

Marinus

Aratus

Strabo

Hipparchus

Polibius

VIRESCIT VVLNERE VERITAS

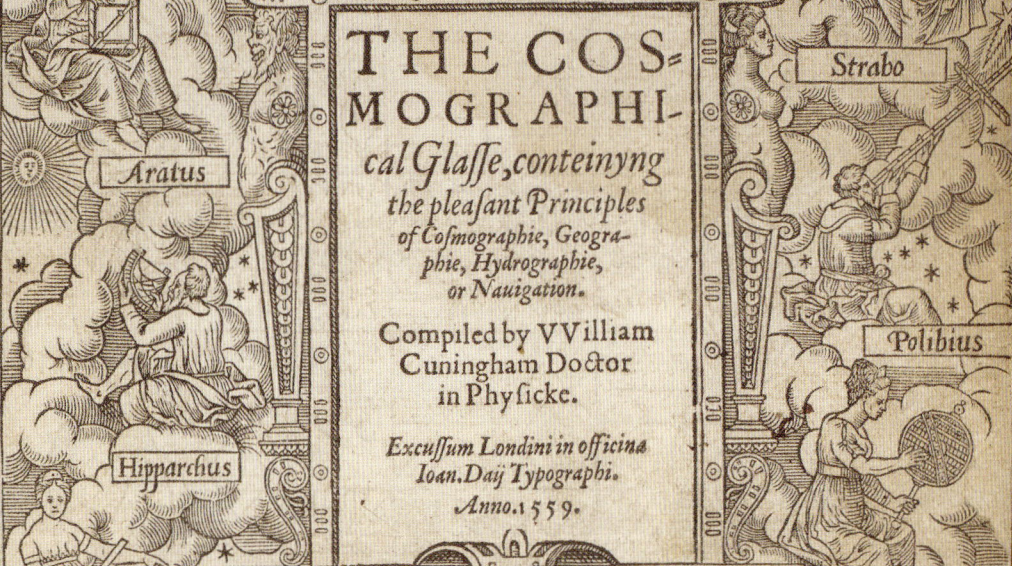

THE COS-
MOGRAPHI-
cal Glasse, conteinyng
the pleasant Principles
of Cosmographie, Geogra-
phie, Hydrographie,
or Nauigation.

Compiled by VVilliam
Cuningham Doctor
in Physicke.

*Excussum Londini in officina
Ioan. Daij Typographi.*
Anno. 1559.

In this Glasse if you will beholde
The Sterry Skie, and Yearth so wide,
The Seas also, with windes so colde,
Yea and thy selfe all these to guide:
What this Type meane first learne a right,
So shall the gayne thy trauaill quight.

Geometria

Astronomia

Arithmetica

Musica

IB F

MERCVRIVS

would convey vital information on diplomatic concerns, military or dynastic strategy and a wealth of other topics to inform Privy Council deliberations. The idea of map use in a variety of circumstances was gaining further traction.

As well as directly practical roles in administration, defence and intelligence-gathering, maps served symbolic purposes, especially through the use of decoration. They were deployed as propaganda for the Elizabethan state and acted as a focus for patriotism. Decoration was not a superficial element of a map, or just used for aesthetic enhancement; it was an important means by which the aims of the map's patrons were realized. An atlas such as Saxton's, with an image of Elizabeth in lieu of a title page, followed by a portrayal of the kingdom as a set of counties with uniform appearance, conveyed a powerful message: the unity of the English state was proclaimed in maps. In being portrayed as a patron of geography, Elizabeth also shows her mastery of it as a tool of image creation. The decorative style of the *Atlas* proclaims England's glory. More generally, the Tudor period was an age of imagery and its conscious manipulation. The first portrait of an English monarch drawn from life in the National Portrait Gallery in London is the first Tudor king, Henry VII.

Maps were also gaining currency at a more intimate scale as a new kind of local plan emerged: the estate map. Property had generally been recorded only by written survey until, as we have observed, the 1570s, when there was a sudden take-off in estate mapping. Indeed, the definition and job description of a surveyor had developed and changed. The traditional estate survey had been the manorial extent, a format first prescribed by statute in 1276. Essentially feudal documents, these terriers or written surveys set out for a lord his income, benefits and obligations, and the services required of his tenants. Much of this non-spatial information simply did not need a map. There was some quantified information about the property, but much of this was based on tradition, estimation and, occasionally, measurement. A surveyor's role was to draw up an inventory of property and make recommendations on its use. The term 'surveyor' was not yet synonymous with map-maker, and a map was rarely the result of the written survey. Maps of landed property only became fairly common, but still far from universal, in the last quarter of the sixteenth century, around the time of Saxton's county mapping. Another kind of local map was the town map. In his 1559 *Cosmographical Glasse* (FIG. 16) William Cuningham produced the earliest surviving printed map of a whole provincial town, a folding woodcut plan of Norwich. Map-making was taking off in a big way.

One word of caution, though, about assuming that using maps would be automatic in past times. To the modern mind all these

FIG. 16 Title page of *The Cosmographical Glasse* by William Cuningham, 1559. Cuningham gives the first account in English of the system of triangulation described earlier in the century by Frisius. The book also includes a map of Norwich, the earliest complete map of a provincial town.

administrative, security and property management considerations would suggest mapping as a useful tool. In spite of the general enthusiasm for maps among the educated classes in Tudor times, the evidence suggests that map-consciousness, the propensity to think in cartographic terms, and carto-literacy are not universal or predictable; they reflect personal choices and precise circumstances. For instance, my study of the estate maps of Christ Church, an Oxford college and cathedral foundation with large landholdings, showed it to be a slow adopter of estate mapping in spite of its economic dependence on its land.[20]

COMPETITORS AND SAXTON'S COMMISSION

The stage was set for Saxton's project, but how would it come to fruition? How did Saxton receive what was essentially a government contract to map Queen Elizabeth's realm? First, the time was right. The 1570s, and just before, was a time of particular cartographic innovation and progress across Europe as a whole. In 1569 Gerard Mercator introduced his eponymous projection, still widely used today. A year later in 1570 the first modern world atlas was published by Abraham Ortelius, the *Theatrum Orbis Terrarum* (FIG. 17) closely followed by the initiation in 1572 of *Civitatis Orbis Terrarum*, the first atlas collection of town plans from across the known world.

Barber draws our attention to several important sixteenth-century regional mapping projects which set Saxton's achievement in perspective and may have served as examples to him.[21] Jacob van Deventer produced wall maps of the northern provinces of the Netherlands from 1536 to 1547, a few decades before Saxton. These were, however, not in atlas form and more importantly did not cover a whole country. Barber also cites Wolfgang Lazius's 'book-sized' surveys of the Austrian duchies in 1561, though these did not appear as one publication.[22] Perhaps the most important precedent Barber notes is Philipp Apian's 1568 printed maps of the duchy of Bavaria at a scale of 1:144,000 or around 2¼ inches to 1 mile. However, Bavaria then was smaller than the German province of today, itself less than half the size of England and Wales. Apian's printed maps of Bavaria did set an important precedent for a detailed map of a whole region commissioned by its ruler: Duke Albrecht V. These were to remain the official maps of Bavaria until the nineteenth century, echoing the longevity of Saxton's surveys. Alonso de Santa Cruz made a map of Spain in twenty sheets at 1:400,000 scale around 1540. These were smaller scale than any of Saxton's county maps and kept in manuscript for security reasons. Saxton was the first to make a printed map at an average scale of a ¼ inch to 1 mile of a whole country and one as large as the Kingdom of England.

FIG. 17 The title page of the 1574 edition of Abraham Ortelius's *Theatrum Orbis Terrarum*, the first modern world atlas, first printed in Antwerp in 1570. This appeared just before Saxton started his survey amidst a flurry of cartographic innovations; an atlas of town plans across the world was soon to follow.

THEA TRVM ORBIS TERRA RVM

Opus nunc denuò ab ipso Auctore recognitum, multisquè locis castigatum, & quamplurimis
nouis Tabulis atquè Commentarijs auctum.

Second, the key individuals were in place. Queen Elizabeth's first minister was Sir William Cecil, later ennobled as Lord Burghley. He was an exceptionally map-conscious individual and was the driving force behind the mapping project which eventually came Saxton's way. By the 1560s Cecil conceived a detailed map of the whole country and was wondering whom to commission. The idea was not new. We know that there was a widely held ambition to make a detailed map of England and its parts as early as 1524, when the German Nicholas Kratzer wrote of such an idea to Albrecht Dürer, his associate.[23] Kratzer was an astronomer and maker of scientific instruments; map-makers were often skilled in cognate areas. He established connections with the English court and by 1521 he was in the service of Thomas More, then treasurer of the exchequer. We do not know of Kratzer's cartographic ambition being realized, but it put a marker down.

Third, there was a range of suitably skilled and experienced contenders for the mapping endeavour. John Elder, mentioned earlier, was a possible early candidate to make a map of England.[24] This colourful figure from Caithness was a map-maker and propagandist. Having been a clerk to the Scottish King James V he was forced into exile in England by 1543 due to his conversion to Protestantism. Soon afterwards he presented Henry VIII with a number of manuscripts, one of which was a map, perhaps the first accurate map of Scotland, for so long crudely drawn as a rectangular afterthought at the margin of maps. In the words of its immodest maker, it showed all the main towns, castles and abbeys together with all ports, lochs and havens. Like many contemporaries, Elder did not confine himself to map-making; another of his manuscripts for Henry was a letter advocating the marriage of Prince Edward to the infant Mary of Scotland, allowing Henry to achieve his rightful destiny as king of both England and Scotland. It seems he had close court connections. In the mid-1550s Elder converted back to Catholicism and propagandized for Mary and Philip. They may have commissioned him to map England.[25] We have seen that word-of-mouth recommendations were very important in the chain of patronage. The senior statesman Sir Nicholas Throckmorton, diplomat and Member of Parliament, recommended Elder to Sir William Cecil as a very able mapper of countries and their coasts. Nevertheless, having been given several ecclesiastical preferments in the Scottish church by the mid-1560s, Elder seems to vanish from history and hence from the circle of available map-makers.

Another contender was John Rudd, whom we have already encountered. From 1561 to 1563, at Elizabeth's request, John Rudd took leave from his clerical duties as vicar and prebendary canon to map the country. Rudd was a keen

FIG. 18 The Nowell–Burghley Atlas of 1564. This extract shows William Cecil, and we may surmise this is to flatter his anticipated patron and persuade him to sponsor a larger mapping project. Cecil is reputed to have taken this pocket atlas around with him on his travels.

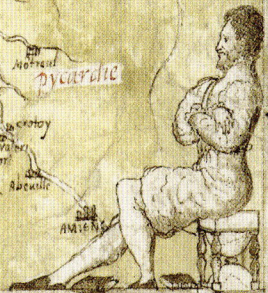

early proponent of maps and in keeping with Renaissance ideals emphasized the importance of original survey rather than compilation of the labours of others or recourse to ancient sources. We learned in the last chapter that he made an original survey at the queen's express wish, but there is no evidence that the work was finished, and the reasons for this are unclear. As his mentor, Rudd was a generation older than Saxton and so was probably out of the running.

In 1563, in the wake of Rudd, Laurence Nowell, a member of Burghley's household, emerged as a contender for the mapping enterprise. Nowell had matriculated at Christ Church, Oxford, and by 1550 was a lector there in mathematics.[26] A noted antiquarian and Anglo-Saxon scholar, he had travelled widely round the country, often with William Lambarde, who shared his interest in its topography. Nowell had become part of Cecil's circle through the personal recommendation of Thomas Randolph, another ambassador under Elizabeth. Nowell appealed in a letter to his new master to commission a similar survey to Rudd's scheme with him as the map-maker. In 1564 Nowell produced a map of the British Isles (excepting northern Scotland) as part of a pocket-sized atlas (FIG. 18); also, surprisingly, containing a map of Sicily. The map of Britain and Ireland included great improvements to the shape of Wales and elsewhere and carried a graticule (network of lines) of longitude and latitude. A blatant sales pitch is suggested by the decoration. A

reclining figure with a barking dog, a perennial hazard for surveyors, seems to be Nowell: the initials *L.N.* appear on the base of the pedestal. At the opposite corner is the seated figure of Cecil on an hourglass, presumably his anticipated patron for a bigger project. It is clear that Burghley used this book, as it bears itineraries in his hand and it is commonly referred to as the Nowell–Burghley Atlas.[27] An ancient but presumably later annotation on a flyleaf reads 'Ld. Burleigh carried this map always about him.' Whether that is true or not, Burghley's strong connection with the atlas is clear. Yet, for reasons which have never been satisfactorily explained, it was not Nowell who was commissioned to map England, county by county. If we assume there was no firm commitment to make the survey until Saxton did so in the 1570s, then it seems that Nowell departed the scene too early. He travelled to continental Europe around 1567 to improve his languages and widen his cultural experiences. The trouble is that by 1571 various attempts at communicating with him from the home country had failed. The beneficiaries of his will were keen to have him declared dead, for obvious reasons. This declaration was made in 1571, and never disproved.

Other candidates for national map-maker existed. The learned mathematician, antiquary and astrologer John Dee, mentioned earlier, was one (FIG. 19). He met Mercator and Gemma Frisius in the Netherlands in 1547 and brought mathematical instruments back to his Cambridge college.[28] Gemma Frisius was a multitalented Dutch polymath who applied mathematics to surveying, improved surveying instruments and pioneered triangulation. Dee made maps with an intricacy and precision that reflected these connections and his scholarly personality. He built up one of the greatest libraries of sixteenth-century England. However, Saxton may have had the edge over Dee, being about fifteen years younger. We may assume that the gruelling task of making a national survey in this era was seen as work for a young man.

There was also Humphrey Llwyd (or Lhuyd), a Welshman who made small-scale maps of England and Wales. Like many contemporary map-makers, he was also a polymath: he wrote medical treatises, studied astronomy and music and was one of the leading antiquaries of his day.[29] Llwyd made a map and description of his native Wales for Abraham Ortelius, the Dutch geographer, to include in his *Theatrum Orbis Terrarum* of 1570, after having met him in the Netherlands. This was a posthumous inclusion though, as Llwyd died rather young in 1568, a few years before Saxton's mapping project.

Reyner Wolfe may also have been considered for the project. Originally a publisher, then a printer, he came over to England from Strasbourg in around 1533. Much of his output was of evangelical and school books, but he did have an interest in topography and maps: owning, annotating and possibly making the 1539 map showing a possible route for Anne of Cleves' journey from Calais to England. Appointed King's Printer by Edward VI, he went

on to be master of the Stationers' Company on several occasions. He was working on a series of regional maps when he died in 1574.

Although there were a number of competitors, the driving force for the project was the highly map-conscious William Cecil. His ennoblement as Lord Burghley in 1571 may have emboldened him to commission more ambitious projects. The crucial intermediary in the mapping project, as it developed, was Thomas Seckford, who held various lucrative posts under Elizabeth, including Surveyor of the Court of Wards and Liveries; Burghley being the Master. It is possible that Burghley had engaged Saxton at the start of the 1570s, but

FIG.19 Portrait of John Dee in a nineteenth-century likeness by William Pengree Sherlock, after an unknown artist. Dee was equally at home with mathematics and astrology. He knew Mercator and Frisius and advised Queen Elizabeth on exploration and navigation.

by 1574 or at the latest 1575, as evidenced by his coat of arms being on the maps, Seckford was employing Saxton to continue the work, and importantly he had the means to underwrite the project as necessary. A financial crisis for Saxton may have necessitated the involvement of this new wealthy patron. A 1574 grant of a lease of land to Saxton compensated him for his charges and expenses, whereas later rewards are for his labour alone. This would seem to imply that Saxton himself was covering the costs at first but may have run out of funds to do so as the survey progressed.

Why Christopher Saxton was commissioned has never been convincingly explained. Like many other things, it probably comes down to a lucky coincidence of circumstances and having the right contacts at the right times. We have seen that many of his competitors had either died or were too old to be considered suitable for the arduous work of a national survey. Christopher Saxton received 'letters' or a commission from the queen on 28 July 1573 according to a notebook by Dr John Favour, discussed later.[30] It seems quite possible that an ageing John Rudd would have recommended his able and youthful pupil Christopher. With this connection, we might suppose that young Saxton already had his foot on a ladder of royal support and patronage.

FIG. 20 Humphrey Llwyd's (Lhuyd or Lloyd) 'Angliae Regni Florentissimi Nova Descriptio' in Abraham Ortelius's *Theatrum Orbis Terrarum*, edition of 1580. This exemplar is appended at the end of a Saxton *Atlas*. Llwyd was a polymath, like many other map-makers of his era.

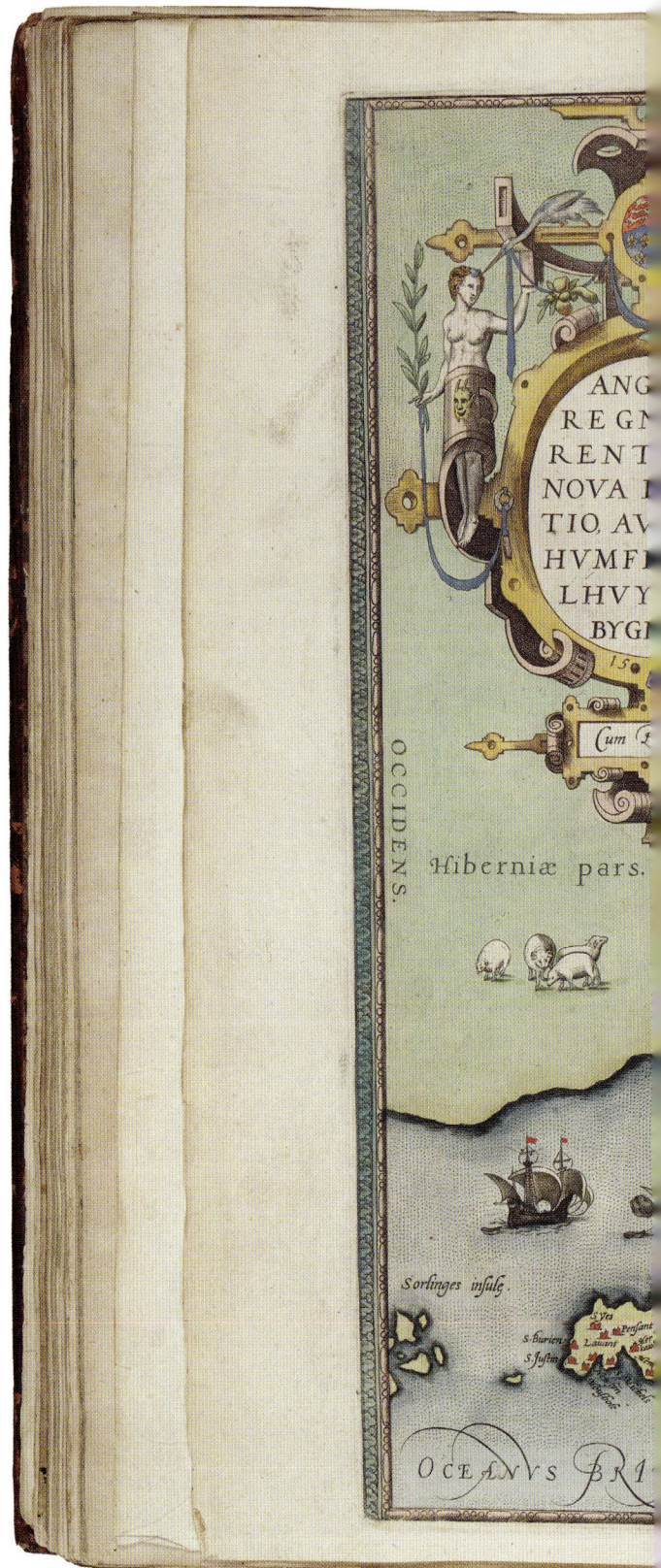

SEPTENTRIO.

Scotiæ pars.

Anandalia

OCEANVS GER

MANICVS

MARE HIBERNICVM.

WALLIS.

ORIENS.

MERIDIES.

Wijght

Scala miliarium Anglicarum.

Wenhaston · Bliborugh · Walderswick · Sowowlde A

Linsted magna · Huntigfeld · Cokeley · BLITHING HV̄

Laxfeld · Cratfeld · Heuenighm̄ · Walpole · Bramfeld

Vppeston · Sibton · Darshm̄ · Thorington · Dunwiche

radbrok · Dilbye · Brundyshe · Dinnygton · Baddinghm̄ · Pesnall · Voxford · Wesselton

arlingworth · Taynyngton · Brusyeard · Fordley · Midleton

Cransforde · Kelsale · Misnere hauen

ersohm̄ · Framlinghm̄ · Swesflinge · Rendshm̄ · Carleton · Theberton · N V S

Ketleborough · Parhm̄ · Glemhm̄ mag · Stratford · Saxmundhm̄

Easton · Glemhm̄ pua · N̄carlefor · Benhall · Sternfeld · Lays ton

ethering · Wickhm̄ · Hacheston · Farnhm̄ · Knatshall · Sisewell

Lishe · PLOMES · Snape bridge · Friston · Thory · Aldringhm̄

Petistrie · Blaxall · Dunnyngworth · Hasillwod

Dalinghoo · Tunstall · GATE HV̄ · Iken · Aldebrough

Ufford · Rendlesh̄ · Wantisden · Chillesforde · Sudburne

Bredfeld · Eyke · Sudburne

Melton · Brumeswall · Butley · Orforde

Hasketon · Sutton · Capell

ding mag · Boyton · Orford hauen · Scala Miliarium

Sekford · WOODBRIDGE · 1 2 3 4 5 6 7 8 9 10

Mertlesh̄ · Shatsh̄ · WILFORDE HV̄ · Hoseley

raue · Waldringfeld · Rammesholt

RLEFORD · Brightwell · Hemley · Alderton

Foxall · Newborne

Buckleshm̄ · Bawdsey

Kirton · Bawdsey hauen

acton · COLNES · Lenigton HV̄ · Falkenhm̄

ton · Trimleis · Felixtow · Walton · PESTIS PATRIÆ PIGRICIES

Shotley · Langerston

Orwel hauen

dsey · Harwiche
uer court

THREE

MAKING THE COUNTY ATLAS

IMAGINE ONE DAY in the early 1570s. Christopher Saxton must have been daunted by the idea that the whole of England lay before him and that he had to capture its form in a map. A great task in any age, it was much more so in a preindustrial and undeveloped, though evolving, country. Most people in England were ill-educated; transport was limited, primitive and inefficient; and the science and technology which underlay mapping was rudimentary, though fast developing, as was the technology of printing for dissemination of the output. As we have seen, the mapping impulse was by no means an automatic one and there was some resistance to any sort of central government investigation, certainly any that involved a surveyor tramping across the land. Would this be a portent of increased or new taxation or some other kind of government meddling?

England (including Wales) has an area of about 37 million acres and so was not small compared with its sixteenth-century European counterparts. The country is elongated, being over 400 miles north to south by about 300 miles west to east at its southern side, though less than 100 miles wide near the Scottish border: a large area of ground to cover. The coast is fairly indented given the country's dimensions, being over 2,700 miles in length. Much of central and southern England is plains and low hills, the remainder being more mountainous, though with much internal variation. The natural face of the country was further varied by human settlement and endeavour. As we have seen, in many areas the open field system still predominated, especially in counties across the middle belt of England. Enormous fields, sometimes of a 1,000 acres, surrounded villages where land was held in strips. However, around the peripheries of this central belt was much early-enclosed land that lay in small compact fields surrounded by hedges or walls. These many and varied kinds of terrain would present diverse challenges to Saxton. There was also a degree of land-use change at this time: woodland was being cleared, enclosures continued and farming was spreading into areas that could be reclaimed from moorland, woods or marsh. Social changes came in the wake of all this: conversion of land use from arable to pasture usually accompanied the enclosure of open fields, and this led to local depopulation.

We have seen that England in the mid-sixteenth century was still an overwhelmingly rural country. Foreign visitors were struck by the greenness of the land – a country of woods, chases, pasture and parks.[1] It was not noticeably more rural than many European counterparts, but its climate made it more verdant. The population of England and Wales is estimated at around 60 million (2022), about seventeen to twenty times the likely population in Saxton's time. The much lower mean population density than today left much room for colonization and expansion. Towns were small and compact and sheltered a small minority of the population, though many more people than lived in them had contact with them from their rural hinterlands.

The country also seems different when we peer below the surface to see how it was perceived. Landscape was seen very differently in Saxton's day; indeed, the term only came to replace 'country' in the 1590s. The very idea

of scenery and an aesthetic appreciation of the wilderness is a more recent one. The late Tudors clearly valued the manicured elegant gardens and parks which were coming into vogue as settings for their new and expanded great country houses. In contrast, areas of forest, moor and waste that lay beyond cultivation were often regarded with fear, or with disdain as areas of little economic value and accordingly were not prized. What Saxton 'saw' was very different from what and how we might see today.

Saxton's England was not a free country in the modern political sense, nor an equal society; characteristics which both constrained and empowered Saxton at the same time. Local sensibilities and the dignity of the Crown loomed ever present. The localities were dominated by the gentry, the nobility and the church. England in those days has been called a community of communities, with a great lord and his officials being the local equivalent of the king and his government.[2] At the same time, armed effectively with a royal warrant to map, Saxton was in a powerful position as he went on his way.

Saxton's task was to map this complex, fairly large country county by county and, arguably, to lend it visual unity. For this purpose, he would make a series of medium-scale maps showing individual settlements and other major landscape features like rivers, hills, parks and forests (though not separate buildings and fields, as would be drawn on the still rare large-scale estate plans). No commission for Saxton survives, and perhaps one was never issued, so we do not know his exact orders, but we can deduce much from the finished product and the various passes and privileges he was given to assist and reward his work.

THE PATRONS

Saxton had royal patronage, but this did not necessarily amount to direct financial support from the Crown. His project was supported by private finance from a courtier, as we shall see. In this case we can identify Burghley's and later Seckford's individual initiative and keenness on maps to explain their production rather than some nebulous impersonal historical forces. Elizabeth's father Henry VIII had inherited a very wealthy Treasury from his father, augmented later by the vast spoils of the monasteries. As we have seen, he was able to pay directly for extensive coastal mapping. In contrast, Elizabeth's funds were more meagre, significantly constraining royal power and largesse. Hence, the Crown's role was to create a favourable environment for map use, both by example in commissioning maps as funds allowed, and more often by encouraging its clients to produce them acting as proxies for the queen.

Royal power was channelled through the queen's principal counsellors, most prominently William Cecil, who became Lord Burghley in 1571 (FIG. 21). He had long been in royal service, working for the Duke of Somerset, Lord Protector, early in the reign of the boy king Edward VI.[3] He administered Princess Elizabeth's properties in the reign of Mary. Cecil was made Secretary of State on the first day of Elizabeth's reign, 17 November 1558, and raised to Lord Treasurer from 1572 until his death in 1598. Whatever formal titles he held, he was always the queen's right-hand man. Though Elizabeth's will could never be taken for granted, Cecil was almost literally the power behind the throne. Indeed, some think he was the model for the king's calculating minister Polonius in Shakespeare's *Hamlet*.

Burghley was an obsessive bureaucrat, working relentlessly in the interests of his country and adopting a methodical and systematic approach to any issue that crossed his desk. He spent long hours annotating state papers and writing memoranda, and it seems he loved collecting facts and compiling lists.[4] Perhaps maps can be seen as a kind of list, information inventoried and organized in a spatial sequence. To a 'control freak', maps may have had a particular appeal in providing an instant graphic view of any issue with a spatial characteristic. The administration of a whole country with the aid of maps was a tempting prospect for Burghley.

As with Christopher Saxton, we know much more of Burghley's work than his personal life. We do know that he was a committed though not overzealous Protestant. Learned from an early age, he was always more a pragmatist than an idealist in politics and religion. If zealous in anything, it was in his commitment to the Elizabethan state and its religious settlement. Everything would be done to protect it. To this end, he worked very closely with Sir Francis Walsingham, the queen's spymaster, who controlled an extensive information network, pivotal to Elizabeth's security (FIG. 22). Walsingham was a fellow map enthusiast, as were many of the important educated people of the time, and, crucially, those close to royal power. We have seen that through Burghley's work and influence, his extensive use of maps – even drawing some himself – became firmly entrenched as a tool of statecraft.

Burghley had motives beyond the practical and aesthetic for favouring map use. He was a propagandist, producing copious tracts, for instance, after the 1569 Northern Rebellion of Catholic earls in favour of Mary, Queen of Scots' claim to England.[5] He wrote covert and open pamphlets warning of the enemy within and aiming to vilify the perceived Catholic threat. Burghley's role as Secretary of State gave him access to, and control of, all state papers. He knew that information was power and he knew how to manipulate that power. Maps were to be a key part of his propaganda toolkit, as graphic images conveying an argument, view or point, potentially subliminally on sight. A map of all England might suggest its territorial integrity, unity, stability and give an impression of uniform sovereignty across the whole country.

Burghley was the most powerful of Elizabeth's subjects. His power came from the trust the queen placed in him, which he amply repaid, and from the many sinecures and other offices he held and could disburse. Burghley was the man that his countrymen went to when they wanted a favour, support in a dispute or lucrative employment. In this era, rewards were frequently not paid in cash or wages, but in the form of land grants, profitable offices, monopolies and other privileges. Saxton was to be rewarded in this way for his map-making. It was necessary to have someone like Burghley behind a project like Saxton's for it to prosper, but he was an extremely busy man charged with the administration of the whole country. It would take an individual patron to see the project through, and importantly to finance it.

This man was Thomas Seckford (FIG. 23), an administrator and barrister, born into the gentry.[6] His family held the lordship of the manor of Great Bealings in Suffolk and had recently rebuilt Seckford Hall there, the family seat since the time of Edward I. Seckford studied at Cambridge, but at which college it is not known, and was admitted to Grays Inn in 1540, a contemporary there of William Cecil. The two men probably kept in contact thereafter. Seckford was called to the Bar and attained the distinction of being Lent Reader at his Inn for a term: a senior barrister of the Inn chosen to lecture on a legal topic for that term.[7] He served as a Member of Parliament from the

FIG. 21 Portrait of William Cecil, Lord Burghley, circa 1588, seated on a mule. Burghley was Queen Elizabeth's right-hand man. As well as being involved with the inception of the work, he took a close interest in Saxton's project, receiving and annotating proof maps as Saxton completed them.

1550s onwards. Clearly, he had become part of the establishment, a senior lawyer or 'man of business', the term used of such professionals. At the start of Elizabeth's reign in 1558 Seckford became deputy chief steward of the Duchy of Lancaster and in the same year one of the two Masters of Requests, serving the Court of Requests, which provided cheap access to justice, especially for the poor. As a Master he assisted the Court's head, the Lord Privy Seal. This Court followed the queen around on her progresses and received poor men's petitions. Seckford went on these excursions and must have learned much of the country from them, perhaps fostering an interest in topography and maps. Seckford also kept close to the queen through travelling with her: valuable proximity for an ambitious man. Although the Court heard primarily the submissions of the poor, its officers had no compunction in profiting from it. Seckford received £100 a year for attending the queen on these royal progresses, and other remunerative and important offices came his way.

Seckford's preferment was possible only with the support and patronage of Burghley. This continuing link between the two men is confirmed by Seckford's appointment in 1579 as general surveyor to the Court of Wards and Liveries under Burghley's mastership. Thomas Seckford was known for his integrity, a rare characteristic in an era where corruption was unremarkable. The contemporary topographer William Harrison greatly praised him for his help and good nature in a dedication in his

FIG. 22 Portrait of Francis Walsingham, circa 1589, attributed to John De Critz the Elder. Walsingham was Elizabeth's spymaster and was one of many of the queen's courtiers who were keen on maps, covering the walls of his residences with them. Walsingham's copy of the Saxton *Atlas* is the only known copy on vellum.

Description of Britain. If Burghley was looking for someone with the personal qualities to see through an ambitious project such as Saxton's county mapping, he needs to have looked no further.

Clearly, Thomas Seckford was a very wealthy man. He had considerable independent inherited wealth judging by his landed assets, swelled in 1575 by inheriting his father's estates. His government roles and offices, as well as his legal career, would undoubtedly have further greatly enriched him. Biographical sources confirm that he had a considerable fortune at his death, in part through his ownership of lands in Suffolk and other counties, and through buying and being granted by Elizabeth valuable land at Clerkenwell, then just outside London. In 1587 he established himself as a philanthropist by getting letters patent from Queen Elizabeth to establish seven almshouses at Woodbridge in Suffolk to relieve the distress and need of the aged, using funds from his Clerkenwell property.[8] This charity and its buildings still exist today. He also improved his house known as Great Place, one of the adornments of Tudor Ipswich, and built himself mansions in Woodbridge in Suffolk and Clerkenwell. Seckford was, therefore, very likely to be able to fund a project such as Saxton's county mapping.

We do not know precisely the chronology of Seckford's role in Saxton's survey; our evidence is mainly circumstantial. It seems likely that Burghley, the initiator of the county mapping, called in Seckford to take it forward at an early stage in the enterprise. It would seem that Seckford was involved at least from 1575, as his coat of arms was included on the proof states of the maps from then. Having taken on the financial burden, quite understandably he would want his armorial bearings on the product, together with those of the queen. Christopher Saxton appears to be cast as cartographic servant; his name only appeared on the proof maps from 1577 when he was granted a ten-year copyright on them. The Tudor social pecking order is ever-present.

THOMAS SECKFORD ESQ.ʳᵉ
Founder of the Alms Houses near Woodbridge in Suffolk.
A Master in Chancery in the Reign of Queen Eliz. lived in Clerkenwell.
Engraved from an Original by Thomas Prattent.

FIG. 23 Portrait of Thomas Seckford, by Thomas Prattent, in a late-eighteenth-century etching after an unknown artist. Seckford was an administrator and barrister, owning properties, including in Suffolk and London, and holding lucrative offices under the Crown. He became the patron for Saxton's project, his coat of arms appearing on the maps.

THE SCIENTIFIC AND INTELLECTUAL BACKGROUND

Just as Christopher Saxton was dependent on patronage and funds for his project, so he was reliant on the developing technology and supportive attitudes to innovations such as mapping. Whilst maps were still not commonplace, we have observed that by Saxton's time there had been a significant recent increase in their production, accuracy and use. Many factors made the uptake of mapping a self-propelling phenomenon. The increasingly literate population of sixteenth-century England created a demand for books and graphic images, including maps. Increasing availability of such maps would tend to enhance map-consciousness and carto-literacy, in turn raising demand and so production of even more maps. Such demand for maps would probably stimulate developments in scientific surveying techniques, thus improving map quality and reliability, and so on in a virtuous circle.

Technical developments in map-making were part of a wider scientific and mathematical revolution of which Saxton and his collaborators were part. Sixteenth-century theoreticians and practitioners referred to a group of kindred disciplines as the 'mathematicalls', a generic term for astronomy, navigation, surveying, gunnery, mensuration and architecture.[9] Some mathematicians of the day acted as self-appointed advocates of the practical utility of such mathematically related disciplines. They went into print to advance these ideas, and their number included some writers of surveying texts which recommended a mathematically based approach to map-making; specifically depending on arithmetic and geometry. Such a public-relations exercise was necessary, as to many contemporaries the mathematical arts were seen as tedious, self-contained and self-indulgent, as well as just too difficult for many to master. Worse, some regarded mathematics as somehow connected in a nebulous conspiracy with Catholicism and its alleged occult and superstitious practices in this time of religious strife.

Scientific work was also challenging established knowledge. For instance, in 1576 Thomas Digges published *A Perfit Description of the Cælestiall Orbes,* giving the first published account in English of Copernicus's thesis of a heliocentric system. This reversed the medieval notion that the Sun and all heavenly bodies revolve round the Earth, and proved Aristotle mistaken. Such revolutionary challenges to established learning reflected empiricism, the view that knowledge should be based on sensory experience, taking hold among natural philosophers, as scientists were then known. Tastes in mapping were changing to reflect these scientific and intellectual developments. Scale and geographical fidelity based on direct observation shifted the emphasis to practical utility. These were becoming the standards of excellence in map-making, though decorative and symbolic elements were still evident. This is the intellectual underpinning of Saxton's county-mapping enterprise.

SURVEYING TECHNIQUES AND TEXTS

Until the early sixteenth century the most commonly used method of collecting information for regional maps was the itinerary, or list of places written in the sequence of a journey. The prime exemplar is the circa 1250 map of Britain by Matthew Paris showing pilgrims how to get to Dover en route to Rome (FIG. 24).[10] Such a method was not suitable for Saxton's project to compile detailed county maps. A more scientific approach was to make maps from detailed calculation of latitude and longitude. Anthony Ascham, brother of Roger Ascham, the then Princess Elizabeth's tutor, made some maps in this way in the 1520s, apparently using data from Ptolemy's *Geography*, and included the maps in a manuscript on astronomy. However, this method needed more observations than were usually available, was costly, and relied on significant mathematical knowledge and skill.[11]

The relatively new method in Saxton's time was triangulation, as mentioned in the last chapter. This is simple in conception but requires skill, accurate instruments and an understanding of the revived Ancient Greek geometry of Euclid. The technique depends on the accurate construction of a measured baseline and then measurement of accurate angles from its ends to a third point which completes the triangle. Triangulation, therefore, uses

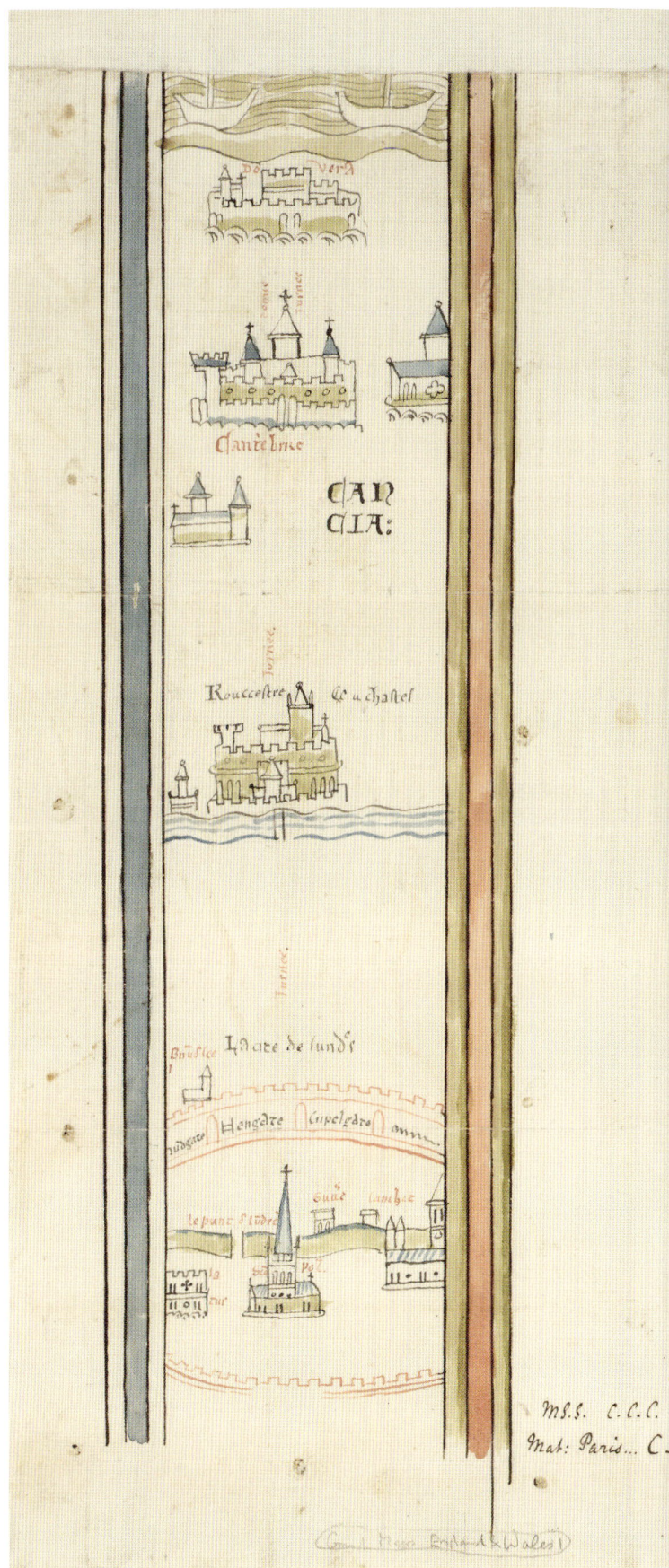

FIG. 24 Section of Matthew Paris's *Itinerary*, covering the journey from London to Dover, from a later manuscript copy of an original of circa 1250. An itinerary was a list of places forming a simple linear route map, a common predecessor of detailed surveyed maps of the wider landscape.

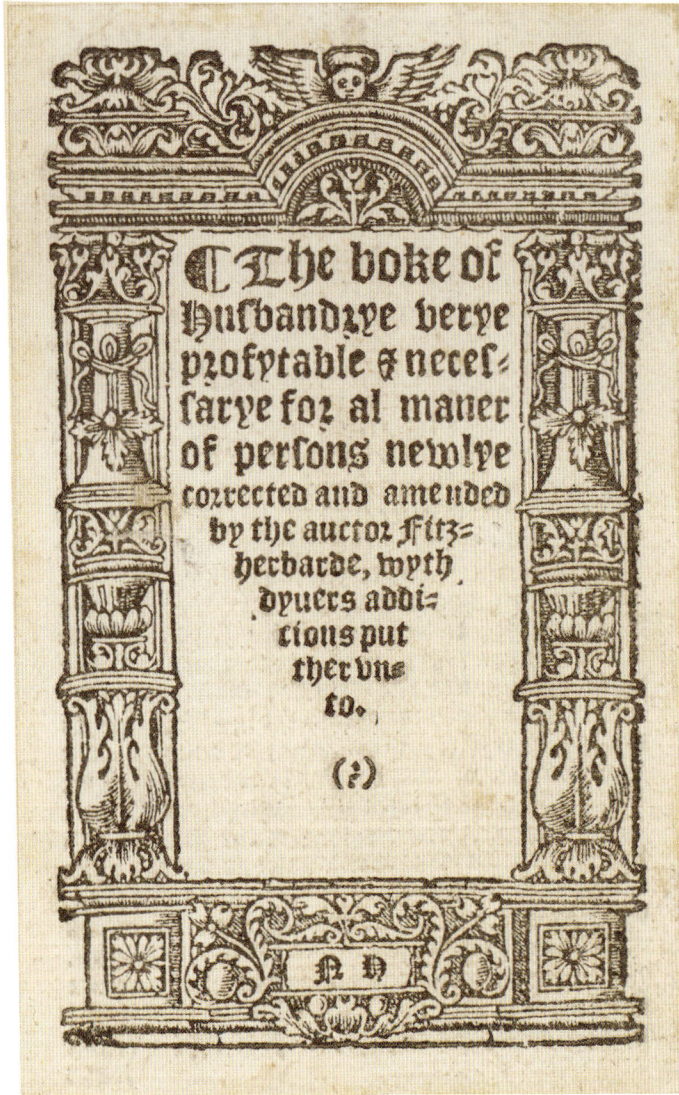

trigonometrical functions by which the sides of a right-angled triangle may be worked out when one side and two angles are known. This process is extended to a large array of triangles to cover the area to be mapped, putting a premium on accurate distance calculation, angle measurement and trigonometry, but not requiring any external information such as longitude or latitude. It is thus a self-contained exercise, though requiring mathematical knowledge and aptitude.[12] Triangulation was developed and advocated by the Dutch polymath Gemma Frisius in his 1533 *Cosmographia*. William Cuningham in his 1559 *Cosmographical Glasse* gave the first English-language account of Frisius's system. Trigonometric surveying using triangulation was greatly to boost the quality and quantity of sixteenth-century map-making.

In the later part of the sixteenth century treatises on surveying started to describe and advocate such scientific methods for mapping, especially triangulation, reflecting the changing expectations of surveying as synonymous with map-making. We may get some idea of how Saxton proceeded from the various treatises and textbooks on surveying available at the time, such as that by Cuningham. We have observed that in this period there was a gradual change in the role of a surveyor from mere oversight

FIG. 25 The title page of John Fitzherbert's *The Boke of Husbandrye*, 1547. Early texts like this and his earlier *Boke of Surveying and Improvements* treated surveying in the traditional sense of land management as understood at the time, without a measured cartographic survey.

FIG. 26 The title page of *A Geometrical Practise, named Pantometria*, published in 1571 by Thomas Digges posthumously for his father Leonard Digges. This small book could be taken into the field and was aimed at convincing practitioners of the merits of a scientific approach to map-making.

A GEOMETRICAL

Practise, named PANTOMETRIA,

diuided into three Bookes, *Longimetra*,

Planimetra and *Stereometria*, containing Rules manifolde
for menſuration of all lines, *Superficies* and *Solides*: With
ſundry ſtraunge concluſions both by inſtrument
and without, and also by Perſpectiue glaſſes, to
ſet forth the true deſcription or exact plat of
an whole Region: framed by *Leonard*
Digges Gentleman, lately finiſhed
by Thomas Digges his
ſonne.

Who hathe also thereunto adioyned a *Mathematicall* treatiſe of
the fiue regulare *Platonicall* bodies, and their *Metamorphoſis*
or transformation into fiue other equilater vniforme
ſolides *Geometricall*, of his owne inuention, hi=
therto not mentioned of by any *Geometricians*.

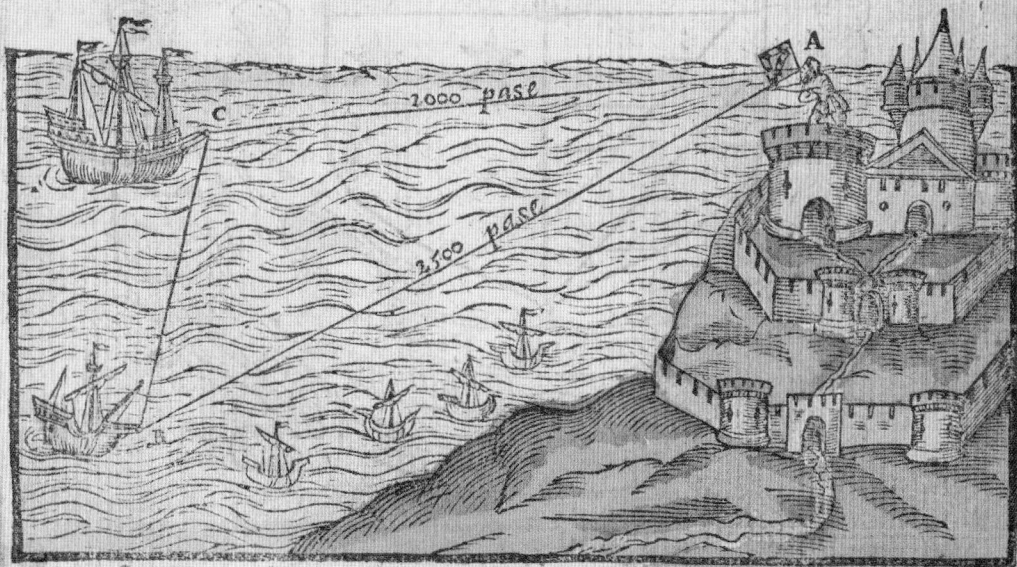

Imprinted at London by Henrie Bynneman.
ANNO. 1571.

of the lands and boundaries of an estate to the incorporation of cartography, usually using scientific instruments. Early surveying textbooks reflected this original priority. For instance, John Fitzherbert's 1528 *Boke of Surveying and Improvements* treated surveying in the old sense, without recourse to a measured cartographic survey. His book was concerned with giving advice to overseers of manors and land stewards. Even though this included setting out the boundaries of landholdings, there was no mention of map use. Similarly, Richard Benese in his 1533 *This boke sheweth the maner of measurynge of all maner of lande...* does not advocate cartography for the purpose. Although these surveying treatises concerned detailed local surveys, their message would also influence contemporary makers of maps at regional scales in the early part of the sixteenth century. The map had not yet come of age.

In contrast, working later in the century, Saxton was emphatically the new kind of surveyor: primarily a maker of maps. Just before his time, surveying texts like Leonard Digges's 1556 *A booke named Tectonicon, brieflie shewing the exact measuring, and speedie reckoning all manner of land...* were advocating maps as the finished product of a survey and explaining how to make them. Digges's third chapter is entitled 'Howe to measure all maner of triangled lande' using diagrams and text. In 1571, just before Saxton started his county survey, Thomas Digges published posthumously his father's *A Geometrical Practise, named Pantometria* (FIG. 26). Leonard Digges died when Thomas was thirteen, after

which he became a ward and pupil of John Dee and later became a leading Copernican astronomer.[13] Saxton moved in the same scientific world and it is highly likely he was familiar with Leonard Digges's work. Indeed, Digges's books were intended for widespread use and not mere ornament. Unlike the large gilded, decorated and expensive tomes, often in Latin, which graced the shelves of a gentleman's library, Digges's works were aimed at utility and convincing practitioners of the value of a scientific approach to map-making. His books were small enough to take into the field. They served as instruction manuals on the assembly and use of scientific surveying instruments. In the preface to *Tectonicon*, Digges states that, unlike large elegant library books, his is not 'locked up in straunge tongues', such as Latin.[14]

Contemporaneously with Saxton's survey, in 1577 Valentine Leigh wrote *The Most Profitable and Commendable Science, of Surveying of Landes...* advocating the commercial value of surveying, as well as promoting its technical aspects (FIG. 27). Leigh annexes a treatise on measuring lands which gives an account of triangulation with diagrams showing a range of worked examples. Although mainly directed at large-scale estate mapping, the advice was applicable also to medium-scale mapping like Saxton's.

FIG. 27 A page from *The Moste Profitable and Commendable Science, of Surveying of Landes...*, published by Valentine Leigh in 1577. In this book, Leigh both advocates scientific methods of surveying and provides a practical guide to them; this page shows triangulation instructions.

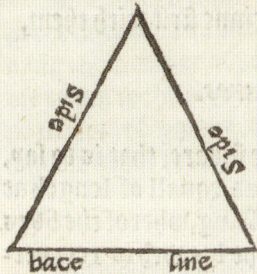

Ut before I enter into the declaratiō of any exāples, I must first enforme you, That whē any line (which cutteth any side of a Triangle oz suche like euen crosse) maketh the thinge it deuideth, like vnto a Carpenters squire, I do alwaies tearme, suche a line to fall, light, oz hit, squierwise. And I name that line, the depēding line, and sometime I call it hereafter, the whipped line, because I haue fourmed it, in all the Figures like a littell whipcozde, that by suche difference ye may know it from the other lines, being also the principall wozker foz the learning of all quantities . And that side oz parte of euerie thzee cornered oz triangled peece of Lande, whiche the saide dependyng oz whipped line cutteth, to bee called the base line. And note also euery peece of Lande is named a Triangle, when it hath oz is supposed to haue only thzee corners oz angles, and thzee sides, whether the sides be equall oz not: and likewise they be called squares , that haue foure sides oz foure corners, whether they differ in widenes oz not.

Note also that howsoeuer your péece of lande be fourmed oz fashioned, be it square oz partly square, rounde oz partly rounde, triangled oz partly triangled, oz a hill mountyng, oz a valley descending (of some of al which figures ye shall hereafter see examples) Yet alwaies must suche peeces of Lande whatsoeuer it bee, bee reduced into one certaine bzeadth and one certaine length , oz els it can neuer bee collected oz summed into a perfecte contente oz number of Acres , and other odde quantities . The findyng out of whiche Lengthes and Bzeadthes, my examples ensuyng shall thzoughly shewe you.

¶ The firste Rule, called the Rule of Squares.

Now because the euen Squares bee the easiest to be measured

SURVEYING INSTRUMENTS AND THEIR MAKERS

Scientific surveying needed a ready supply of instruments, and books such as Leonard Digges's posthumous 1571 *Pantometria* promoted a range of these for the specialist surveyor. These included a vertical quadrant to measure heights, and a circular plate divided into degrees with a centrally mounted alidade: a sighting device to determine direction. The latter he termed 'theodelitus', an early theodolite which Digges is credited with inventing. He also refers to the creation of an 'instrument topographicall' combining several instruments as of such perfection that it would serve for all kinds of mensuration.

The practical realization of the idea of a theodolite had been a scientific ambition for much of the sixteenth century (FIG. 28). In Saxton's time, simple versions had been developed and were becoming available. The basic theodolite is a portable surveying instrument used for precise measurements of angles between chosen visible points. For the early versions this meant horizontal angles only. This simple theodolite had a circular plate divided into 360 degrees and a rotating alidade to determine directions. This metal alidade would have apertures at either end for sightings. The instrument

FIG. 28 An Altazimuth Theodolite, an early theodolite of 1586, signed by Humfrey Cole, lent by St John's College, Oxford, to the Museum of the History of Science, Oxford. Theodolites were state-of-the-art surveying technology in Saxton's day, and it is likely, though not certain, that he used one.

would be fixed to a tripod with adjustable legs. Telescopes were later added, but not known until 1608.

The plane table is a device simpler than a theodolite, but far more commonly used in Saxton's time. First mentioned in the mid-sixteenth century, though probably having older origins, it was originally termed a 'plain table' for its simplicity. It is a flat wooden board mounted on a tripod, with a detached alidade or sighting rule. For orientation, a compass is used on the side of the board. Paper is fixed to the board so that plotting can be done directly in the field rather than back at the office. Lines of sight are drawn to distant features to be mapped. The plane table is then taken to the next surveying point and the distance is measured with a chain and the position is drawn at scale further along the sight line. Subsequent positions can be calculated using triangulation or another traverse.

This graphical method avoids the need to measure the degrees of angles. However, Thomas Digges in the posthumous 1591 edition of his father's *Pantometria* saw the plane table as inferior to the theodolite, the former being an instrument only for the unlearned and ignorant with no knowledge of numbers.

For this reason, those 'ignorant' surveyors valued the plane table for its simplicity in requiring minimal mathematical skill, as well as being relatively cheap and easy to set up and use. In practice, and with less purist sensibility, many surveyors used plane tables and theodolites alongside each other as appropriate.

Scientific map-making stimulated a market for the production of instruments, ensuring their availability for map-makers. The trades were often interlinked. Thomas Geminus, an early printer of copperplate maps in England, also made surveying instruments. Engraving was needed both for printing and for showing calibrations on instruments, so it was a transferable skill. Probably the first and most prominent English instrument maker in Saxton's day was Humfrey (or Humphrey) Cole, who was also an engraver of dies for stamping coins at the Royal Mint.[15] Furthermore, he made and sold surveying instruments from his house near the north door of St Paul's Cathedral in London, probably to augment his income from the Mint, which he claimed was insufficient. Cole was versatile in his skills, making a map of Palestine in 1572 to illustrate Archbishop Matthew Parker's *Bishops Bible*, perhaps to advertise his instrument-making skills. Cole was a prolific instrument maker: even today, twenty-six of his instruments survive, including theodolites, astrolabes, compasses and quadrants. We do not know if Saxton used Cole's instruments or similar, but he must have been influenced by the growing profusion of such technology.

We know that Saxton was in contact with John Dee, who in 1570 wrote his *The Mathematicall Praeface to Elements of Geometrie of Euclid*, where he sets out the value of the mathematical arts and skills. He refers to land measuring as

'geodesie', saying how much wrong and injury has been done by untrue measurement and surveys of lands. Indeed, Dee claims that the difference in value between the inadequate and the good surveys made would pay in perpetuity for two mathematical readerships, one in Oxford and one in Cambridge.[16] This attitude that maps should meet a clear standard was evidently well ingrained by 1582 when Edward Worsop wrote, just after Saxton's *Atlas* was published, *A discouerie of sundrie errours ... committed by lande-meaters...* The extensive full title of this volume continues: 'Euery one that measureth land ... is not to be accounted therefore a sufficient Landmeater, except he can also prooue his instruments, and measurings, by true Geometricall Demonstrations.'[17] The term 'landmeater' is derived from the Flemish for surveyor: probably because so many map-makers, instrument makers and engravers came from there.

SAXTON'S SURVEYING PRACTICES

So, how did Saxton survey his county maps? The answers have to be found mainly from circumstantial evidence: he left no working papers or instruments. We may assume that Saxton read and was influenced by most of the contemporary surveying treatises mentioned. Although Sebastian Münster in the 1550 edition of his *Cosmographia* advocated that all surveyors' measurements should be taken by triangles, his advice was not necessarily followed.[18] Some notion of Saxton's working practices may be deduced from his maps and the common working practices of the time. The best evidence we have suggests that Saxton did use triangulation. It has been convincingly argued by Ravenhill that he could have relied on the national network of beacons as survey-ing stations.[19] This network was developed for state security, and access to such sites, though carefully controlled, would have been given to Saxton as his work was deemed to be in the national-security interest and was state-commissioned. Any surveyor needed help from people with local knowledge, and the watchers at these beacons could have directed his open sights with his theodolite to known neighbour-ing beacons, making an unfamiliar landscape intelligible to Saxton. Ravenhill finds from his sample counties of Devon and Cornwall that both had a sufficient density of beacons to allow triangulation and suggests this finding could reasonably be extended nationwide. It seems likely that triangulation from inter-visible beacons would have made it possible to plot towns and villages and other features, and complete the survey in the time Saxton took. This time was, incredibly, probably only five summer seasons, meaning an average of less than one month to map each county.

It is also possible that Saxton used the traverse method in combination with triangu-lation. Unlike triangulation, traverse means literally crossing the ground to make the survey. This is the older tried and trusted ap-proach using a compass and a length measurer like a pole, as well as a 'waywiser': a device used to measure distance travelled on foot, such as a pedometer. In a traverse, distances are measured from one point to the next, though errors can obviously accumulate. The traverse method is time-consuming and so it must have been used selectively. Saxton did not map any roads, and yet in traversing would often have needed to use them. Perhaps the prominence of rivers on his maps not only reflects their relative importance as a means of transport but may indicate that Saxton used them as survey routes.

Whilst the theodolite was the instrument of choice for the scientific surveyor in Saxton's day, it is not clear whether he used one. They were available and being made and used in England in the late sixteenth century, and with a rich patron like Seckford a theodolite would be affordable. Given that he was working, indirectly, for the queen, surely Saxton would want to show he had used state-of-the-art technology? Saxton, through Dee, was connected to a network of scientific surveying enthusiasts. John Dee met Gemma Frisius in Louvain in 1547 and brought back surveying books to his house in Mortlake in 1551.[20] Digges used Dee's library there to write his 1556 *Tectonicon*. Dr William Cuningham was at Cambridge on Dee's return there and says he brought scientific instruments, which may have included a theodolite. Dee probably inspired these men to innovate, and this spirit is likely to have influenced Saxton too.

At a literally down-to-earth level, we should remember that hands-on land surveying and mapping in the field were especially hard physical work in Saxton's day. Philipp Apian was only in his twenties when undertaking measuring work across Bavaria in the 1550s to produce his survey of the whole province, in some ways comparable to Saxton's.[21] This survey took seven years but was restricted to the suitable summer seasons. Mercator was in his fifties in 1563 when he undertook his measurements in Lorraine, but it all proved too much for him and he never did any more outdoor work, sending his sons and grandsons in his place.[22] Travelling around in the sixteenth century was arduous and could also be dangerous, with villains of diverse kinds lying in wait for unsuspecting and unfamiliar travellers. England was densely populated in some parts and had complex landscapes; all these factors provided more difficulties for the measurer of lands. All in all, it was as well that Saxton was still in his thirties when he mapped the kingdom.

OTHER MAPS, OTHER DOCUMENTS?

How did Saxton complete his surveys so quickly? Actual observation was almost certainly only part of Saxton's data. Much other information was already available to guide him around the counties and to help him compose his image of the country. One problem in assessing Saxton's sources is the poor survival rate of maps. Map historians agree that the majority of sixteenth-century maps are no longer with us and so we must allow the likelihood that rather more detailed data may have been available to Saxton in the 1570s than are extant. Such information, cartographic or written, may have needed only to be verified rather than surveyed anew.

Of the maps we know today, there were accurate maps, recent in Saxton's time, as has been seen, but there were none anything like as detailed or comprehensive as Saxton's, which show almost every settlement, usually by its spiritual and social centre: the church, as well as a range of significant landscape features like rivers, bridges, hills, parks and woods. Existing maps provided skeletal outline information at most and only for some areas, often mainly along the coasts, though at least he would arrive in an unfamiliar county with the head start of a general cartographic framework.

Several slightly earlier maps may have served this purpose. The 1564 map of most of Britain by Laurence Nowell was much too generalized to have provided more than outline data. Its small scale only permitted a handful of places to be shown. Nowell also produced a set of thirteen schematic maps of England showing generalized outlines of the coast and far fewer settlements than Saxton. Mercator's 1564 map of the British Isles similarly shows only a few names and county labels, and it is thought that some of Mercator's information is taken from Rudd's unpublished surveys. Since Saxton was Rudd's apprentice, a common thread of information is likely.

As we have seen, a series of maps depicting parts of England's coasts and planned fortifications made from 1539 survive in the Cotton Manuscripts in the British Library. An example is a plan for the fortification of the north coast

of Somerset from the early sixteenth century. Also, from 1574 there is a plan of the Isle of Sheppey, and earlier in the century a map of a proposed fort at Harwich. Many more examples could be given, but all are coastal or near coastal area maps and would not have served Saxton in England's hinterland. Furthermore, many of these maps were made for defensive purposes and so are either very small-scale and limited in topographic detail or very large-scale and focusing, for example, on a single planned fortress in detail, and so were of little use for comprehensive county surveys of the whole country. Saxton may have had access to some other detailed regional maps. In the Burghley Atlas is a map of County Durham by John Rudd made in 1569. We know that Saxton was his apprentice and so he was possibly involved in making this map. Overall, however, it seems most probable that existing maps were just a starting point and that much of Saxton's cartographic information was primarily sourced.

Saxton would complement existing maps as sources with written topographic surveys and accounts. As well as offering a contemporary travelogue, these presented much of antiquarian, historical and archaeological interest as though the past and present were all one. The first notable English exponent was John Leland, who wrote many volumes of *Itineraries*, the original manuscripts being now in the Bodleian Library (FIG. 29). Leland, a poet and an antiquary, was concerned to preserve books that were rapidly being dispersed as a result of the dissolution of the monasteries.[23] It seems he made about five journeys around the country in the 1530s and 1540s, sometimes making distance measurements and maps along the way and consulting local people and documents for topographic information. His itineraries were published by others after his demise, and it seems highly likely that Saxton would have found in them a useful source of data as well as an inspiration for a national survey.

Mirroring cartography, antiquarianism, a strong element in topographies, was becoming more rigorous and empirically based in Saxton's era. It was similarly harnessed to an agenda of patriotism and the promotion of a national iconography, evident in contemporary mapping, most notably Saxton's county maps. It seems that Elizabethans had greater awareness of their place in history than their medieval ancestors: that they were, and knew that they were, fundamentally different from them. This also brought to mind a sense of a world lost, a sense that prompted some contemporaries to rescue and record as much of its material and documentary evidence as they could. Perhaps this prompted Saxton and others to record a fast-vanishing landscape. Leland's work encouraged others such as

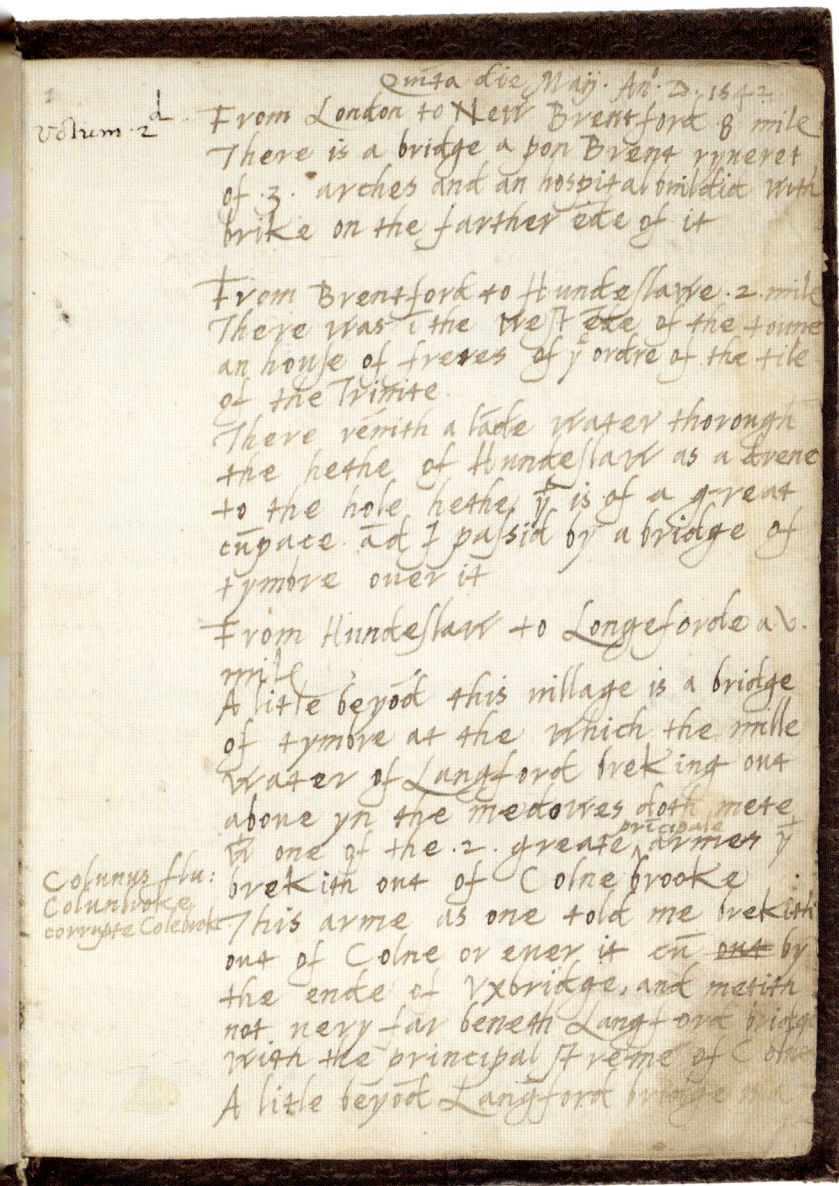

FIG. 29 A page from John Leland's *The Itinerary of England and Wales*, describing the Brentford area in Middlesex, dated 1542. Leland, the poet and antiquary, travelled extensively around the country in the 1530s and 1540s collecting and recording detailed topographical information. His *Itineraries* are likely to have been among Saxton's sources.

William Lambarde, whose 1576 *A Perambulation of Kent* was the first individual county topography. In 1577 Raphael Holinshed's *Chronicle of England, Scotlande and Irelande* appeared, incorporating William Harrison's *Description of England*, incidentally an important source for Shakespeare in writing his history plays. These topographies were being published at the very time of Saxton's survey and it seems highly likely he would have drawn on them.

As well as topographic information, these antiquarians are thought to have used maps, now lost, which Saxton may also have had access to. Lambarde inherited many of Nowell's maps and drew maps himself to prepare his *Topographical Dictionary of England* in the late 1560s and 1570s. It is also thought that maps made by the printer Reyner Wolfe for Holinshed's *Chronicles* may have been available to Saxton.[24] It is clear that by the 1570s, although Saxton was prominent among them, work was being done by several men on the mapping of England, its topography and antiquities.[25] There was probably a symbiotic link as collection of topographical information would quite probably suggest its graphic presentation in map form, and such maps might further inspire explorations of local topography and antiquities.

THE CHRONOLOGY OF SAXTON'S SURVEY

Our first clues as to the order of Saxton's county mapping come from the sequence of his engraved maps. It seems likely that he proceeded county by county; this was the main unit of local administration and social and sentimental affiliation. It would be the easiest basis to organize the work as county authorities from lord lieutenants downwards would be called upon for assistance and permission for Saxton to enter land. We can assume that Saxton worked in logical progression through the counties, going from one to its next neighbour. This sequence could be interrupted by prior needs of military security, so that a county thought more at risk by foreign invasion might be mapped earlier, out of turn. Such a sequence makes sense when we look at the order of maps suggested by the date of engraving. Maps would probably be engraved in the order that they were surveyed, this being soon after fieldwork and plotting had been completed.

Saxton's first county map was of Norfolk, printed in 1574. This was closely followed that year by a combined map of Oxfordshire, Buckinghamshire and Berkshire, suggesting a focus on eastern and midland England. Attention moved in 1575 to some southern counties and Suffolk, the East Anglian neighbour of Norfolk, and the home county of the project's patron Seckford. Then came counties such as Devon, Dorset, Hampshire, Sussex and Kent, which with their English Channel coasts may have

FIG. 30 Map showing the progress of Christopher Saxton's county mapping based on the dates on his maps. It is assumed that engraving and publication followed fairly swiftly after survey. All English and Welsh maps were issued between 1574 and 1578, and the *Atlas* first came out in 1579. Note: The Northumberland map is undated, its date inferred from its neighbours.

Progress of Saxton's survey
(dates of map publication)

▦	1574
▦	1575
▦	1576
▦	1577
▦	1578

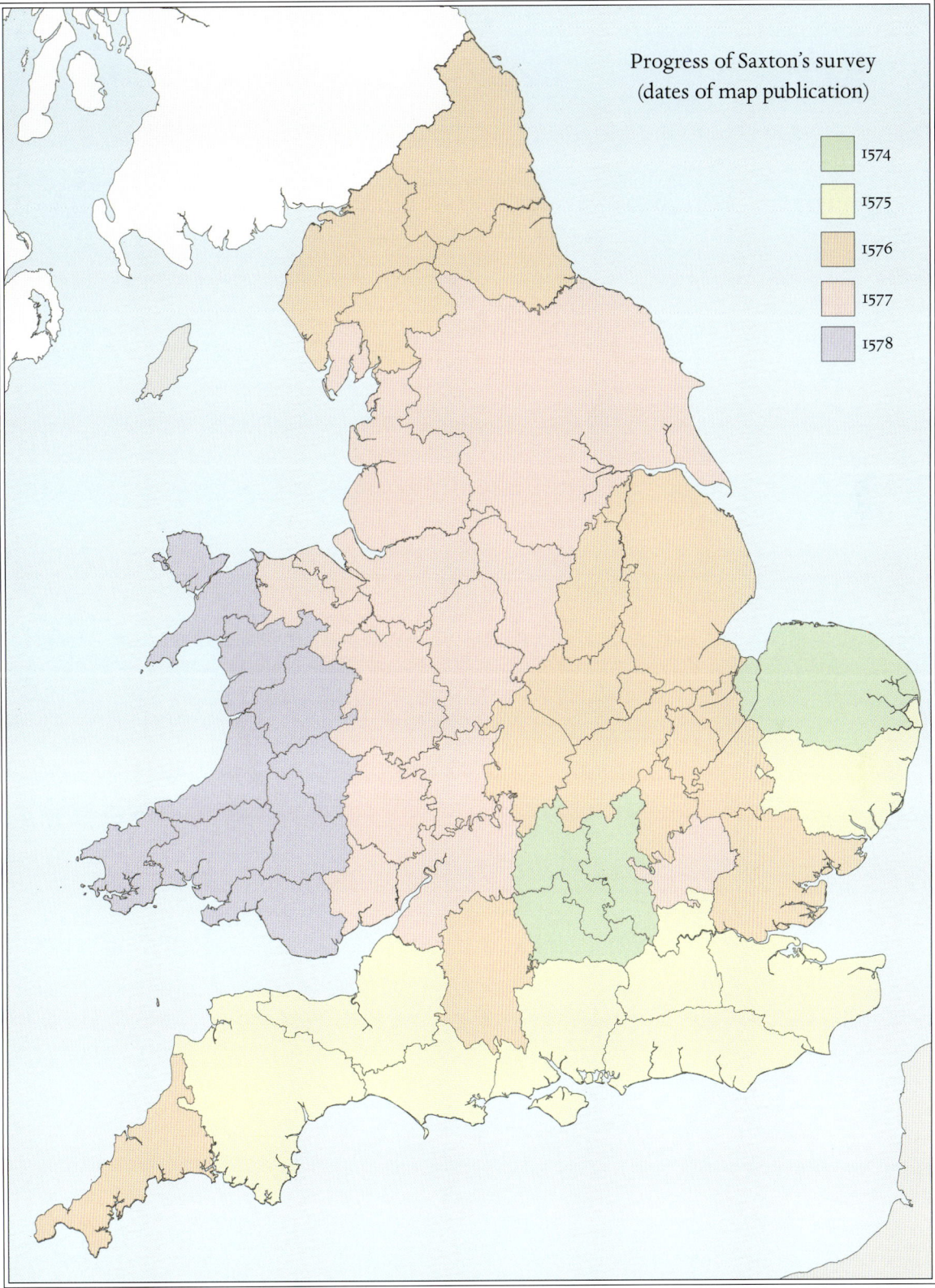

been judged more prone to invasion. A variety of counties were engraved in 1576, including northernmost England, some midland counties and others elsewhere. The northern counties bordering Scotland had strategic significance, with a potential adversary on the other side. A similar geographical concentration on particular areas, suggestive of a logistically organized sequence, is apparent in 1577, and in 1578 most of the counties of Wales were completed, as was the whole survey. The *Atlas* itself appeared the following year, 1579, but Lord Burghley received proofs as the maps were made.

More evidence on the chronology of Saxton's mapping comes from documents showing the assistance and privileges he was given along the way. These also give important clues to his operational practice and also of his increasing recognition and rising status. A pass was issued to Saxton on 11 March 1575 described as 'A placart to ___ Saxton, servant to Mr. Sackeford, Master of the Requestes, to be assisted in all places where he shall come … to describe certein counties in cartes [maps] being therunto appointed by her Majesties bill under her signet.'[26] Clear evidence that the survey was under way, and with royal favour, is the grant of a lease of land to Saxton at Grigston in Suffolk, also Seckford's county, on 11 March 1574.[27] From this point, the proof maps bear the royal coat of arms. This lease consolidated Saxton's status as a member of the landed gentry and made him an agent of the queen. It is likely that he received payment in kind in this way throughout the whole survey.

The above is a transcription of a 'Placart' or proclamation of 1575 ordering that Christopher Saxton be assisted in his survey, issued in the name of the queen. Saxton is now described as working for Seckford. Such a pass gave Saxton's work royal backing and was indispensable in overcoming local reluctance to assist in information-gathering.[28]

A short time later, on 10 July 1576, the queen gave Saxton an order for assistance in Wales, which he began mapping the following year.[29]

The order is an open letter to all Justices of the Peace and mayors across Wales, stating that 'the bearer hereof, Christopher Saxton, is appointed by her Majestie under her signe and signet to set forth and describe in coates [maps] particularlie all the shieres in Wales.'[30] This letter is invaluable in confirming Saxton's royal command and authorization for his work and indicates his likely working methods, much of which would have been applicable across England as well. The local officials are instructed to assist him in getting to any tower, castle, high place or hill to view the country, and he is to be accompanied by two or three 'honest men' who best know that area, for the 'better accomplishement of that service'. When Saxton finished in one locality the letter orders 'the said towne do set forth a horseman that can speke both Welshe and Englishe to safe conduct him to the next market towne, &c.' This last clause anticipates the difficulties of surveying in unfamiliar parts. It is assumed that this English map-maker may face hostility in Wales, but an outsider like Saxton making detailed local investigations may be likely to arouse suspicion in England too. Local knowledge was clearly at a premium and would be invaluable all across England and Wales. In the case of the latter, the possible language barrier may be overcome by an accompanying native speaker in a land where many still spoke only the mother tongue, who might also perhaps help with the spelling of local names in Welsh.

Further important validation, security and reward for Saxton came in a ten-year exclusive licence to publish his maps granted by Elizabeth on 20 July 1577; essentially an early form of intellectual property protection.[31] It is significant that Saxton's own name appeared only on the proof maps from this time, though it was added to all maps in the published *Atlas* of 1579. Copying was rife in Saxton's era and there was no legal copyright system until the first relevant statute in 1710. In lieu of this, the queen's licence was the best protection available and a valuable commercial safeguard for its bearer. The licence refers to Christopher Saxton as the servant of Thomas Seckford, the Master of Requests. The term 'servant', of course, would probably mean employee or even contractor in modern terms, without necessarily any demeaning connotation. Nevertheless, the power structures were clearly in place and plainly expressed. The licence explicitly rewards Saxton's profitable and beneficial enterprise 'to all manner of persons', so recognizing the utility of the set of county maps well beyond the queen and court circles, as a national asset; 'hieghe indignacon and displeasure' would befall any violators; and more specifically a fine of £10 (about £3,300 in 2024) and forfeiture to Saxton of the whole stock of any offending maps.[32]

MAP ENGRAVING AND THE ENGRAVERS

Having completed each survey, it seems likely that engraving and printing of proofs followed quite swiftly. Though printing in the Western world had been established for over a century by Saxton's time, recent technical advances, especially in copperplate printing, permitted the fine production of his *Atlas*. We can assume that Saxton passed his drawings, which have not survived, to engravers, with his instructions for the appearance of the finished map. The plain and minimally decorative style of many of Saxton's estate maps, however, suggest he was little interested in embellishment and his instructions may have been mainly limited to the topographical content.

Stylistic variations suggest that those engravers added many design elements of their own. It is suggested by some that Saxton may have engraved some of the maps himself. We know that six named engravers produced Saxton's maps, and that the remainder were unsigned: possibly Saxton engraved some of these? The making of Saxton's *Atlas* linked the patron and commissioners, the surveyor and cartographic draughtsman, through to the engraver and printer and finally to the map sellers and customers. Christopher Saxton was at the centre of a large network of information diffusion.

The life stories of the engravers are interesting in their own right, some being colourful larger-than-life figures, and others little known beyond their work for Saxton. Whilst the surveying was home-grown, the engraving process, at least at first, involved engagement of skilled workmen from continental Europe. Of the six named engravers of Saxton's maps three or perhaps four were Dutch or Flemish, and they produced the majority of the maps. The Low Countries had become a new centre of excellence for map engraving by this time and it is possible that some of the foreign engravers may have been fleeing religious persecution on the European mainland. The engraver of what was probably Saxton's earliest county map, the 1574 map of Norfolk, was Cornelis de Hooghe. Born in the Hague, he had a colourful life, or at least life story, claiming to be the natural son of the Holy Roman Emperor Charles V. He was one of many engraving pupils of the Dutch publisher Philip Galle. De Hooghe made just one map for Saxton. Perhaps his life was too frantic to stay in England to make any more. He was executed by the Dutch for treason in 1583, accused of plotting with imperial Spain.[33] Leonard Terwoort, who signed his maps as 'of Antwerp', engraved four of Saxton's county maps, and possibly also the unsigned Suffolk map. Little is known of him beyond these English maps. More prolific was the Dutch engraver Remigius Hogenberg, who signed nine maps, the most of any one engraver, and from stylistic evidence the *Atlas* frontispiece of Queen Elizabeth is commonly attributed to him. He is known also as an engraver of portraits of the Archbishop of Canterbury as well as kings and queens of England.[34] Remigius was part of a family highly involved in map engraving; his brother Frans Hogenberg was the engraver of many of the over 500 maps of world cities in the major contemporary city mapping project *Civitatis Orbis Terrarum*.

Next to enter the field was the first of the English engravers engaged by Saxton, who was also to establish an international reputation for his skills, which also included instrument making. Augustine Ryther made four county maps and the general map *Anglia* covering England and Wales. He was possibly a Yorkshireman like Saxton, which if true may have made contact between them more likely; although, as much of the engraving was probably done in London, there is some doubt about this.[35] Ryther was distinguished enough to be the first of the many Elizabethan instrument makers to be given freedom of the Grocers' Company, the London guild which came to incorporate the profession. Proud to proclaim his English nationality in a field hitherto dominated by Continental engravers, he signed his maps

Anglus Sculpsit. Two other engravers were engaged. Francis Scatter engraved only two English county maps, and possibly one of a group of Welsh counties. These are the only testimony to Scatter's work and we know no other biographical details; nor whether he was certainly a countryman of Saxton. It has been suggested that Scatter was most likely to be the Dutch Franhoijs Schatter, associated with correspondence of 1581 from Haarlem to the Dutch Church in London.[36] Finally, there was Nicholas Reynolds, who only engraved one map for Saxton. He signed the map 'Londinensis sculpsit' and so English nationality seems highly likely. Reynolds had a track record in cartographic engraving, having been employed by Reyner Wolfe.[37] Reynolds was well connected and accomplished. He was a correspondent of Ortelius and also engraved the very influential 1562 map of Muscovy.[38] There remain twelve unsigned maps; the reasons for such reticence remain unclear.

THE TECHNIQUE OF MAP ENGRAVING

The first printed map was made in 1472, only two decades after the first use of movable type text in the West. Until then, all maps, and anything else written or drawn, were manuscript and therefore usually unique or produced only in small numbers; and, if copied, often imperfectly so. The first century of

FIG. 31 A woodblock French navigational chart by Guillaume Brouscon, fifteenth century, showing southern Britain. Woodblock printing was used for many early maps, but does not allow the fine line detail possible using copperplate printing.

printing in the West is seen by many print historians as one of trial and error interchangeably between two main methods: relief or woodblock, and intaglio or engraving. Woodblock printing, such as used by Gutenberg, involves cutting wood so that the details to be printed stand out in relief. Intaglio printing is the opposite, using a smooth polished surface, usually copper in Saxton's time, on which the map detail is incised in a recessed mirror image.[39] The metal plate is heated and then ink is forced into the engraved lines. The plate surface is cleaned and dampened paper is placed on it. The paper and plate are then pushed together on a rolling press to produce the image.

The adoption of printing was a vital part of the opening up of knowledge in Renaissance Europe, transforming closely guarded, often unique, manuscript production to widespread dissemination through publication. As well as text, printed images were becoming commonplace and maps were a notable form of these. Graphic images, maps among them, were visually powerful, and it is clear that this power was realized and deployed by Saxton and those involved with his mapping. That visual power was spread far and wide by the medium of printing, which allowed relatively cheap, exact and repeatable reproductions to be mass-produced, or issued in limited numbers if they were to carry the cachet of exclusivity or serve the purpose of secrecy and state security. Accurate and detailed maps require fineness of line, the ability to revise detail, and dimensional stability for the paper or other medium on which maps are printed, lest scale be distorted. Skilled copperplate engraving, which could achieve far finer results than woodblock methods, was vital to the elegant and refined appearance of Saxton's maps.

Copperplate printing started soon after woodblock production, but for a long time had a relative cost disadvantage. In the early sixteenth century the

The map labels visible include: SHORDICH, FYNNESBVRIE FIELD, Fynnesb Courte, THE SPITE, S. Mª Spitel, MOOR FIELD, Dogge house, Bushoppes gate Streete, Blak house, Bedlame, Bedlam Gate, Giardin di Pietro, S. Butolfe, MOOR GATE, All holyes nº the Wall, BVSSHOPPES GATE

FIG. 32 A section of the copperplate for City of London map, circa 1559. There are no known copies of the printed map taken from it, but the plate suggests the fine detail which could be reproduced using it. As well as topographic detail, the map depicts people engaged in their daily activities.

Fugger family of Augsburg had a near monopoly on copper ore in their mines in the Tyrol. This costly dependence on overseas supply lessened in mid-century as the Companies of the Mines Royal and of the Mineral and Battery Works were established in England. There were also great advances in smelting of copper ores and furnace technology, and a new method of rolling copperplates allowed production of a much more perfect surface than with hand beating.[40]

The copperplate process had thus become more widely affordable by Saxton's time. It has several advantages for map printing. Larger printing plates could be used than for woodblock printing, vital for large-format maps. Finer lines for map detail and lettering were also possible. Furthermore, the copperplate could be re-engraved, allowing map revision. Though more expensive than woodblock, the copperplate process was far more versatile for map production and probably more cost-effective in the long run.

Map engraving epitomizes map-making as a collaborative process. The cartographer makes a manuscript cartographic drawing and the engraver's skill transforms it into a finished printable map. For a map to be legible, and thus effective, it requires careful graphic design, as we would now term it, and the engraver plays a part in this alongside the cartographer. Copperplate engraving allows for fine lines, tones, lettering and emphasis of detail. For example, the skilful use of hill shading can convey a three-dimensional impression on a two-dimensional sheet. Engraving also produces a slightly raised image on the paper, which adds to the visual impact. Most surviving editions of Saxton's *Atlas* have coloured maps. However, they were printed in black ink only, with the colour added by hand to enhance geographical features and add elegance. Contemporary opinions varied as to whether these aims were fulfilled, as for some the colour washes obscured the carefully engraved detail.

FIG. 33 Saxton's map of Southamtoniæ (Hampshire), mid-1570s. This monochrome copy shows the fine detail copperplate printing allowed. Some contemporaries preferred uncoloured prints for their clarity. This may be an early proof as Saxton's name and Seckford's motto do not yet appear and it is undated.

ARTE OF BARK SHIRE

WILT PARS

PART OF SURREY

GODALMYNGE

PART OF SOUTHSEX

MIDHERSTE

GYLEFORDE

Newbury Enborne Kingesclere BASINGSTOKE Basing ODIHAM FERNHM

Andover Whitchurche Overton Auston

WINCHESTER STOCKBRIDGE ARESFORD PETERSFEELDE

RYMSEY BISSHOPS WALTHM SOUTHWICK FARAM HAVANT CHICHESTER

SOUTHHMTON PORTESMOUTH

Calf hot castel Hurst castel

OCEANVS

WIGHT INSVL

SOVTHAMTONIÆ
Comitatus (preter Civitatem
Wincestriam) habet Oppida mer-
catoria 18 pages et villas 248.

MERIDIES

FIG. 34 From the Burghley Atlas, the map of Dorset, 1575. Lord Burghley received proof copies of Saxton's maps prior to publication and annotated them, especially with security information. Here, he adds marginal notes on dangerous places of descent along the coast.

We have a unique detailed glimpse into how Saxton worked in an 'atlas' now held among the Royal Manuscripts in the British Library. The Burghley Atlas, so called, is a compilation built around proof copies of Saxton's thirty-four county maps and the map of 'Anglia' sent to William Cecil, Lord Burghley, before publication.[41]

We have already met Burghley, surely one of the most map-conscious men of his age, requiring and using maps for all manner of government business. This atlas is essentially a scrapbook compiled by Burghley which also contains twenty non-Saxton maps, eighteen in manuscript and two printed, as well as a great many lists and itineraries. Like many other early maps or groups of maps we have seen, the Burghley Atlas combines cartographic with written records of topography in a single volume.

Burghley's principal aim of national security sets the agenda, as evidenced by his copious annotations of Saxton's county map proofs. For instance, the 1575 map of Dorset has marginal notes on places vulnerable to enemy landings. The Devon map of the same year adds to this detail the store of ordnance earmarked to be kept in each corporate town, and the powder, match and lead and so forth remaining in the hands of the Lord Lieutenant. On the Northumberland map Burghley lists the names of the main lordships and lords in the Middle March: the border area with Scotland. This region was characterized by conflict, and the loyalty of families on either side of the border could vary, so they had to be monitored. As we would expect, the most annotated of Saxton's maps are vulnerable coastal counties and those near the Scottish border.

As well as external threats, Burghley is concerned with internal security: the Catholic enemy within.

Bound after Saxton's proof map of Lancashire is a slightly later (circa 1590) manuscript map of the county, which has basic topographic detail supplemented with the names and residences of about 150 local gentry or nobles. Twenty-eight of these have crosses added, it has been claimed, to mark their Catholic status. The map also marks out the homes of several leading Puritans, either as they were also seen to be a threat or because they were considered to be possible allies.[42] There is a 'List of trained and untrained men within every Session of Lincolnshire',[43] showing the importance in Burghley's mind of defensive readiness. There are also lists of Justices of the Peace for each county, individuals forming the very basis of local administration, and law and order.

The atlas continued to be augmented by its owner, sometimes in abstruse and eccentric fashion. Alongside the list of Justices of the Peace for Essex is a Latin verse 'The title of the lawles Courte in the Honnour of Rayghle', dated 1588.[44] Burghley has also added a rhyme comparing some great houses in the county, concluding that Copthall is the best. The estate of Copthall was given to Sir Thomas Heneage by the queen and she visited the great mansion he built there.[45] Elsewhere in this miscellany are historical and topographical notes by Burghley, covering the country's history from 'Anno Mundi 2390, when Brutus came to Britain'.[46] The catalogue date of the atlas, 1574–92, indicates use and addition of materials by Burghley at least over a decade after Saxton published his atlas, suggesting their continuing currency and value in his plan to preserve the strength and peace of the nation.[47] This volume provides an invaluable window into the perception and use of the maps by their ultimate commissioner.

Clemens et Regni moderatrix iusta Britanni
Hac forma insigni conspicienda nitet.

Tristia dum gentes circum omnes bella fatigant,
Cæciq; errores toto grassantur in orbe.
pace beas longa, Vera et pietate Britannos:
Iusticia moderans miti sapienter habenas.
Chara domi, celebrisq; foris, longævaq; regnu
Hic teneas, regno tandem fruitura perenni.

An. Dñi 1579

FOUR

THE NEW PICTURE OF ENGLAND AND WALES

CHRISTOPHER SAXTON'S *Atlas of England and Wales* appeared in 1579. It was the first detailed national atlas of any comparably sized realm and the largest and most elaborate volume printed in the British Isles to date.[1] The atlas allowed people to see an intimate picture of the whole country and its parts for the first time. The revolutionary significance of this is not easily overstated. Only very recently had technological and social changes made the production and reception of such an ambitious, comprehensive and large-scale cartographic project possible. The country would never be perceived in the same way again. It was now possible to view it cartographically from the armchair: the virtual reality of the day.

FIG. 35 The magnificent frontispiece to Christopher Saxton's *Atlas of England and Wales* showing Elizabeth enthroned under a canopy, probably engraved by Remigius Hogenberg circa 1590. The queen is shown surrounded by figures representing geography and astronomy. She was the ultimate patron of the *Atlas*, some referring to it as 'The Queen's Atlas'.

It is thought that Christopher Saxton himself was the publisher; there is no evidence of his involvement with any member of the book trade. It was, after all, Saxton who was given the ten-year exclusive publication privilege a couple of years before, presumably in anticipation of the imminent completion of the project. Saxton's name appears on all the final published versions of the maps; no separate publisher is indicated; so, in a sense, he was publishing in his own name and by royal appointment.

1579: THE *ATLAS* IS PUBLISHED

The Saxton atlas had no standard format, although from 1590 it seems to have assumed a definitive appearance.[2] Indeed, it is possible that it was not at first conceived as an atlas, but as a series of maps; the idea of a book perhaps coming from the recent printed collection of maps in Abraham Ortelius's *Theatrum Orbis*

Terrarum of 1570. It has been suggested that the earliest copies of the maps were meant mainly for local administrators such as Justices of the Peace, due to their non-standard format. They could be assembled on request, accounting for the varying order of content. This raises the intriguing possibility of a policy of restricted circulation on security grounds; that the maps were only selectively issued on a 'need to know' basis. This parallels detailed mapping projects in Spain and Italy, where for similar reasons maps actually remained in manuscript. In England power was executed using Justices of the Peace and Lord Lieutenants, so only printing could produce sufficient numbers of maps. In more centralized Continental states manuscript production would have sufficed.

Further evidence of limited familiarity with Saxton's *Atlas* appears in a letter of December 1585, probably from Elizabeth's ambassador in Paris, Sir Edward Stafford, to Sir Francis Walsingham, noting there is a book of colour maps of every shire costing £5.[3] Stafford had long been acquainted with the *Atlas*. This high price further suggests a security restriction using price stratification: only the wealthy and powerful, who were also the political elite, could afford it. Such a limitation proved unnecessary as time went on and the information became widely known, Philip II having later obtained a copy.[4]

Carto-bibliographers have devoted considerable time to describing and enumerating the varieties of presentation: there are, however, some general patterns.[5] In the absence of a modern-style title page, most exemplars start with a portrait of Queen Elizabeth I, usually attributed to Remigius Hogenberg, and bear the date 1579 (FIG. 35). The queen is enthroned below a canopy and surrounded by figures symbolizing astronomy and geography. Astronomy is indicated by a figure holding an armillary sphere, a spherical arrangement of rings round the earth representing astronomical features; and geography by figures taking a sighting, using a compass and drawing a map.[6] These figures are conventionally represented by women, but in this case, and in contrast, it is men who surround the queen, the centre of power. The royal arms appear above the canopy along with images of peace and righteousness.

The symbolic power of this frontispiece shines out from the page. Elizabeth appears as the patron of these scientific forms of measurement and as one who has successfully harnessed their power as a prince. It is notable that the portrayal of the queen herself underwent a very early alteration. At first she is shown with her dress elaborately bejewelled, with its drapery in a straight line across her lap. After just a very few surviving impressions, this was replaced with simpler jewellery and the drapery shown in more natural-looking folds.

FIG. 36 The Index to this Bodleian Library exemplar of Saxton's *Atlas*. This list provides unity and organization to the volume, showing the links between its components: county maps and a general map. It names and gives locations of judicial circuits, confirming that the maps were partly geared to administration.

Indicem huic operi tripartitum adiecimus. Primo, Alphabetico ordine singulos Comitatus. Secundo, nostræ distributionis ac tabularum seriem. Tertio, Iudicum itineraria, Initia, & dierum Iuridicorum ac Locorum ad Iudicia tam Ciuilia quam Criminalia exercenda constitutorum definitum tempus (Vulgus Circuitus ac assisas vocat) reperies.

Ordo Alphabeticus
A. & fol. numerus.

Anglia.	
Anglesey.	34.
B	
Bedfordia.	14.
Berceria.	10.
Buckingham.	10.
Brecknock.	30.
C	
Cantium.	1.
Cantabrigia.	14.
Cestria.	22.
Cumberlandia.	26.
Cardigan.	30.
Caernaruan.	34.
Caermerden.	30.
Cornubia.	7.
D	
Dunelmes. epis.	25.
Derbia.	21.
Dorcestria.	3.
Denonia.	6.
Denbigh.	33.
E	
Eboracum.	23.
Essexia.	8.
F	
Flint.	33.
G	
Glocestria.	11.
Glamorgan.	29.
H	
Huntingdonia.	14.
Hartfordia.	9.
Herefordia.	19.
L	
Lancastria.	24.
Lecestria.	15.
Lincolnia.	20.
M	
Merionidh.	32.
Montgomery.	32.
Monumetha.	28.
Middlesexia.	1.
N	
Nottinghamia.	20.
Northumbria.	27.
Northamptonia.	14.
Norfolcia.	13.
O	
Oxonium.	10.
P	
Penbrok.	31.
R	
Rutlandia.	14.
Radnor.	30.
S	
Salopia.	18.
Somersetus.	5.
Southhamptonia.	2.
Southsexia.	1.
Staffordia.	16.
Suffolcia.	12.
Surria.	1.
W	
Warwicum.	15.
Westmorlandia.	26.
Wigornia.	17.
Wiltonia.	4.

Tabularum series.

Anglia.	
Cantium, Southsexia, Surria & Middlesexia.	1
Southhamptonia.	2
Dorcestria.	3
Wiltonia.	4
Somersetus.	5
Denonia.	6
Cornubia.	7
Essexia.	8
Hartfordia.	9
Oxonium, Buckinghamia & Berceria.	10
Glocestria.	11
Suffolcia.	13
Norfolcia.	12
Northamptonia, Bedfordia, Cantabrigia, Huntingdonia, & Rutlandia.	14
Warwicum & Lecestria.	15
Staffordia.	16
Wigornia.	17
Salopia.	18
Herefordia.	19
Lincolnia & Nottinghamia.	20
Derbia.	21
Cestria.	22
Eboracum.	23
Lancastria.	24
Dunelmensis episcopat.	25
Westmorlandia, & Cumberlandia.	26
Northumbria.	27
Monumetha.	28
Glamorgana.	29
Radnor, Brecknok, Cardigan, & Caermarden.	30
Penbrok.	31
Montgomeriæ & Merionidh.	32
Denbigh ac flint	33
Anglesey, & Caernaruan.	34

Iudicum Circuitus. / Initia. / Dierum numerus. / Loca.

Iudicum Circuitus.		Initia.	Dierum numerus.	Loca.
1	Cantium.	Iouis.	3.	Roffæ, Cancuariæ, Maidstoniæ, vel Dertfordiæ.
	Southsexia.	Lunæ.	3.	Horshamiæ, vel Grimstediæ.
	Surria.	Iouis.	3.	Suthuariæ, Croydonit, Kingstoniæ, vel Guilfordiæ.
	Hartfordia.	Lunæ.	3.	Hartfordiæ, vel Wariæ.
	Essexia.	Iouis.	3.	Chelmesfordiæ, Burntwodiæ, vel Colcestriæ.
2	Southamptonia.	Lunæ.	3.	Wintoniæ.
	Wiltonia.	Iouis.	3.	Salisburiæ.
	Dorcestria.	Lunæ.	3.	Dorcestriæ.
	Somersetus.	Iouis.	3.	Tauntoniæ, vel Chardiæ.
	Denonia.	Lunæ.	6.	Exoniæ.
	Cornubia.	Lunæ.	3.	Lanstoniæ.
3	Buckinghamia.	Lunæ.	2.	Alisburiæ, vel Brichhilliæ.
	Bedfordia.	Mercur.	2.	Bedfordiæ, vel Dunstabuli.
	Huntingdonia.	Vener.	2.	Huntingdoniæ, vel Neotis.
	Cantabrigia.	Lunæ.	2.	Cantabrigiæ.
	Suffolcia.	Mercur.	4.	Buriæ sancti Edmundi.
	Norfolcia.	Lunæ.	4.	Nordouici, vel Thetfordiæ.
4	Berceria.	Lunæ.	2.	Abbingtoniæ.
	Oxonia.	Mercur.	3.	Oxoniæ, vel Burfordiæ.
	Glocestria.	Lunæ.	4.	Glocestriæ.
	Monumetha.	Iouis.	2.	Monumethæ.
	Herefordia.	Lunæ.	3.	Herefordiæ.
	Wigornia.	Iouis.	3.	Wigorniæ.
	Salopia.	Lunæ.	3.	Salopiæ, vel Bridgenorthiæ.
	Staffordia.	Mercur.	3.	Staffordiæ, vel Wulnerhaptoni.
5	Northamptonia.	Martis.	2.	Northamptoniæ.
	Warwicum.	Vener.	2.	Warwici & Couentriæ. Lunæ.
	Lecestria.	Martis.	2.	Lecestriæ.
	Derbia.	Vener.	2.	Derbiæ.
	Nottinghamia.	Lunæ.	2.	Nottinghamiæ.
	Lincolnia.	Iouis.	3.	Lincolniæ.
	Rutlandia.	Lunæ.	1.	Bradcroftiæ.
6	Eboracum.	Lunæ.	6.	Eboraci.
	Dunelmensis epis.	Lunæ.	3.	Dunelmi.
	Northumbria.	Iouis.	3.	Nouocastri.
	Cumberlandia.	Lunæ.	3.	Carlioli.
	Westmerlandia.	Iouis.	3.	Kendaliæ, vel Applebeiæ.
	Lancastria.	Lunæ.	6.	Lancastriæ.
7	Middlesexia.			Notandum quod omnes querelæ & placita, quæ in isto comitatu oriuntur, in cuius Aulæ Westmonasteniensis quolibet termino discutiuntur.
8	Cestria.			Notandum quod Cestria comitatus est Palatinus & Assisas magnas Cestriæ bis quotannis habet. Speciales huic Comitatui Iudices Regio diplomate designantur.
9	Denbigh. Flint. Montgomery.		North Wallia.	
10	Caernaruan. Merionidh. Anglesey.			Quilibet horum Comitatum Assisas sex dierum bis quotannis habet. Dies Lunæ semper dies Assisarum primus. Loca & tempora in vnoquoque Comitatu edicto publico declarantur quindecim ad minus diebus Assisas precedentibus.
11	Radnor. Brecknok & Glamorgan.		South Wallia.	
12	Caermarden. Penbrok. Cardigan.			

(right margin)

Nomina Ciuitatum & oppidorum quorundam, quæ illis Comitatibus nominibus insigniantur.

Ciuit:
Londinium.
Eboracum.
Nordouicum.
Cantuaria.
Lincolnia.
Exonium.
Couentria.
Lichfeldia.
Glocestria.
Bristollia.
Cestria.

Oppid:
Southamptonia.
Nottinghamia.
Nouû castrum super tyne.
Kingstone super Hull.
Poole.
Hauerford west.

Termino Hillarij & Trinitatis, billa positibus in Aula Westmonasteriensi, affiguntur ad pedem graduum ascendentium versus Cancellariam & Regium Bancum, quibus Loca assisarum & certi mensium dies declarantur.

NEC VI, NEC FRAVDE

In most copies of the *Atlas* an index of the maps follows, the only page in the *Atlas* printed using movable type. The sheets are listed alphabetically and in order of appearance, with folio references. Some earlier editions were restricted to just a list of county maps, but most later versions are more elaborate, adding a column with details of judicial circuits and assizes in each county, lending further utility to the volume. The pages reproduced on pages 89–159, which probably represent the settled definitive state of the *Atlas*, are dated circa 1590.[7]

Further evidence for this dating is the inclusion of the next pages of preliminary matter: a set of coats of arms and then a tabulation of information about all the counties, engraved and included in copies from 1588–89. There are eighty-three numbered coats of arms and one left blank. The first sixty-five are the peers of the realm in hierarchical order, from the sole marquess, of Winchester, down to the barons including Lord Burghley, the remainder comprising officers of the realm such as chancellor. Hence, the whole of the top-level political elite was listed at the start of the *Atlas*, the cartographic and heraldic display of power being united by their proximity. The tables itemize numbers of cities, bishoprics, market towns, castles and parishes in each county; and numbers of rivers, bridges, chases, forests and parks: a comprehensive enumeration of the physical and human geographical imprint on every part of the country as shown on the succeeding maps.

ANGLIA AND THE COUNTY MAPS

The main event, the thirty-four county (or group of counties) maps, follow the map of *Anglia*, which shows the whole of Elizabeth's realm. The order of the maps is broadly south to north, not the order of survey date. The first map combines the counties of Kent, Surrey, Sussex and Middlesex, the seat of the capital. The last English county map is Northumberland, followed by the Welsh counties, also from south to north. Of the thirty-four county maps, twenty-five appear as single counties and nine as combinations, though the reasons for the combination are not always clear. From the *Atlas*, all the kingdom can be seen at a glance or in detail.

The most apparent feature of the maps is the image of the county, the unit of mapping. *Anglia*, the map of all England and Wales, depicts and differentiates each county with a thick border coloured distinctly from its neighbour, making the counties stand out.[8] Every county on the county maps is similarly edged with a prominent coloured border, and for groups of counties the name, such as 'Kent', is written prominently across its extent. Although the maps were printed in black ink only, most editions were then hand-coloured; the sensory impact is to bring the administrative geography to the fore.

Although the county maps differ a little in scale and content, there are many common features. They are at a scale intermediate between the smaller scale of a national map and the larger scale of an estate plan. They range in scale from the map of Kent and so on, Lancashire, Lincolnshire and so on, and Northumberland at 1:313,783, to that of Monmouthshire at 1:146,432, or between about 5 miles to 1 inch up to about 2⅓ miles to 1 inch respectively.[9] The median is around 4 miles to 1 inch, the 'quarter-inch' scale later quite fashionable for mapping, such as by the Ordnance Survey.

There is no obvious reason for the grouping of counties; it does not produce maps of equal scale – quite the reverse. For example, the Kent group includes the counties of greatest political importance around Westminster and London. It might be that economies had to be made as the project progressed. Barber argues this might have prompted Burghley to call on Seckford at this point to bring the project back on track, lest increasingly crowded and less informative maps were to follow.[10] As a saving grace, it might have been thought that this significant group of what now are termed the 'Home Counties' should be seen at one glance: they were closely connected to London, the seat of power, which might also make this map a bestseller. To show Kent, Surrey and Middlesex separately would divide the environs of London between maps. Sussex is perhaps grouped with them to make a neat block of territory. The edges of Essex are shown as a neighbouring county, but the environs of London near the River Lea and the important riverine and coastal settlements along the Thames are depicted allowing these economically and strategically vital adjuncts

to the capital to be seen alongside the county group. The reason for some other combinations is harder to imagine.

The relatively small scale of the maps made generalization and simplification of reality essential. This was achieved, in part, using signs and symbols, often pictorial; their meaning thus obvious without a legend. It was not usual to include keys to maps in the Renaissance period; indeed, even the early Ordnance Survey 1 inch maps, over two centuries later, did not carry legends. Saxton's county maps show a range of elements of the cultural and physical landscape.

The main cultural element is the large array of settlements, from the largest cities down to villages and some hamlets. Cities and large towns are named in capitals and shown as a cluster of churches and buildings; where there is a cathedral a cross is shown. Smaller towns are named with large bold letters and indicated by a couple of spired church symbols. Villages and hamlets are indicated by their parish churches, drawn as single-spired buildings. Chapelries and hamlets, as well as prominent

FIG. 37 OVERLEAF *left* The coats of arms of peers and statesmen in the initial pages of Saxton's *Atlas*. This array captures the political elite of the country and symbolizes their power and connection with the territory represented. Many of these major landholders would probably acquire a copy of this expensive and exclusive atlas.

FIG. 38 OVERLEAF *right* Table of counties (*Catalogus*) giving a spreadsheet of Tudor geographical information. A plethora of details are enumerated, allowing the reader to see data including the number of castles, market towns, parishes, forests and parks in any county: a useful addition to the atlas and invaluable for administration.

M. Winton.	C. Arundeliæ	C. Oxoniæ	C. Northūbr.	C. Salopiæ	C. Kantiæ	C. Surrey.
C. Derbeiæ	C. Wigorniæ	C. Rotelandiæ	C. Cūberlandiæ	C. Suthfexiæ	C. Huntingdoniæ	C. Bathoniæ.
C. Warwici	C. Southāptoniæ	C. Bedfordiæ	C. Pembrochi	C. Herfordiæ	C. Leicestriæ	C. Essexiæ.
C. Lincolniæ	V.C. Montacuti	V.C. Bindon	D. Abergaveny	D. Audley	D. Zouche	D. Willughbye de E.
D. Berkley	D. Morley	D. Dacre	D. Cobham	D. Stafford	D. Grey de W	D. Scroope.
D. Dudley	D. Stourton	D. Lūmley	D. Montioy	D. Ogle	D. Darcy. B	D. Sandes.
D. Vaux	D. Wandsore	D. Wentworth	D. Borough	D. Mordant	D. Cromwell	D. Eure.
D. Wharton	D. Riche	D. Willughby de P	D. Sheffeld	D. Paget	D. Darcy de C	D. Howard de E.
D. North	D. Chaundos	D. Hunsdon	D. Saint Iohn	D. Buckhurst	D. de la Warr	D. Burghley.
D. Compton	D. Norreys	C. Hatton Can	F. Knolles Th	I. Croft Compt	T. Henege Vice C	F. Walsingh P.S
W. Dauison S	W. Mildmay Can	A. Poulet	I. Woollay	C. Wrey C. I	G. Gerrard C.R	E. Anderson.
R. Manwood C.B.S	T. Selsford L.M	P. Dale L. I. M	R. Rookeby	I. Herbert L. I. M	I. Forescu L. M	

CATALOGVS *Urbiū, Episcŏ, oppido Mercŭ, castrŏ, Eccle, parochialiŭ, Fluuĭ illustriŭ, Pontiŭ, Lucorŭ, Saltorŭ, Septorŭ, omniŭ, quæ per totam Angliæ Walliæq, in vnoquoq comitatŭ continentur, quemadmodŭ suis locis in Chirographico Angliæ Walliæq tabulis (vbi suis cuiuq nomē reseritur) illustrissime reseruntur. Numerus vero eorum omnium quæ in hãc serie colliguntur, ad imum huius indicis distinguntur, sicuti infra videre licet.*

Comitatus	Vrbŭ	Episc.	Op.M.	Castr.	Ec.Pa.	Fluui.	Pon.	Luco.	Salto.	Septo.
Cantium	002	002	017	068	398	000	014	000	000	023
Southsexia	001	001	018	001	312	002	010	000	004	033
Surria	000	000	006	000	140	001	007	000	004¼	017
Middlesexia	002	001	003	000	073	001	003	001	000	004
Southamptonia	001	001	018	005	248	004	031	000	009	029
Dorcestria	000	000	018	006	248	004	002	001	002	012
Willtonia	001	001	021	001	304	005	031	001	004	022
Somersetus	003	002	029	001	385	009	045	000	002	018
Deuonia	001	001	040	003	394	023	106	000	000	023
Cornubia	000	000	023	006	161	007	031	000	000	009
Essexia	001	000	021	001	415	007	028	000	001	046
Hartfordia	000	000	018	000	120	001	024	000	000	023
Oxonium	001	001	010	000	208	003	026	000	001	009
Buckinghamia	000	000	011	000	185	002	014	000	000	015
Berceria	000	000	011	001	140	003	007	000	004	013
Gloecstria	001	001	020	001	280	012	022	001	002	019
Suffolcia	000	000	028	001	464	002	032	000	000	027
Norfolcia	001	001	026	000	625	003	015	000	000	000
Rutlandia	000	000	002	000	047	000	001	000	000	004
Northãptonia	001	001	011	002	326	005	024	000	003	023
Huntingdonia	000	000	005	000	078	001	005	000	000	007
Bedfordia	000	000	010	000	116	001	006	000	000	012
Cantabrigia	000	000	006	000	163	001	007	000	000	005
Warwic	001	001½	012	001	158	007	021	001	000	016
Lecestria	000	000	011	002	200	001	010	000	002	013
Staffordia	001	001½	012	005	130	013	019	001	001	038
Wigornia	001	001	007	003	152	005	013	001	002	016
Salopia	000	000	013	013	170	018	013	000	007	027
Herefordia	001	001	008	007	176	013	011	001	002	008
Lincolnia	001	001	026	002	630	009	015	000	000	013
Nottinghamia	000	000	011	000	168	005	017	000	001	018
Darbia	000	000	008	004	106	013	021	000	001	034
Cestria	001	001	009	003	068	009	019	000	002	018
Eboracum	001	001	046	014	563	036	062	004	008	072
Lancastria	000	000	018	006	036	033	024	000	001	030
Dunelmensis	001	001	005	004	062	011	020	000	000	021
Westmorlandia	000	000	004	006	026	008	015	000	002	019
Cumbria	001	001	008	015	058	020	033	000	003	008
Northumbria	000	000	011	012	040	021	016	000	001	008
Monumetha	000	000	006	007	142	015	014	001	000	008
Glamorgan	000	001	007	012	151	016	006	000	000	005
Radnov	000	000	004	005	043	013	005	000	003	000
Brecknok	000	000	003	004	070	027	013	000	000	002
Cardigan	000	000	004	000	077	026	009	000	004¼	000
Caermarthin	000	000	006	004	081	020	016	000	004¼	002
Penbrok	000	001	006	005	142	006	007	000	002	003
Montgomere	000	000	006	003	042	028	006	000	000	000
Merionidh	000	000	003	002	034	026	007	000	000	000
Denbigh	000	000	003	003	053	024	006	000	000	006
Flint	000	001	003	004	024	004	002	000	000	002
Anglesey	000	000	003	000	083	008	002	000	000	000
Caernaruan	000	001	005	003	073	017	006	000	000	000
Shires 52	25 Cities	26 Bisho.	641 Mar.To.	182 Cast.	9725 Paroch.	554 Riuer.	986 Brid.	11 Chase.	68 Forr.	781 Parc.

manor houses and castles, are shown by a single house only. All these places are coloured in red for prominence. The overall appearance, then, of the county maps is an array of places across a well-settled and colonized realm, except in mountain and moorland areas.

Roads do not appear; perhaps a surprising omission. Prominence in the rural landscape is given to the mansions of the rich and their parks surrounded by pales. Another important facet of the cultural landscape is the administrative divisions. Whilst most maps just show the county, a few maps show main subdivisions of counties, usually hundreds, very important for the administration of justice. The map of Norfolk dated 1574 shows hundreds by alphabetical letter on the map cross-referenced to a key; other maps, like Cornwall of 1576, show the hundred names on the face of the map. On some early county maps, the numbers of market towns and parishes are indicated in a small text panel. Little is shown of neighbouring counties except their name and a few settlements close to the boundary, though rivers are continued across the extent of the map reflecting their importance. The administrative geography was less neat than today. Many counties existed in partially fragmented form, with some detached outliers.

Natural features include rivers shown very prominently as broad blue lines, important as means of transport, as well as the bridges built over them. Hills are shown as brown mounds, with varying sizes broadly representing extent and altitude. Woods and forests are shown similarly naturalistically with varying-size groups of trees coloured green; as are chases, royal hunting preserves like forests. Marshes are shown as empty open land and named; or, in some cases, like 'Chatmosse' in the county of Lancaster, their extent is shown by reed-like symbols. Estuaries, normally described as havens, are depicted on coasts. All features are shown with size of lettering indicating their extent.

It is not easy to separate the decorative or iconographic features from the practical; both serve the utility of the map as a means of conveying information and ideas. The *Atlas* as a whole is elegant and ornamental. The bound versions often have leather covers and gilt lettering, though some of these may be later additions. All maps, including *Anglia*, have a decorated title cartouche with a variety of floral, human, animal and mythical figures and the name of the county in Latin, such as *Wiltoniæ* for Wiltshire, a brief description in Latin and the date. The map edges have decorated border strips with the four compass points in Latin: *Septentrio*, *Oriens*, *Meridies* and *Occidens*. Other marginal details are more purely decorative, such as ships, boats, large fish and other sea creatures in the seas off coastal counties. Empty and unadorned map space was not attractive to potential customers. Technical and authorship information is provided in the margins, such as a scale of miles and the names of engraver and Saxton the cartographer, all in decorative form.

The royal coat of arms appears on every map, with the motto *Dieu et Mon Droit* reminding the peruser of the queen's divine right to rule. Saxton's *Atlas* could even be viewed as the queen's title deeds to the realm: an explicit record of property and possession. Importantly, the royal coat of arms appears as a corollary to the royal portrait on the frontispiece. Its presence is a heraldic reminder of the power of the queen over every county; the royal writ ran evenly across the whole territory. Indeed, some referred to Saxton's *Atlas* as 'The Queen's Atlas'.

Saxton's maps are above all about status. A clear hierarchy of names is evident from the queen at the apex. Royal heraldry is augmented by the page showing arms of the nobles of the kingdom in an atlas which maps their territorial associations. As paymaster, Seckford also made sure his arms and motto were prominent on all the maps. Lowest billing is given to the engraver, where indicated, and to the mapmaker. Meekly, in small letters, 'Christophorus Saxton descripsit' is written inconspicuously somewhere on each map. His name became much more prominent on maps later on, ironically after his death.

The emphasis on certain features reveals the map-makers' priorities. For instance, parks feature prominently, ringed by circular enclosing pales (wooden or iron fences). They were areas of exclusive hunting by nobles; a privilege only the monarch could grant. As spaces for recreation and display, they conspicuously demonstrated the privilege and landed wealth of the nobility. The emphasis of parks also reflects their significance as potential military resources. Parks were particularly important as places where troops could be mustered, and so a cartographic overview of their locations was indispensable. Their importance as breeding grounds for horses, an important asset to be requisitioned by the Elizabethan government in times of conflict, had been recognized by legislation since the time of Henry VIII.[11]

Saxton set not only the geographical image of England for nearly two centuries, but also the standard style of county mapping for some time to come. Though he did not originate all his schemes of representation, his maps served to establish a reasonably consistent model for the future, with hand-colouring conventions like blue for water, green for trees, red for settlements, and distinct colours for the boundaries of adjoining counties. Styles of marginal adornment of the kind Saxton used also became the norm.

The resulting maps, shown on the following pages in the order in which they appear in the Bodleian Library's exemplar (Map Res. 80), are clear and vivid evocations of Elizabeth's kingdom.

THE COUNTY MAPS

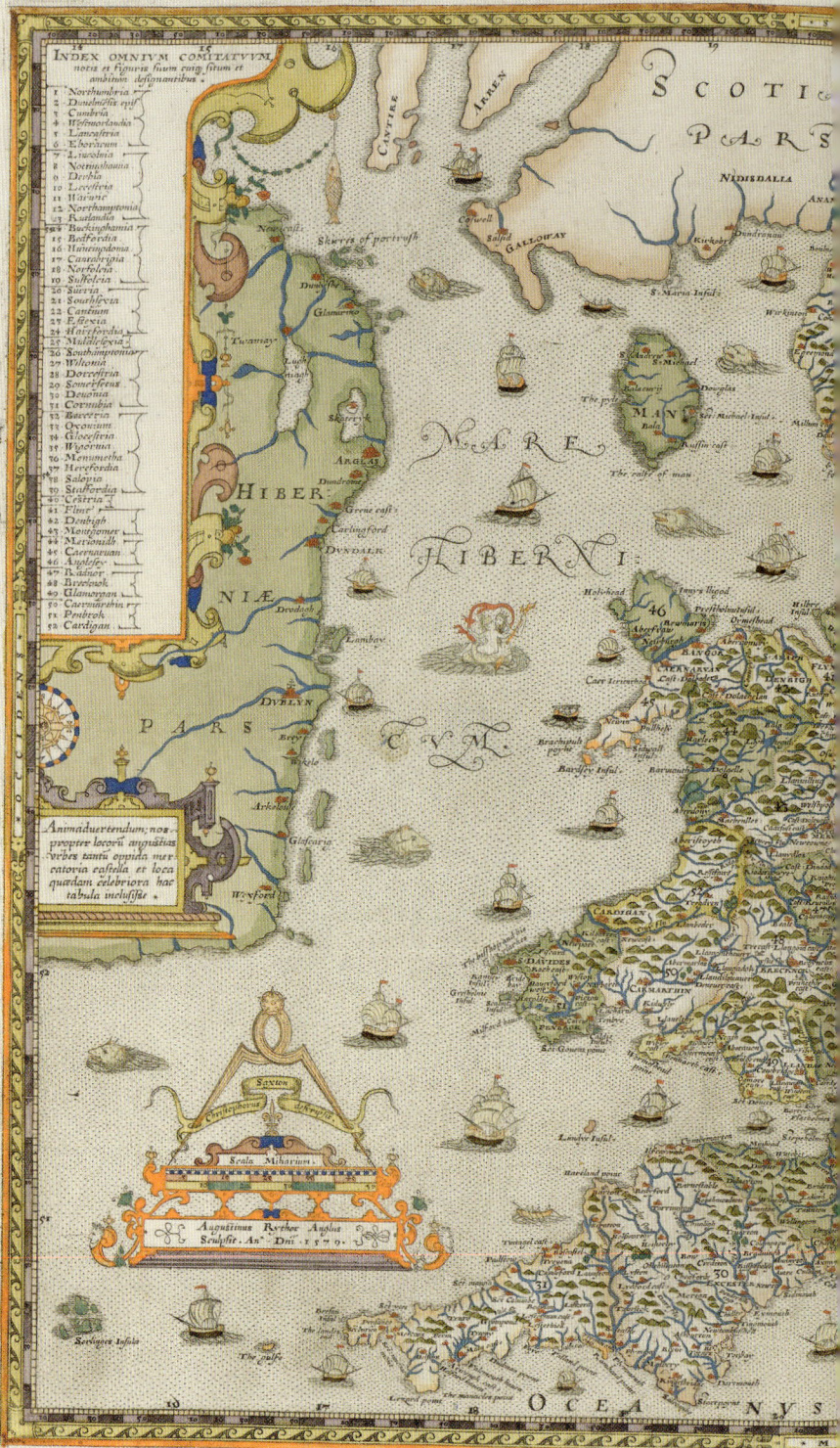

FIG. 39

INDEX OMNIVM COMITATVVM
notis et figuris suum cuiq, situm et
ambitum designantibus

1 Northumbria
2 Dunelmensis epis
3 Cumbria
4 Westmorlandia
5 Lancastria
6 Eboracum
7 L. incolnia
8 Notinghamia
9 Derbia
10 Leicestria
11 Warwic
12 Northamptonia
13 Rutlandia
14 Buckinghamia
15 Bedfordia
16 Huntingdona
17 Cantabrigia
18 Norfolcia
19 Suffolcia
20 Siluria
21 Southsexia
22 Cantium
23 Essexia
24 Hartfordia
25 Middlesexia
26 Southamptonia
27 Wiltonia
28 Dorcestria
29 Somersetus
30 Deuonia
31 Cornubia
32 Baceria
33 Oxonium
34 Gloucestria
35 Wigornia
36 Monumetha
37 Herefordia
38 Salopia
39 Staffordia
40 Ceftria
41 Flint
42 Denbigh
43 Montgomer
44 Merionidh
45 Caernaruan
46 Anglesey
47 R. adnor
48 Brecknoc
49 Glamorgan
50 Caermardhin
51 Pembrok
52 Cardigan

Animaduertendum; nos
propter locorum angustias
vrbes tantu oppida mer
catoria castella et loca
quædam celebriora hac
tabula incluisse

Augustinus Ryther Anglus
Sculpsit. An° Dni · 1579

Scala Miliarium.

SCOTIÆ PARS

NIDISDALIA

GALLOWAY

HIBERNIÆ PARS

MARE HIBERNI: CVM.

OCEANVS

ANGLIA
hominū numero, rerumq̃; ferè
omniū copijs abundans, sub mi:
tissimo Elizabethæ serenissimæ
et doctissimæ Reginæ, imperio,
placidissima pace annos iam
viginti florentissima.

An⁰ Dñi
1579

OCEANVS

GERMA:

NICVS.

GAL:
LI Æ
PARS

BRITANNICVS

PARTE OF HERTFORDE SHIRE

PARTE OF BUCKINGHM SHIRE

PARTE OF BERKE SHIRE

PARTE OF HAMSHIRE

MIDLESEX

LONDON

KENT

SURREY

SUSSEX

THE DOWNES

THE DOWNES

The Forreste of St Leonerds

Word forest

Ashdowne forest

Altshole forreste

The forrest of Windsor

Windsor

Blackwater

OCCIDENS

OCEAN

Watforde

Uxbridge

Burnhm

Colbrok

Madenhead

Amersham

Beaconsfelde

Staines

Kingeston

Croydon

Guildford

Horshm

Peterfeld

Aldherst

Chechester

Arundel

Lewes

Brighthelmston

New Dorchill

Enfeld

Highberue

Waltham St crue

Romford

FIG. 40

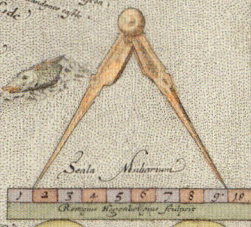

FIG. 41

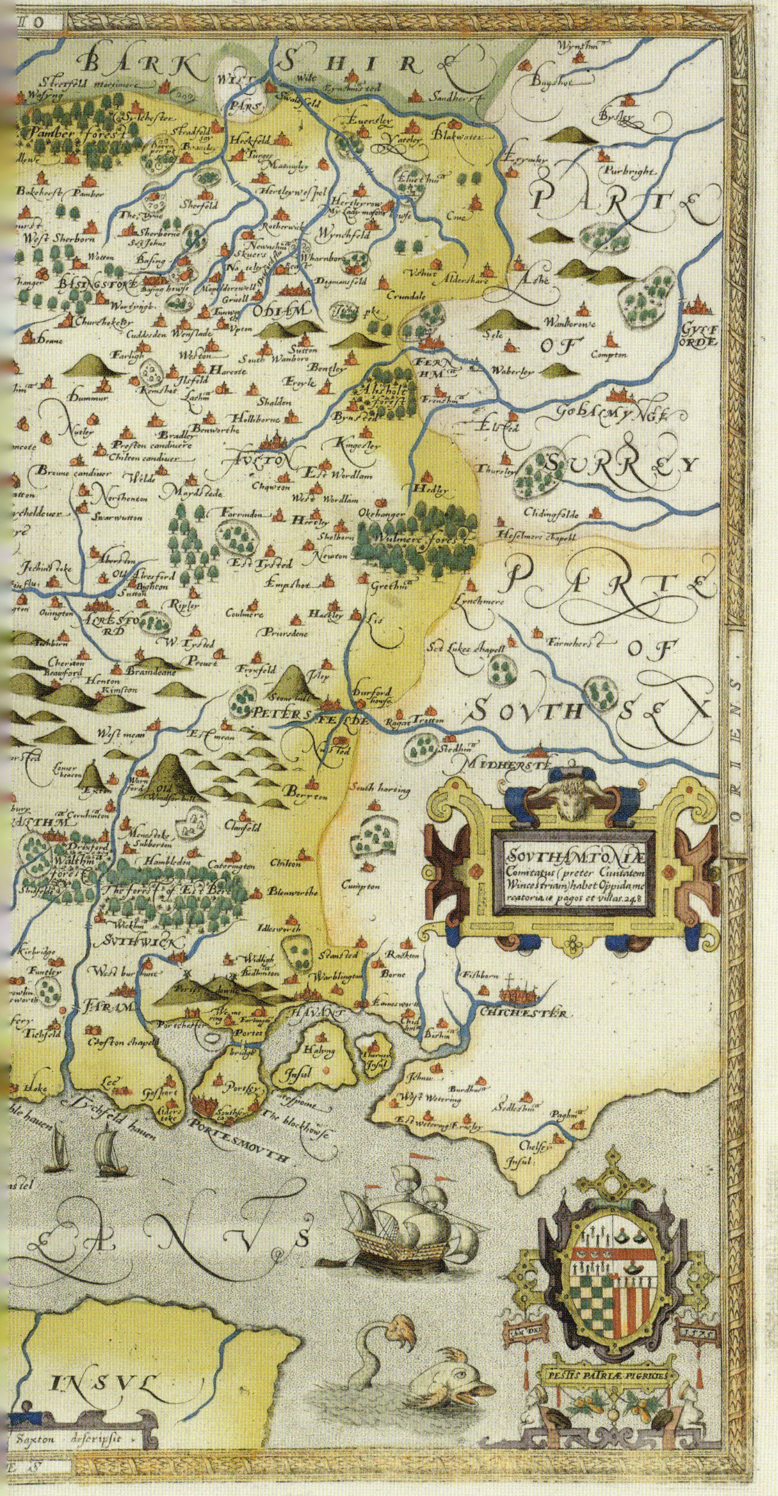

BARKSHIRE

PARTE OF SURREY

PARTE OF SOVTH SEX

SOVTHAMTONIÆ
Comitatus (preter Civitatem
Wintestriam) habet Oppidam mercatoria 18 pagos et villas 248

CHICHESTER

PORTESMOVTH

OCEANVS

INSVL

PESTES PATRIÆ PIGRITIES

Saxton descripsit

DORCESTRIÆ
Comitatus Vicinarumque
Regionum noua veraq; Descriptio
Anno Dni 1575
PARTE OF SOMERSET SHIRE
PARTE OF DEVON SHIRE
OCCIDENS
Scala Miliarium
Christophorus Saxton descripsit
PESTIS PATRIÆ PIGRICIES

FIG. 42

Salesburye Plane

PARTE OF WILT SHIRE

Mere
West Knoikell
Syston
Gillingham
Bugley
Ham
Motcombe
Shaftesbury
Cranborne chale
Cranborne
PARTE OF HAM SHIRE
PARTE OF Ringwoo

Sturmister newtoncast
Blandeford
Blandford marsis
Bere
Wimborneminster
Cantord Lawndes
Christchurche
Sturfeld heathe

Wareham
THE ISLE OF PVRBEK
Corfe Castel

ORIENS

N V S

The point of the race

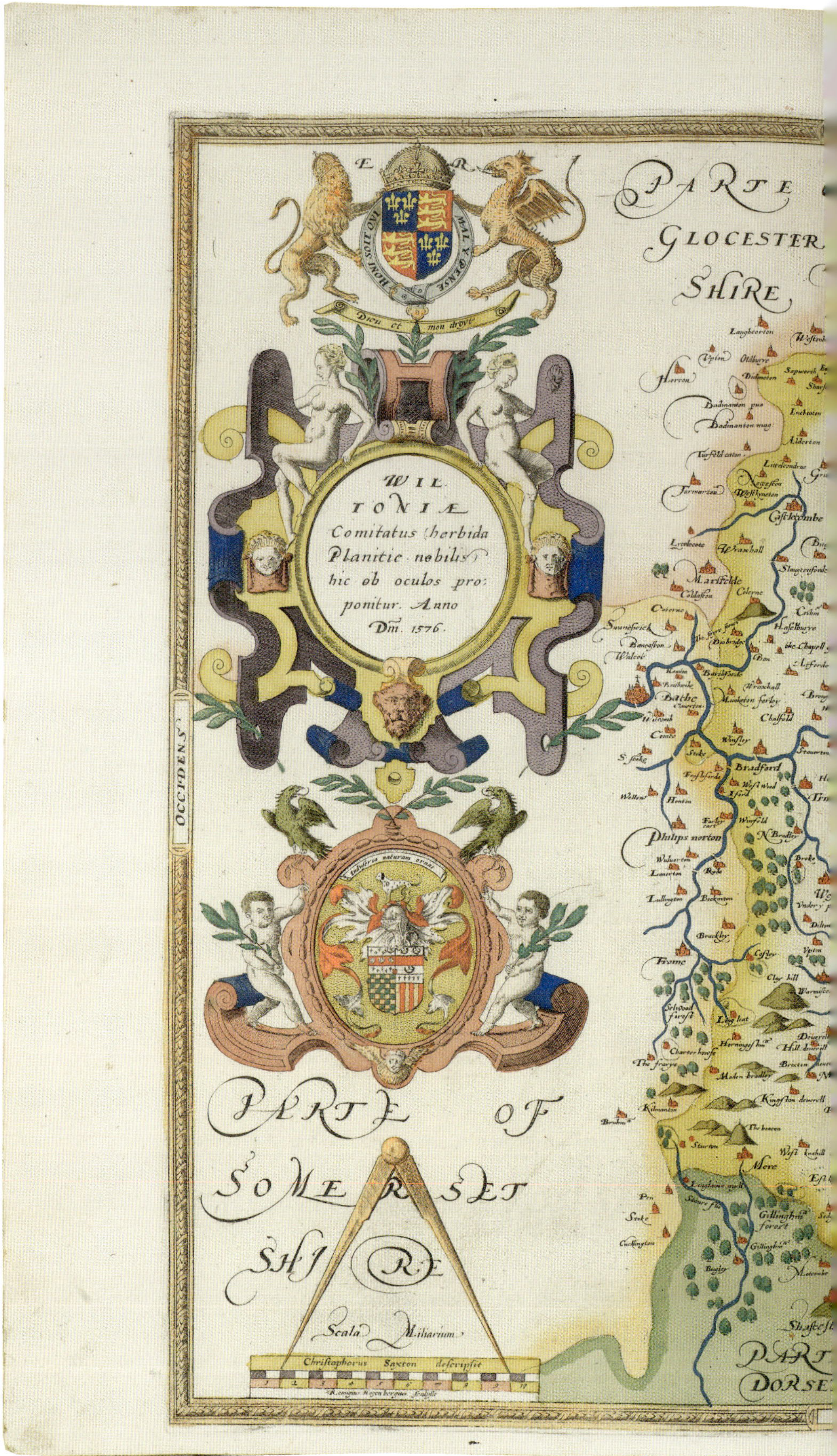

PARTE

GLOCESTER
SHIRE

OCCIDENS

WIL
TONIÆ
Comitatus (herbida
Planitie nobilis)
hic ob oculos pro:
ponitur. Anno
Dm. 1576.

Dieu et mon droyt

HONY SOIT QVI MAL Y PENSE

PARTE OF
SOMERSET
SHIRE

Scala Miliarum.

Christophorus Saxton descripsie

PART
DORSET

FIG. 43

5

PARTE OF BARKSHIRE

PARTE OF HAMSHIRE

ORIENS

Lechlade · Farrindon · Lamborne · Hungerford

Bradon forest · Wotonbassec · Huswathe

Aldburne chase · Sauernak forest

Calne · the Deuyses · Eli Lauington

Black heathe · Salesburye playne

Euerley warren of hares · Chute forest

Ambersbury · Wilton · Salesburye · Salesburye plaine

Cranborne chase

Flatholms Insul.

Stepeholm

SOMERSETENSEM.
Comitat (agri fertilitate
Celebrem) hec ob oculos
ponit Tabula.

DIEV ET MON DROIT

Anno 1575 et D.
ELIZABETHE Regine 17

S

Brefstall point
Stockland

WITCHET

Kelton

Lyston
Sockland Otterhampton Comich
Stockgurfser
Otterton
Perloek bay

L Quantox head
Stowerton
Houfford
Netton
Fowler
Doddington
Comington
Corypole
Chare
Spaxton
Enmore
No

Ower
Calborn
Porlok
Selworthye
MYNHED

Luxton
Weston Curtenay
Smok pere
Timberscombe

Doneter
Set Decombes
Corouton
Old Clevs
Willston

Exmore
Cutcombe
Luxboro
Wichicombe
Nettlecombe
Samford
Combe
Bucknaler
Stoke gomer
Elworthye
Crokan
Leighlands
Trebora
Monkesilver
Exton
Westhill

Exforde
Ex fl.

Wethipole
Winesford
Weston
Brunton roste
Lmeradeshed
Brunton rose
Bashpr
Bromfelde
Combefleyry
Catholston
Weston
Haddon benton
Hewishe
Clatworthye
Tollande
Deus Brok fl. m
Haukeridge
DULVER TON
Badcecombe
Bifshops
GLEDIARD
Kyngston

Tuchen
Molland
Weft Austie

Est Auftie

Comb
Barhford
Langford
Mwkathe

Bilyate
Chipt table
Ralington

WIVELESCO
Etsheade
Hauise

Hestercombe
Norton
Stapl
graver
Cheddon

Exbridge
Digford
Clayhanger
Peton
Highlry
BAYNTON

MILVERTON
Staoley
Oke
Hothefeld
Hilfarrence
Hilbishop
Wilton
May Ash
TAYNTON

Baddleton
Nymhead
Bradford
Longford
Ratesford

Trull
Orchard
Thurloxhace

Afhbrittell
Helcombe rogus

WELLINGTON
West buxland
Samford
Pounnsfor
Prick

Margaret Thorne
Angostor
Pirry fir Corst
Stapls
Curland

Canons leighe
Burlscomb
Baynton
Recke infi hr

Blak don hill

PARTE OF

DEVON SHIRE

Christophorus Saxton descripsit

Scala miliarum

1 2 3 4 5 6 7 8 9 10

LEONARDVS TERWOORT ANTVERPIANVS SCVLPSIT

Ofertuton
Clay haydon

Yaccombe

Stockland

Ler

MER

OCCIDENS

FIG. 44

FIG. 45

PARTE OF SOMERSET SHIRE

OCEANVS

ORIENS

PARTE OF DORSET SHIRE

PARTE OF SOMERSET SHIRE

Duluerton

Baunton

Wellington

Tauton

Backpclowne

Charde

Columbton

Honyton

Axmitter

Lyme

Excester

Sidmouth

Newton

Chudley

Torbay

Dartmouth haven

BRITANNICVS

Devoniæ Comitat: Rerumqvæ omnium in eodem memorabilium ve: cens, vera pticulariſ deſcriptio.
Anno Dn. 1575

Scala Miliariarum

Christophorus Saxton descripsit

R. remigius hogenbergius sculp

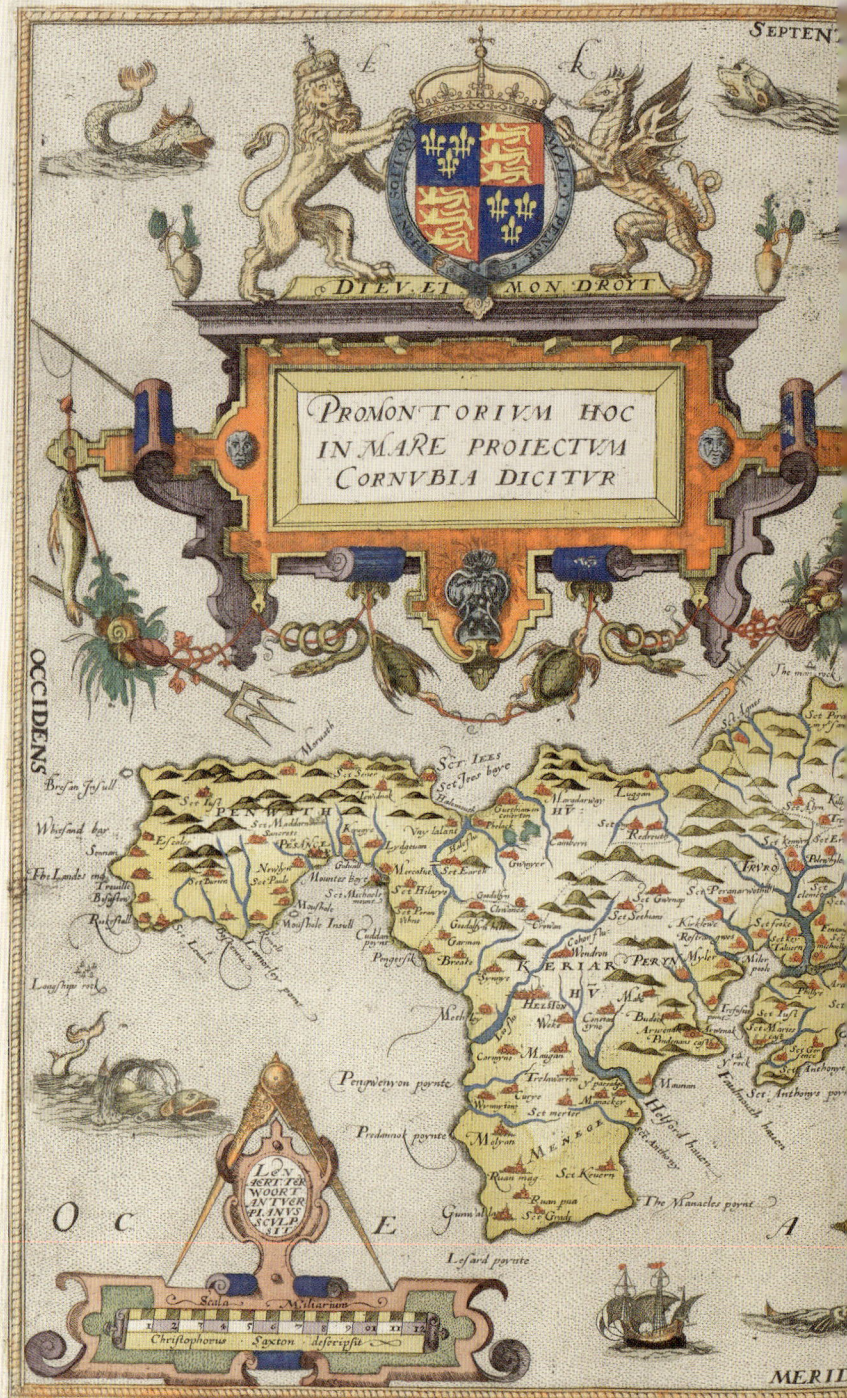

DIEV ET MON DROYT

PROMONTORIVM HOC
IN MARE PROIECTVM
CORNVBIA DICITVR

OCCIDENS

OCE

Scala Miliarium

Christophorus Saxton descripsit

MERID

FIG. 46

8

Map of Cornwall (1576)

Factum est hoc opus An° Dni 1576 et D Elyzabethe Reginæ 18

PESTIS PATRIÆ PEGRICIES

Hartland point
Hartland
HARTON
Welcombe   Clauelle
Marwynstow
Tunacombe
North lee
Stow
Kilkhāiton
Norton
Bude haue
Poughill
Efford   Launcels   Broadworthy
STRATTON   Derdnes   Soulden
STRATTON
Whalesbro   Witsbon   Churche   Brickorcuell   Pyworthye   HOLSWORTHYE
Weston   West
Prinstoke   HV: Whiteſtone
Tintagell cart   BOSCASTLE   Set gennys   Set mayre wyke   Vpton Tamerton   Clauton
TREVENA   Tintagell   Tinagell hauen   Iacobstow   Tetcot
TREVENA   Lesnothe   Otterham   Boyton   Laſſencote
LESNOWYTH   HV: Warrington   Set Giles
Set Teathe   Dauidstow   Tremayne   Tremeune   Penhole   North Petherwyn
Set Endelion   Lautegloſe   Treſmur   Egloſkery   Werrington
Set Myrmer   Set Kew   Michelstow   Set Adwns   Eglosherry
CAMLEFORDE   Egtonmg   Treweu   Set Steuen   LYFTON
PADSTOW   Trewen   Redge   LAVNSTON
Set E. Petheryk   Roſter hill   Alternun   Lidaſte
Set Breoke   Bruard   Brommeſbro   Lanconvok   Lewanock   South   Synth Petherwyn   Lanchiton
Treder   Tredinik   hill   Troſke   Petherwyn   Bradston   Dunterton
Iglesaie   Set ymbers   Northhill   Laſant   Myrlon
RIDER   TRIGGE   Bleſand   Treuarden   Temple   Siddenham
HV: Helcgen   Helm   HV: EAST HV: Callacombe
Set COLVMBE MAGNA   Wethill   Worlgon   Steke   DE
Set Wen   Worlgon   Lankenhorne
BODMAN   Cardenhot   Southill   Set Clan
Set Enoder   Lanitet   Glyn   Lamberhewck   Set Neot   Bickton   Kelbogton   LIVESTOK
Set Denys weſke   Royton   Set Ius   Couldrcch   VON:
POWDER   Luxellion   Leſstewe art   Pratt   Carby thar   Cundrie   Newton   Set Deryney   SHI
HV: Lanleuorye   Bocomo   Quethiak   Set Hellier
Set Steuens   Pelynt   Brook   Coyne   Set Sten   RE
Set Blatt   Set me   Myrhoppey   Set Merton   Ceyrnes
LISKERD   Brichton   Blaſlenny g   Bratt
VMPOUND   Merton   Set aust tell   Tobie   Dudes   Treure   Wottm   Trer Erne   Lemalyr
FOYE   Lauende   Merude   Lauente   Set Germins   Shewak   SALLISI   Tamerton solbre
Trewordrath bay   Set Hense   Plymtt   Lancoyll   Trogenit   Zarche   Set budoc
Penthor   Set Vepe   Pelruan   Lantegebe   Pergyhm   Set Marten   Set budoc
Moregifſo   Set Supers   Tallande   Crof hole   West Anſton   Seakadmereun   PLYMMOVTHE
Chappelland   Lansalwes   Low   Set Ichds   Mill   Catwater
Portwel te   Set Michaels Inful   Set Ihns   Rome   Redford   RE
The black rock   Tallande point   Mo

ORIENS
DEVONSHIRE
OCEANVS

The black rock
Padſtow hauen
The Gull rock

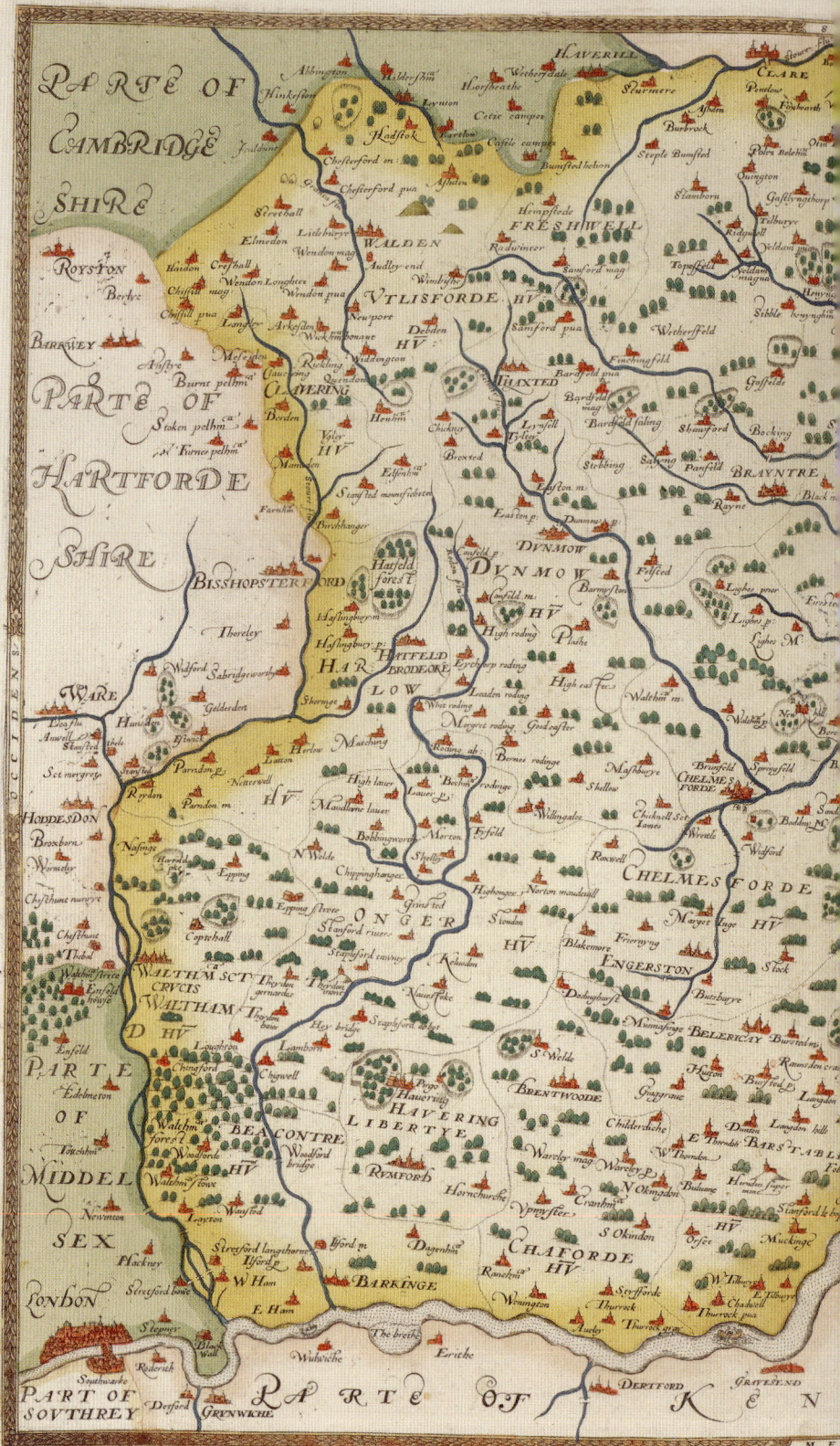

PARTE OF CAMBRIDGE SHIRE

PARTE OF HARTFORDE SHIRE

PARTE OF MIDDEL SEX

PART OF SOVTHREY

RAPTE OF KEN

FIG. 47

9

PARTE OF SVFFOLKE

Ipswiche

SVDBVRY · Cornard pua · Cornard magna · Walton · Wiston · Stoke · Nayland · Higham · Stratford · Est Bargholt · Catwade bridge · Brantham bridge · Sutton · Holbrook · Harkestede · Shotley · Arwerton · Nacton · Lenington · Chempton · Trimlee · Walton · The Orwell river

Horsley pua · Horsley mag · Boxted · Langhm · Dedham · Lawford · MANYTRE · Mystley · Bradfeld · Wrabnesse · HARWICH · Ramsey · Dover · Thorpe

LEXDEN HV · TENDERING HV · COLCHESTER · Lexden · West Donyland · Est Donyland · Wenerbur · Grinsted · Elmsted · Brumley mag · Brumley pua · Wickes · Ockley pua · Ockley mag

Fingringhoe · Brickesey · Langenho · Peldon · Salcot · Wigborough mag · Wigborough pua · Verley · Mersey · The Blokhouse · Est Mersey · Pewit · Frating · Thorington · Bentley M · Wyley · Tendringe · Beamont · Mose · Kirkbye · Walton · Holland M · Frynton · Holland pua · Horsey Insul · The Nase

WINSTRE HV · Inworth · Estthorpe · Layerbretton · Layermarney · Sct Osythe · Clackton pua · Clackton mag

THVRSTABLE HV · Braxted · Toothill · Tolshunt knight · Tolshunt darcye · Tolshunt maine · Tolesbury · Goldhanger

COGGESHALL · Ferring · Copford · Birch pua · Birch mag · Messing · Abberton · Layredelahay

MALDON · Mundon · Wickham · Langford · Hey bridge · Northey · Osey · Bradwell · Sct Peters chapel · Ramsey · Stewgate · Steple · Sct Lawrence · Tillinghm · Asheldam · DENGYE HV · Dengye

OCEANUS GERMA... ... ... ERMA...

DIEU ET MON DROIT

HONI SOIT QUI MAL Y PENSE

ESSEXIÆ
COMITAT' NOVA
vera ac absoluta descriptio
An° Dni
1576

PESTIS PATRIÆ PIGRICIES

ORIENS

Woodham ferris · Stowmaries · Purleygh · Lawling · Lachindon · Althorne · Mayland · Southmynster · Burnham · Crekesey · Crouch flu · WALLOT INSVL · Paulinesse · N Fambridge · S Fambridge · Asington · Canodon · Packlesham · Stambridge · Hall bridge · Rawrethe · Hockly · Hawkewell · Rochford · Stambridge m · Wakeringe Pa · Wakeringe m · Raleghe · Rocheford · Estwood · Sutton · Shopland N · Shoebuye S · Shobuye S church · ROCHEFORDE HV · Pratlewell · Hadlighe · Leghe · Benflete

CANVE INSVL

GRANE INSVL · Albalower · Colnge · Sct Maries · Stoke · Grane · Halsto · Medway flui

Quinboro cast tell · Myuster · Warden

SHEPYE INSVL

Christophorus Saxton descripsit

Scala Miliarium

PARTE OF BEDFORTE SHIR

HARTFORDIÆ
COMITATVS noua, ue-
ra, ac particularis descriptio. Anno Dñi .1577.

HONI SOIT QVI MAL Y PINSI

Occidens
Montmore

Tatternoll   Dunstable

Edgborō   Whipsnade   Kensworth
Wingraue   Stadham   Market   Hardinge
Longe morson   Iuingoo   Gaddes-   Flamsted   Whathors
            Mersworth   den parua   Abresdg   Redborne   Semerle
    Pulnhm   Gaddesdon magna
Buchland   Drayon beacon   Albury   Netleden   S.t.
Aston Clinton   North church   Goramburye   Michael
        Tryng   Wiginton   S.t Steuens   S.t
PARTE   Barkhamsted magna   Hemsted
        Cholsburye   Asrudge   DECORVM
Christoferus   Bonindon   Kinges Langley   Abbotts Langley
    OF   Chesham   HVN: Hunton bridge   Aldenha
        Chesham boies   Latimerse   Maudleine   Sarret
BVC: Nicholaus noldus Londinensis Sculpsit   Cheynes   Watforde   Bus
                        Richmersworthe

Scala   Miliarium

KINGAM   SHIRE

Henlow   Arlesey
    Shefl
Standon   Holwell
    S. billington
        Perton   Hic Kingsford   Lechwor
HYT: Hytchin
    Hexton   Asley
CHIN: Epaletts   W
    Luleg   Templedinsley   Poulos wonder
        Walden regis
HVN:
Luton   Surseed
            Kempton
            Lea   Ayell
        Codington

FIG. 48

10

CAMBRIDGE Royston · Chiffel magna
· Chiffel parua
SHIRE · Morden Lilington Bealee
Rode
DESEY Thaffeld BARKWEY Meseden Clauerringe
Buckland Anstye Berden
Wallington Withiall ED: Burntpelhm
Throckyng Hormed magna Pelhm stokinge Mamden
Rufhden Layston WINSTRE Furnes pelhm
Bradfeld Butingforde Hormed parua Peenbm
HVN: Codrid Afpenden Braughinge Alburyd Birch hanger
Westmill
Yardley HVN: Byfhops
Chesffeld Mundenfurniuall Puckrub Haddam parua ftartforde Hafhingburye
Benington Standon Magna
Afton Hadham magna Thorley Hafhingburye
Shephall Mundenfrewell parua
TER HVN: Sawcombe Thundridge Sabrichs geworth
Knebworth Watton BROVGHINGE HVN:
Dachworth Wadfmyll Geldesdon
Welwin Steglforde Widforde Harlow
Bengeho Huston Eftwick
Digswell Branfeld Ware Amwell Stansted ibels Perndon parua Nettefwell
Hartforde Sct Margrets Shoram Orient
HARTFORDE Hoddesdon Roydon Perndon magna
Hartingford Barkhufted parua Broxburne
burye Bayford Broxbourn wood Nafinge
Tewin HVN: PARTE
Busfhops Hatfeld wood Wormeley OF
Hatfeld Wormeley wood
North Mimmes Cheffhunt park ESSEX
North hall Cheffhunt Wood
LOWE South Theball Cheffhunt
Mymmes Enfelde Chase Walthm: ab:
Ridge Hadly Waltham ftreet
High Bernet The Queenes
N: Enfelde houfe PARTE OF
High Bernet Fateridge
MIDDLESEX

FIG. 49

PARTE OF HAMPTON

PARTE OF WARWIK SHIRE

PARTE OF GLOCESTER SHIRE

OCCIDENS

OXFORDSHIRE

PARTE OF WILSHIRE

BARKSHIRE

VALE OF WHITHORSE

Marleboro

PARTE OF HAM

PARTE OF BEDFORDE SHIRE

PARTE OF HARTFORDE SHIRE

PARTE OF MIDDLE SEX

PARTE OF SVRREY

THE VALE OF AILESBVRYE

BVCK

ORIENS

Scala Miliarium

Christopharus Saxton descripsit

FIG. 50

WARW:
PARS

OXON:

PARS

BERCE:

RIAE

PARS

WILTO:

NIAE PARS

ORIENS

GLOCEST RIAE PARS Shennington

GLOCEST PARS Sutton

GLOCEST PARS Widford

Scala Miliarum

CHRISTOPERVS SAXTON DESCRIPSIT

AVGVSTINVS RYTHER ANGLVS SCVLPSIT AN° DNI · 1577 ·

THE VALE OF EVESHOLME

CAMPDEN

WINCHCOMBE

CHELTNHAM

COTES

CIRENCESTER vel CICESTER

STOW ON THE OWLD

BVRFORD

LECHLAID

CRICKELADE

Thamesis flu.

Windrusht flu.

Echenlode flu.

113

PART OF NORFOLCK

OCCIDENS

OWSE magna flu

Parte of
Cambridgeshire

PART OF ESSEX

SUFFOLCIÆ C
Oppida mercatoria 25
Vna cum singulis H
In eodem Hera
Anno Dom

Wilton   Hackold   Wetinge
Owse pua flu   Wingforde   Downeham
Brandon   Thetford   Rushworth
Lakenheathe   Rushford
LACKFORD HV   Euston   Knattes hall
Litleport   Elneton   Berahm   Cow wene   Ixnorth pua
Ely   Esewell   Honyton
Owse flu   Mildnall   Luremere   Bernentine
Isleam   Ickingham   magn
Wortington   W Stow   Wordwell   Ampton   Ixworthe
Fordhm   Freckenhm   Laca forde   Leuermore mag   Troudworth
Baldingam   Herningswell   Flempton   Rushye   Ixworth
Kennet   Canehm   Fornhm oui   Berton   Norton
Exnign   Fornhm marten
Newmerket   Kensforde   THINGOW   THEDWARE STRE
Gaysesey   HV   Westley   Thurst ton   Tostock
Moulton   Sachm magna   Saxhm pua   Burye   Beighton   Tagget
Ashly   Dalma   Denim   Bareawe   Hepmartelty   Nowton   Bradfelde   Muncke   Drenkes
Cheuelye   Outsden   Ichworth   Hawsted   Bradfelde   Jeffet   Wulpet
Catlinge   Edgate   Chedber   Whelston   Sheffers bradfeld   Gedange
Carterton   Broad   Cowlidge   Hargraue   magna   Rede   Burned bradfeld   Fedshm   Buxhall
Wes ton   Thurlow   Bradley pua   Dens ton   Hausden   Law hill   Cock feld   Thorpe
Thurlow   Stradshell   Brockley   Somerton   Stimington   Kentleashton
Berneda ton   RISBRUGE   Harrys de   Napher   Preston
Fallow   Wrattinge pua   HV   Boxted   Burneuye   Drinst
Withersfelde   Kediston   Honedon   Hartys de   Lanehm
Haue rill   Clare   Giemysfort   S tans ted   Milding
Horshethe   Wickeo   Stoke   Candishe   BABER   Walding feld pua
Sheli campes   Pentlowe   Lachede   Walding fliage   magna
Cat lle campes   Sturmer   Ashdon   belthm   Lyston   Sudburye   Chiton
Burbroke   Ovington   Powers   Borley   Baldington   Cornera pua
PART OF ESSEX   Brundon   Addleton   Henny   Buers

NORWICHE

TE

NOR

KE

yermouth
yermauth hauen

Burgh cast Bradwell
Belton Gorleston
Friston Hopton
Sct Ola' Ashbye
LAN Lounde
Hormiaflete D E Corton
Somerley Blunston
towne Gunton

Wheatacre
Albye Fixton olton Leſtoſt

Geſlton Gillingham
Eſhingham Barsham Worlingham Kirtlow
Shipmeddow Beckles Carleton Pakefield
Denton Rangefeld Jugate Cone MVTFORD
Bungey Metingham Weſton Ellowe Gisleam
Flixton Mutford HV
Sct John WANGFORD Weſton Kushmere
Sct Margaret Sct Andros Weſtown
Harleſton Sct Peters Ratsburn Heneſted
Nedeham Sct Michaell Brampton Sotherton Benacre
Homersfeld Sct maco Stoven Vagethall Coue
Brodiſhe Wetherdall Albane Frostenton Courthall
Wiersdium Sct mergrot Wangford Coue
Thorp Sct James cluſton Sotherton Wangford
Aylan Rumford Spekeall Weſtall
Wayford HOXON HV Willet Blifon Henhm Easton neſſe
Metfeld Lanſtea gua Halefworth Wrnbulton Roydfn
Weybread Pefenfeld Lanſtea magna Bloburgh HV Southwold
Denham Huntingfeld Cokeley Walpole Bramfeld Walderſwick
Losfeld Arrengingum Sibton Thorington Dunwiche
Stradbrok Oppiſton Darſim Weſtelton
Wilbye Brundiſhe Dunniſton Fordey
Redlingfeld Bedingfeld Saxted Cransford Knell Mideton M.ſinere hauen
Southolde Framlingha mag Kelfele Carleton Theberton
Rushangles Kenton Parham Gimham Sternfeld Layſt fon Sibringhill
Kriſton Monewden HV Saxmundhm Sudwold
LOES Sharp Glemha Bruiſall
Brundiſhe Cretingham HV Stratford Sternfeld Knatshall Thorp
Framſden Glemham mag Farnam
Eaſton HV Charsfeld Peſtat PLOMES Sdringhill
Otley Debache Vffort Blaxal GATE HV Hazilwod
Gosbeck Baylie Renaleſham Dunning worth Hafilwod
Eyke Stratford Iken
Brumſwall Butley Aldebroughe
WOODBRIDGE Orforford Orforſet
TREDLINGE Mendham HV Shatsfrid WILFORDE Orford hauen
Petauch Grundeſbrug Boyton HV
Helmingham Bealing mag Boyton
Brackſted Sutton Capell
Stoke Seckford Harkſted Hoſeley
ICLEYDON Clopton Ramfere CARLEFORD Alderton
Westerfeld Kergrave Waldemaſhe Hoſeley
Whinſton Roſemere Bradiſton Dummſhall HV
Burſtall Bromford Newlborne Bawdsey
Wolverſton Mayſord Merteſhm HV
Capel Stoke IPSWICHE Foxall Buckleſton
Chalſthm Capleſton Nacton COLNES Kirton
Brantley Burſted Freſton Legmaton HV Fakemery
Wheefeld pua Wulverſton Brodeⁿp hauen
Tatouaſ ton SAMFORDE Shotley Foxhow
Eaſtberſt Holbrut HV Waldon
Stutton Arnerton Templen
Brantham Markſtea Shootley
Braunfeld Orwel hauen
Manitee Bradfeld Warmuſe Harwiche
Lonford Miſtley Ramsey
Dousy court

O
CE
A
N
VS

ORIENS

Scala Miliarum.
1 2 3 4 5 6 7 8 9 10

PESTIS PATRIÆ PIGRICIES

NORFOLCIÆ comitatus continens in se. Oppida mercatoria 26, Pagos et Villas 625, Una cum singulis Hundredis, & fluminibus in eodem, Vera descriptio.

Cornelius Hogius Sculpsit. Ao Dni 1574.

OCE...

THE WASHE

MERSHE LANDE

OCCIDENS

WISBICH

PARTE OF CAMBRIDGE SHIRE

ELY
LITTLEPUT

PERTII PATRLS BURGH

MILDNEIL

PARTE O...

THETFORD

FIG. 52

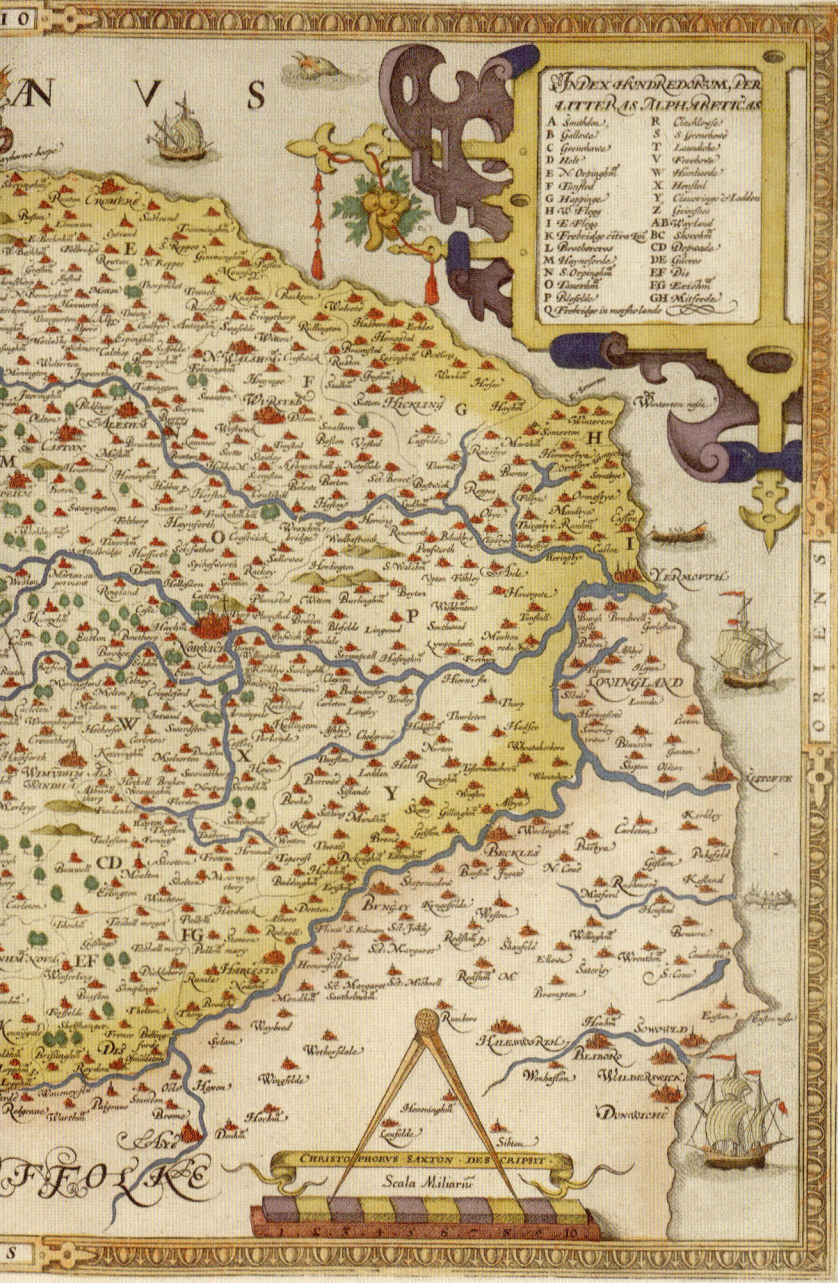

FIG. 53

10

OLN: PARS NORFOL:
Spaldinge
Merket deping Crowland Deuysdale Wilbiche Elm
PARS
Peterburgh Downeshm:
Dember

THE ISLE OF ELY

HUNTING Yaxley Littleport SUFFOL:
Mildnall
DONIA Ely
Brickwillm:
Newberne

PARS Exnyng NEWMARKET

CAMBRIDGE Gogmagog hill

Kimbalton

Biglelwade G

ESSEXIÆ
Royston

Hitchin HARTFORDIÆ
PARS PARS

CHRISTOPHORVS · SAXTON · DESCRIPSIT ·

Scala Miliarium

Tuddington
Dunstable

119

PARTE OF
STAFFORDE
SHIRE

PARTE OF
WORCESTER
SHIRE

PARTE OF
GLOCESTER
SHIRE

WARWIC=
LECESTRIÆQ:
Comtat: Cuitat:
Oppidorú, Villarú,
fluminú, Ceterarumq;
rerum omnium in
eisdem memorabi-
lium. noua. Veraq;
descriptio

PART OF
SALOP
Hales oun
SHIRE

OCCIDENS

Industria naturam ornat

PESTIS PATRIÆ PIGRICIES

LYCHFELD
TAMEW

BROMYCHÁ
COLESHIL
SOLYHUL
HENLEY
STREFFORD
ALCESTER
EVESHOLME
CAMPDEN
SHIPSTON

FIG. 54

DERBYE   PARTE OF   NOTTINGAM   SHIRE

NTRIO

PARTE OF LYNCOLNE SHIRE

LEICESTER SHIRE

RVTLAND SHIRE

PARTE OF OKEHAM

HINKLEY

BOSWORTHE

LVTTERWORTH

RVGBYE

HAVERBVRGH

MELTON MOEBRAY

WALTHAM on the wowld

PARTE OF

PARTE OF ORIENS

SOVTHAM

DAVENTRE

NORTH HAMPTON SHIRE

PARTE OF BANBVRYE HVNDERDE SHIRE

Scala Miliarium

1 2 3 4 5 6 7 8 9 10 11 12

Factum est hoc opus An° Dni 1576 et D. ELYZABETE Reginæ 18

Chryſtophorus Saxton deſcripſit

Leonardus Terwoordus Antuerpianus Incidebat

121

CESTRIÆ

STAFFORDIÆ
Comitatū pfecte et
absolute elaboratū hæc
tibi tabula exhibet
Anno Dni 1577

PARS.

OCCIDENS.

SÆLOPIÆ

PARS.

Scala Miliarium

Franciscus   Scatterus sculpsit

1 2 3 4 5 6 7 8 9 10

Saxton

Christophorus   descripsit

The 3.

Dane fl.

Wharmfort

Bosley

Swathanley Marbrok

Ridycard

Congleton Rushton

Byddle yendon Harrades

Marton fla Delynes

Horton The wall gr

New Chap Cheddleton

Church Lauton New chap

Talke chap Chell Bagnal chap

Bicknalhall Brodewall Tunstall Burslem Hilton ab Weston

Barthumlegh Audley Apedale Chesterton Wilstanton Shelton Bucknell chap

Betley Knutton NEWCAST Stoke Meare

Wrynehill Madeley Kerle Penele Fenton ma

Anneley chap Claton Hanford Blurton chap

Owtre Aeton Trenthã Foust

Whitmore chap Barleston The 7

Knyghton Charleton The beach Darlafton Hila

Bearston The beach Darlafton STONE My

Norton Maer Staune Afton Stoke

Beifton Muckleston Ashby Swynstead Walton Burfton

Black heath Charnes Byshops fley ECKLESHALL Shawford

DRATON Amynton Blore Elenhall Whitorns Marft

Bridgeford Raynton Hoptone

Tunstall High ofley Raynton ab STAFO

Adbafton Stonprã

Chipnall Knightley Stafford caft

Cheswardyne Norbury Gnashall Burton Ruc

Billington chap

Rilston Sutton Haughton Dunft

Chetwin Thegreat Willbrighton Braidle Pne

Meare Acaton Moton Churchealon Lapley

NEWPORT Hyghon On gun Aston chap

Stockton Brynton Hollybuall BREWOO

Woodcote Chatwall Blymhill Hydr

Heathhill Burlaton Weston under lesyart Chellington

Sheryfehales Gnoston

Tong caft Woken

Albrighton Pepperhill Wrotsley

Bonyngale Parton

Patshull Patingham

Trescot Nether

Shipley Sesdon Wam

Tresill

Clanerley

Gattaker Bublynton

Emull

Rawsley Compton Kn

Saberms fla

Baryate Shutte

Quer Arel

Haukebach

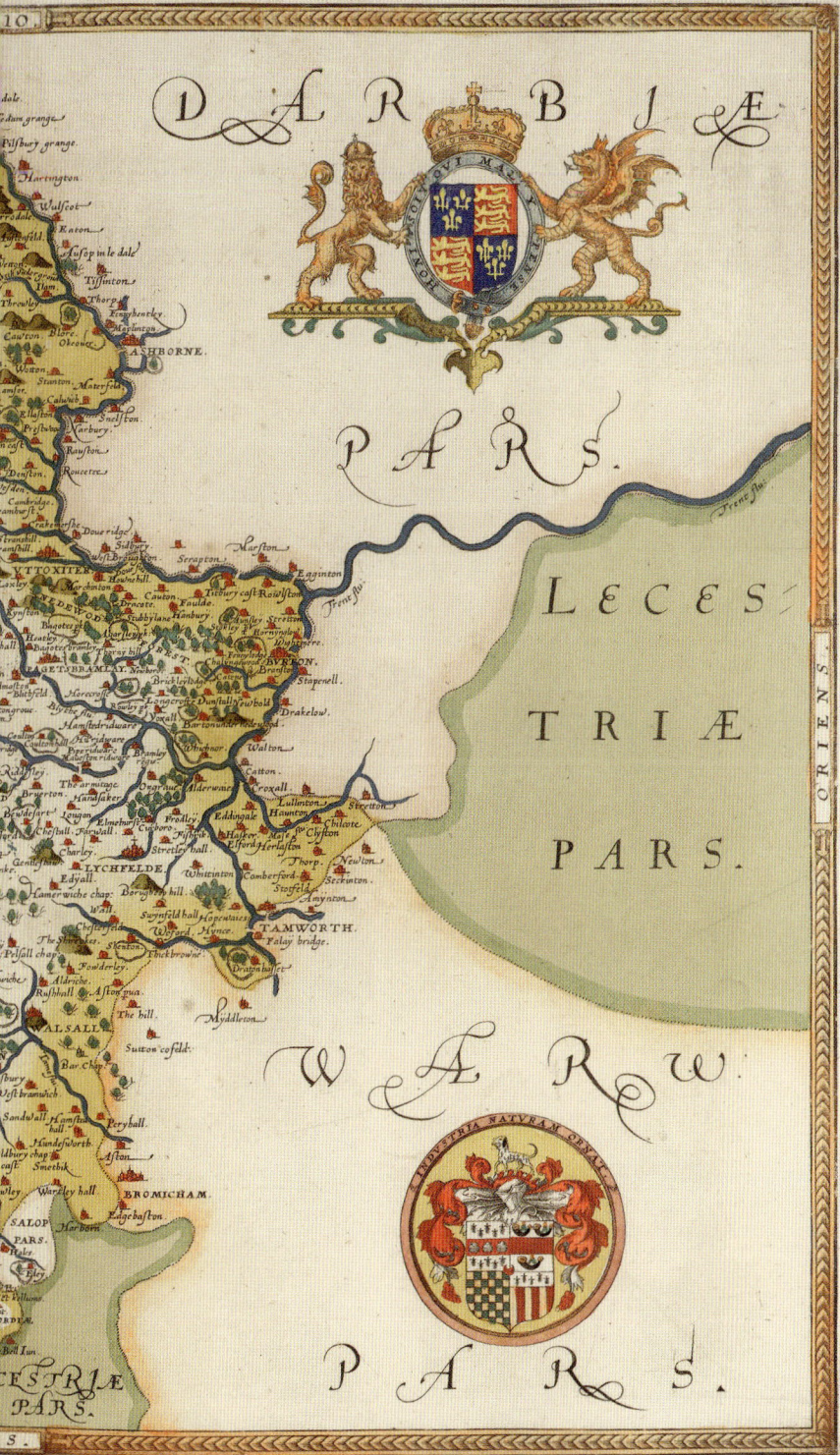

17

10

DARBIÆ

PARS

LECES-
TRIÆ
PARS.

ORIENS

dole
dam grange
Pilsbury grange
Hartington
Wulscot
rodale
ffeld Eaton
Venon Alsop in le dale
Ham Tyssinton
Throwley Thorp
Cauton Blore Ensybentley
Okeover Maylinton
ASHBORNE

Wotton Stunton Materfeld
Camber Calwich
Ellaston Snellston
Preswton Ranbury
Denston Rawston
Roucetre

Cambridge
cambrest
Craxenathe Doueridge
Stramshall Sudbury
cranshill
UTTOXETER Maxfeild Brunston Marston Seragton Egginton
Loxley Marchinton Cawton Titbury cast Rowston
ynton Hylle Dracott Faulde Ansley Stretton
Heatly Begotes Stubbylane Hanbury Horninglo
hall Bagots bromley Abas leygh Sherly Wightmere
Loynton Chulmestwod Newboro Brensby
GETESBRAMLAY Meddow Brich foxbam Stapenell
Moreovrt Longcrost Dunstall Newbold
Byrke Hu Wibaston Foxwall Bartonunderheed wood Drakelow
Hamstdedraware
cron grouse Whichnar Walton
uttons Alrewidrure
Radley Pype Ondray Catton Croxall
Beudesert The armitage Alderwene Stretton
ord Longan Hanslaker Rydley Lullinton Haunton
Elmehurst Fradley Chilcote
ford Chesball Farywall Cuboro Edingale Mayfeld Afstonlafton
Charley Stretley hall Fysbyke Thorp Newlton
LYCHFELDE Whittnton Comberford Seckinton
Hamerwiche chap. Edyall Borowth hill Stowfeld chap
Swynfeld hall Hopenlaskes Amynton
Chesterfeld Myuce TAMWORTH
Pellall chap Wyfes Stenton Falay bridge
Shenstone Chickbrowin
Fowderley
runche Aldriche Afston qua Dranhousee
Rushhall chap
WALSALL The bill Myddleton
Sutton cofeld

WARW.

PARS

SALOP
PARS.
Wales

CESTRIÆ
PARS.

S

S

SALOPIÆ

STAFFOR

PARS

PARS

OCCIDENS

INDVSTRIA·NATVRAM·ORNAT

HEREFORDIÆ

· Christophorus   Saxton   descripsit ·

Scala Miliarium

1 2 3 4 5 6 7 8 9 10

PARS

FIG. 56

18

WIGORNIENSIS
Comitatus Sabrinæ
Fluminis Amœnitate
nisissmis descriptio
An° Dm 1577

DIÆ

SLOP:

Smethik

Westleyhall

Harborne

Edybaston

Castle bramecke

Kingeshurst

Sheldon

Hodnedon

Selybull

Moseley

RS:

Frankley

Norfeld

Northweeld

Kingesnorton

Luckey beacon

Cofton

Withe chap

Alchurche

Hewellgrange

Shuter

Feckenham
Forest

Teckenium

Bradley

Inkebarow

ROVE

Tardbik

Burley

Fedter

Colnlaton

Bachith court

AVLCESTER

Arrow

Rugley

Moreton

Wetheley

Beyenten

Grafton

Flyford

Abberton

Samford

Deffordon

Clue

N. Eytelton

Penworth

priories

Piddle

Rosselrucke

Churcheloeche

Netton

Harminton

Naunton

Byshington

Thregmarton

Hyll

Lenchewicke

Piddle

Fladbury

Charleton

Defforton

Myddle Eytelton

South lyrleton

PERSHORE

Wike

Craythern

Boyelyn

Wike Byse

Wihensed

ELVESHOLME

Hampton

Aston

Barlinghll

Bricklahum

Commertoppe

Commer

Querton

Birlingham

Welley

Pandey castle

Hampton

Eluesholm

Childes wikan

Willerfey

Somerffedas ton

Hayston

S. Andree

Bredon hill

Cumberton

Ashton underhyll

Werwynton

Norton

Bredon

Kemmerton

Boctford

Tewell

WORCESTRIÆ
PARS Wass pars qua
Ausleton

GLOCES

Overbury

Alchurch

NEWKESTVRYE

TRIÆ PARS

Jusseler

Goldesthorp

WORCES
TRIÆ

Aldevingaston

Whitewyck

Laventen

Newhall

PARS

Tredecton

Hunyton

Alnecfort

Blakoll

SHIPTON

Darbagefrete

Tidcomton

Stratton in the
vousse

Danford

Hangingerston

WORCESTRIÆ
Nerehek
Pars

Brackley

Lemyngenton

WORCESTRIÆ
PARS
Ausleton

WORCES
Euersde
TRIÆ
PARS

OXON:

TER

W:

R

RW:

A

S

ORIENS

PA

RS

The Vale of Eueshom

GLOCES

TRIÆ PARS

PARS

125

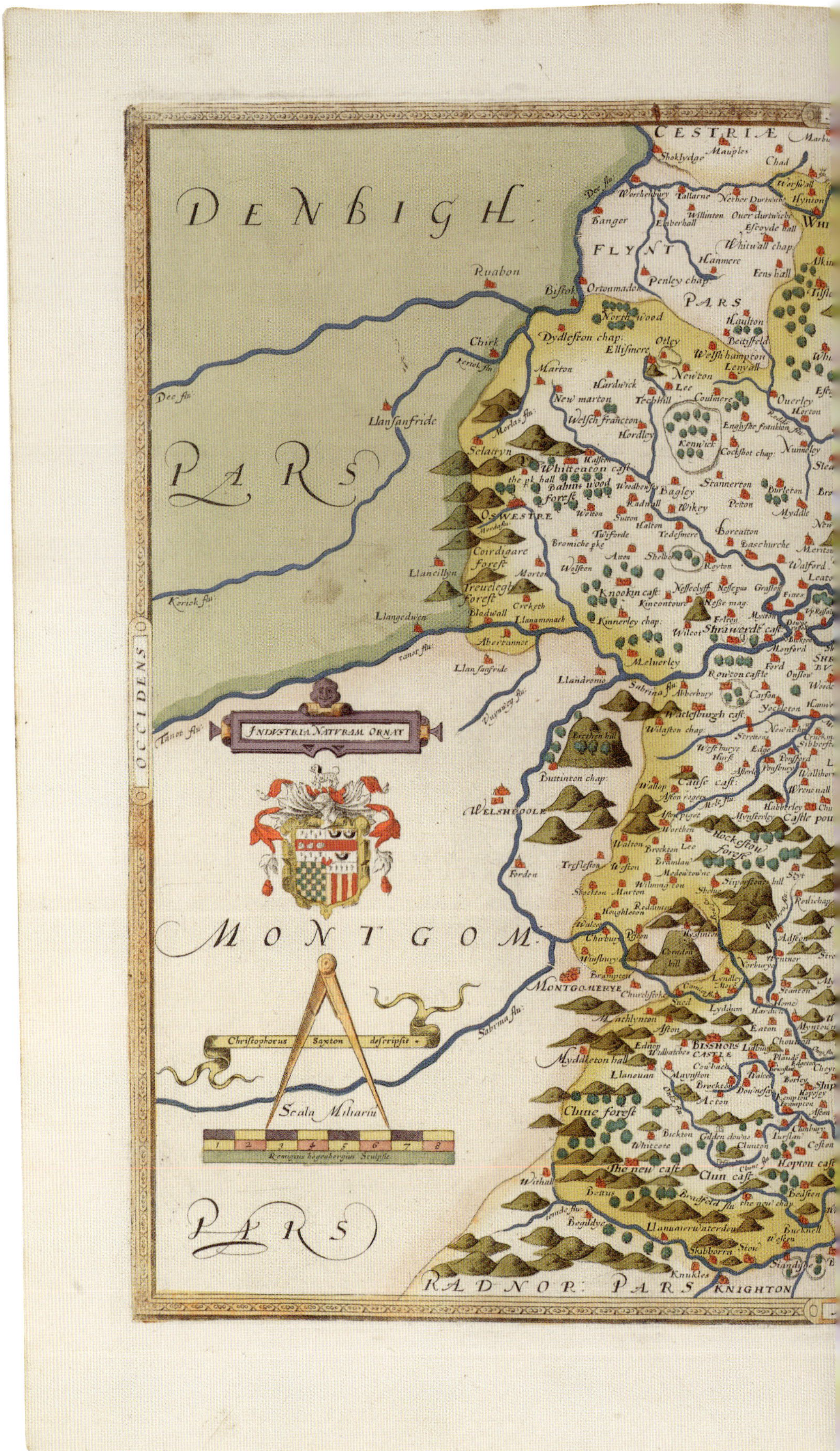
DENBIGH
PARS
CESTRIÆ
FLYNT
PARS
OCCIDENS
INDVSTRIA NATVRAM ORNAT
MONTGOM
PARS
Christophorus Saxton descripsit
Scala Miliariu
1 2 3 4 5 6 7 8
Remigius hogenbergius Sculpsit
RADNOR PARS
KNIGHTON
Ruabon
Chirk
Dee flu
Keriok flu
Llansanfride
Llancillyn
Llangedwen
Tanot flu
Llan sanfride
Sabrina flu
Welshpoole
Forden
Montgomerye
Bisshops Castle
Clun cast
Oswestre
Whittenton cast
Ellismere
Shrawerde cast
Caurse cast
Chirbury
Corndon hill
Clune forest
The new cast
Hockestow forest
Knookin cast
Coirdigare forest
Treueleglh forest
Aberrannet
Llandrono
Buttinton chap
Myddleton hall
Stiperstones hill
Bangor
Ortonmaden
Northwood
Haulton
Penley chap
Hanmere
Welsshampton
Marton
New marton
Selattyn
Kenwick
Cockshot chap
Stannerton
Kinnerley chap
Melverley
Abberbury
Wattlesburgh cast
Westbury
Wallop
Trefleston
Worthen
Walton
Snede
Lydham
Llanewan
Acton
Whitcote
Bettus
Knukles
Stow
Skabborra

FIG. 57

19

STAF

SALOPIÆ COMITATIS,
summa cum fide, cura et dili-
gentia descriptionem hæc tabula refert. A.Dñi. 1577.

SVIT QVI

MAL Y PENSE

FOR
DIÆ
PARS

ORIENS

WOR
CES
TRI
Æ
PARS

SALOP
Hales
PARS

Anneley
Andlem
Audlem
Bure
Bourston
Terne fl.
Knighton
Yrley
Belaport
Nerten
Muckleston
Shenton
Aberley
Benot
Blore
Annyston
Stanly
Adbasston
Mauerley
Moreton
Longford
DRATON
Dlechley
Terne fl.
Adbasston
Chipnall
Wullerton
Tyrley
Cheswardyne
Hatton
Hodnet
Hynheck
Pickstoke
Peplew
Childes acell
Chetwin
Meare
Stanton
Allerton
Edgemond
NEWPORT
Stechen
Ellerdon
Keynton
Tibberton
Chatwen assen
Horbet eaft
Belris
Longford
Churchaston
E.Edgebalton
Newton
Watercyph
Aldeny
Brockton
Woodcott
Muckleton
Cheryton
Chatwall
Walton
Aftaston
Stepe
Heathhull
Chelmston
Roden
Rodinton
KINGES WOD
Dunnyton
Weston under lesfiart
Burlaten
Shervffhyley
Cotall
Longchappel
Morton
Hadley
Wombridge
Draton
Adbaston
Resadyne
Rytmostsoveril
Woodhonses
Codsall
Wrethton
Orleton
WELLYNTON
Olerpate
Pryors holt
TONG caste
Scenten
Albrighten
Wrensley
Charleton caste
Halcot
Haughton
Shestull
Elston
Hatton
Beynnall
Peplesale
Dasley pua
Laley
Laley
Hurdyton
Strechley
Wike
Euclyn
Beckbury
Parshull
Ruston
Vendok put
Bratton
Hymyten
Roycon
Leghton
Eldas moor
Haddey
Sucten
Hissord
Wost fl.
Eatonsip sabcna
Bellas put
Sabney
Norton
Badath
Driston
Gressfledston
Stockton
Shipley
Cunde
Harpridge grange
Wike
Acleton
Aitonhurnell caste
Chapron
Lynley
Hanns
Hylton
Harley
Vervill
Claverley
Kenler
Burton
Norley
Afsley
Ringleford
Tucksen
Langley
Prenchap
Howlee
Presson
Muckley
Harles
Whil
Ploshe
Sponell
Rowndunt
Tasley
Morfe
Gatacker
Whentennaston
Whitton
Bridgenorthe
Wuatford
Dubhviten
Easfey
Munkehopton
Vndersore
Medeley
Didmasten
Morthinsses
Upton
Chenton
Fanten
Marken
Emull
Cota
Chelmarsh
Hempton
Compten
Shipton
Longstanton
Glassley
Skemnshuydolleton
Ravesley
Wowgate caste
Neynton
Prioersditton
Tenwkessall
Iueley
Bradston
Rickton
Sidbury
Muslfey
Tugsord
Billingesfley
Hanoarsfwort
Abton
Iugley
Munflow
Hawes
N. Cleburye
Shugersord
Hedley
Cleouer chap
Dodderels aston
Oner Arcley
Cramerofe caste
Browne
Boreaston
Earyate
Trimple
Hoanes
clee hull
Staterton
Dudlesbury
Corshin caste
Whettle
HEREFORD PARS
Kynlet
Conster
Sutton
Westton chap
Mylburnstoke
Sidington
Hanchall
Cleobrye
Shefton
Whichcote chap
Haytons
Silington
Hoonderton
The forst
The forst WYRE
Ticknns
DEWDELEY
Stanton lacye
Lodon
Staterstones hull
Hopton wafry
Cleobrye
Myddleton chap
Coreley
Mylton
LVDLOW
Henley
Buiterley
Newotabrey
Bayton
Ereno
Lefwiche
Laggealghun
Nashe chap
Cenan
Whitton chap
Bruegewod chale
Ashford
Kirkenall
Grete chap
Rackeford
Burfard
Burley
Deam ph.
Knyghton
RD.
Richardes caste
Ashfordbeaudeft
Herefordshyre
Henburye
HERTFORD PARS
Temd. fla.
Wooferton
Cambertton
Burrinton
Bruneld

SÆLOPIÆ

LVDLOW PA...

RADNOR PARS

OCCIDENS

BREKNOK

PARS
Christopherus Saxton descripsit
PARS
Scala Miliarium.

1 2 3 4 5 6
Remigius hogenbergius.

HEREFORDIÆ PARS
The fothok

MONV...
PA...

PRESTAYNE
LEMSTER
PEMBRIDGE
WEBLEY
KYNETON
HAY

Old radnor
Glaſtre
Huntyngton
Brilley
Mychaelchurch
Whitney
Bettus chap
Clifford caſt
Hardwick
Keueſop
Craſwall chap
Llancony
Cledok
Michael church
crucorne

FIG. 58

20

VIGOR
NIÆ

PARS

ORIENS

GLOCESTRIÆ

PARS

MONMOVTH

FRVGIFERI
AC AMENI
HEREFORDIÆ
COMITATVS
DELINIATIO
Anno Dñi 1577

INDVSTRIA NATVRAM ORNAT

BRAMYEARDE

LIDBVRY

NEWENT

ROSSE

Rochford
Ouerhanley
Kyre
Stokebly
Ouerfapye
Clyfton
Shelley welfhe
Wulferlow
Nether fapye
Nethwood
Collynton
Tedfton dela mere
Edwinloche
Tedfton wafers
Whitborne
Thornbury
Edwinrafe
Knightwick
Teme flu:
Wackton chap.
Burdenbury
Grendon epi
Suckley
Grendon warren
Auenbury
Marfton
Pencombe
Newton
Stanford epi
Cowley
Monderfeld
Cowarnpue
Acton beachm
Cradley
Stoke lacye
Byfhfrome
Mathern
Hullyngwick
Eaftnache
Cowarne magna
Morton Iefferey
Caftle frome
Pitchers ocul
Bofbury
Felton
Ingleton
Canfrome
Coddinton
Ocull
Styuiton
Colwall
Dynehill
W. Hyde
Yarcle
Munfley
Wethinton
Afperton
Effmor
Beggerfweeton
Taddington
Pixley chap.
ab tarrington
Brayfill eaft
Stoke edyr
the Worldes end
Dormington
Ayifton
Marcle pua
Longwart
Sufton
Dunynton
Campton
Killinafton chap.
Branfhorgh
theràs chap
Mordeford
Well hope
Preffon
Dimmok
Dinedor
Faune hope
Tutley chap.
Marcle magna
Hamlacye
Salers hope
Yaiton
Kempley
Boulfton
Brockanton
Dew'churche pua
Ballenghm
How capl.
Fawley chap.
Inkefton
Vpton
Tregel
Horewethye
Lynton
Afton
Aull regis
Fox
Harwood
Sellek
Bridfton
Brampton
Ecklefwall
Landinabo
Wilton caft.
Rudhall
Wefton
the Lea
Pencoyde
Heatland
Peterftou
Mychael church
Thewearefend
Penthard caft
Treuire
Ham
Conghirm chap.
Sci Wancrs
Hayf Manefell
Garran pua
Langarran
Glewfton
Waifton
Penrofe
Goderich caft
Marfton
HONOME
Pembridge caft.
Whitchurch
Welche bicknor
Wefhe newton
LENSIE
Llanrothall
Gunnore'e
Sci Michaell
Englifhe bicknor
Meughan

P A R T E   OF

YORKE

SHIRE

DIEV ET MON DROIT

LINCOLNIÆ NOTINGHAMIÆQ;
Comitatum noua vera et
accurata descriptio. Anno
Domini 1576

OCCIDENS

PAR TE

of

DÆRBY

SHIRE

Christophorus Saxton descripsit

Scala Miliarium

PART

OF LECES

SHIRE

FIG. 59

21

Hull

Humber

The Spornheade

Salfleet haven

OCEA

NVS

ORIENS

LINDESEY

KESTEVEN

the fen

Boston

Donyngton

the Wasshe

HOLLAND

Spalding

Holland fenn

Crowland

PARTE OF RVTLAND SHIRE

PARTE OF NORTH HAMPTON SHIRE

PARTE OF CAMBRIDGE SHIRE

PARTE OF NORTH FOLKE

FIG. 60

LANCAS
TRIAPARS

CESTRIÆ

PARS

OCCIDENS

VNIVERSI
Derbiensis Comitatus
graphica descriptio
1577

NON · SINE · CAVSA

Tame flu.
The Woodhead
Errufell   Mossesin   New chap.
Hollingworth   Woodland
Motterain   Glossop   Barwenslow   Edall
                 Chalesworth   Newstede   Bare
Mellor chap.   Tharset hall   hill rareslin
Merpull chap. Bothomsall   Nether bouthe
Egre flu.   Outherset Heathfield   Monhill
               Beardhall   Casterion Hope flu. Dut
                                              The Castle in y peake Broadwall
Yerdesley   Elhmork
hall   The Chapelling The chamber in y forest Huckless qua
Wolgebrid   Marshhall firthe Steake forest   Huckley
            Ridgehall Wedneswell   magnus
Tinkhall   Eaterfield Harditshall Westm Middelwall Gyr
                 Tinsted Merthonslow Wardlow
Overton   Bixton well Kingsfcarndale Wormhill
Gorston   ferlhouses Staden Conlon New medow Wac
Goytbouse Epeholes Crowdale Blakewell
            Chelmerton Taddington
            Flaghenifor Shelton
Thorlesbouth   Mag ish
           Bouchead Sharudale   Roddall flu
            Cronafton
           Longnor Medangraige
Wharnford   Pillsbury grange
              Shrue   Herbtcte
                            Hartyngton
                     Wolster
                     Narrodale   Raer
                              Po
                   Auffenfeld   Lg

STAF

FOR

DIÆ

Ellgfton   Rowsley
             Cambidgle Mar
             Crichfam Eato
             Vttoxater
                       Mar

PARS

Scala Miliarium
1 2 3 4 5 6 7 8

Christophorus · Saxton · descripsit ·

MER

22

CENSIS PARS

Sheafeld

Treeto

Hanforth

Aston

Henderbridge

Beghton Wales

Gleder H. Wrboll

Kilmarshe Thorpfalter De shire oke

NOT

Bechif nb. Norton

Barlbrugh Whitwell

Eckinton Cloune Belphe Welbek

Wodhowse Drondfeld Whittento Staley Wodlhorp Netherthorp Ehneton Norton cuckney

Morehowse Dunfton Sprowefa Clowne church Holbek

Newbold Heimeliall Dronpton Dickmanto Woodhowse Whaley Nether Langwich

Chesterfeld Bowfewer eaft Ouer Langwith

Walton Farlandhall Sutton Normanton Palterton Sherbrok Scarclef

Wingerworth Williamfthory Heuthe Houghton

Harwood grange N. Wynfeld Stanefire Glapwell Pleafler Nettlewrth

Roefleyhall Wedbery Hardwick Hackney Maunffeld Woodhouse

Stretley Afhauer Anton Tifller Rawthorp

Darly hall Hanley Morton Terbfhelpe Teuerfall

Wollet Oefton H. Iohn Blakwell Suttnny Afhfeld

Taylby Myllnetowne Pentrych Hucknall

Marlok Drakenyds S. Normanton Kirkby

Deddikhall Wighton Norland Carbyngwhatehall

Wheatcroft Alfreton Prynton

Cromsforn Wakebridge hall Somercotes Selfen

Myddleton Winfeldmanor Sumerwck Wanfley

Wolftamewebridge Preifley Codner caft Branfley

Aldenvafh Pentridge Codnor

WIRKEWORTH Cromlhey Butterley Heur

Afhby hay Ripley Codnor

Anton Shotley pk. Langley

Kirk Iereon Belper Denbye kidlegip pk. Effwood Graifley caft

Turndrehil Wyndlylhill Kilborn Smalley Shipley

Mugginton Holbrek Horfley Cafiall

Mircafton Pefton Vnderwood Horfemcaft Maperley Alkefton Streeley

frogegnos Danfley Halam Trewell

Yednafton Breafeleton Kedlhefton Offer Morley Stanley Kirkhalam

Darby Lonwdhall Allifter Stanton Stapleford

Hellymon Langly Maikwoton Bradfall Dale Atherton

Chefter gyne Gibfaker

Danbery leies DARBYE Litchurch Ockbrok Horfell Rifley

Redborne Ofmafton Spyndon Chadeften Longeaton

Our gun Alnafton Breafton Chyfton

Thornafton Barwardcote Synfalle Bowlton Elluefton Weibe Sawley

Offafton Normanton Ambafton Trentflu Barten

Afhe Elwall Arkefton Chelafton Sharleut Welne magn Thrumpeon

Burten Broughton Findeme Ingleby Wefton Afton

Superton Tedford Mylton Spuen Newton Lockinton Hemington

Hoone Hilton Eggineton Enwarke Caft. Dunyngton

Roufflon Mylton Melborn caft

Fauld Tirbuy caft Repton

Stretton Newton fon Bredon fug inont

Wighenton Brathye Tickmall

Burtonlup Pyfhill Hartfhorn Staunten

trent Caukc Worthington

Newbolde Stapnell Smethik Colerton

Drakelow Shuggen Swadlincote The greabee

Caldwall Grefley Blangthorpe Afhbyedelazouche Packinton

Waleon Lynton Caft greifley Normanten

Catton Raufflaton Netherfeo Olkethorp Swayfton

Caton Ludlington Stayt orange Swarfeton Normanton

Edingale Chilcet Stretton magn Swarflon

Thorfilton Hanteon Appleby

TIN GAMIÆ PARS

LECESTRIÆ PARS

ORIENS

Trent flu

LAN ...

OCEA

NVS.

OCCIDENS.

CESTRIÆ Comitatus (Romanis Legionibus et Colonijs olim insignis) vera et absoluta effigies.

INDVSTRIA NATVRAM ORNAT.

FLINT

PARS

DENBIGH PARS.

FLINT PARS.

DELA MERE FOREST

Leuerpoole hauen
Crosbye pua
Crosbye magna
Bowtle
Bankehall
Kirkdale
LEVERPOOLE
Wallasee
Poton
Seacombe
Bydston
Claghton
Tramnole
Oxton
Morten
Vpton
Ouer Church
Saw commaste
Meisse mag
Newton
Woodchurch
Nesse pua Grange
Grosefley
Frankbye
Westkirkbye
Cauda
Irbye
Thurstenton
Oldfeld
Brunston
Thornton
Branston
Prenton
Bebinton
Stourton
Ouerbebinton
Brumbro chap
Pooton lanceler
Eston
Heswall
Gayton
Leghton
Hooton
Childrenthorn
poole
Neston mag
Willaston
Nesse
The neuheye
Sutton court
Whibye
Stanney
Sloke
Croughton
Burton
Puddington
Ledsum
Capenhurst
The lea
Shotwick
Shotwick cast
Mulynton
Bloconhall
Tho hcitre
Howl
Newton
CHESTER
Plemstan
Traford mag
Gildenfutton
Hardin cast
Broughton
Bretton hill
Ecclefton
Dodlefton
Eaton
Pooton
Pouford
Kynnerton
Burton
Aldford
Alton flu
Golborne
Hanley
Churton
Aldersey
Coddington
Clutton
Farnedon
Holt cast
Dee flu
Tylfton
Malpas
Sholych
Kidinton
Old cast
Worthenbury
Chad

Hilbre Insul.
Balla burtab
Holiwell
FLINT
Dee flu.
Yewloy cast.

Wartre
Garston
Speakhall
Hale
Halewood
Weston
Rock sauage
Sutton
Aston chap
Frodfhm
Nether
Woodhoufs
Helsbye
Elton Thornton
Auonley chap
Mauley
Manlay
Dunham
fup mons
Mouldesworth
Barefton
Barefford
Vpton
Charleton
Bridge trasfor
Ashton
Terwyn
Kelsale
Hecknelplat
Vckinton
Clotton
Duddon
Staplesford
Burton
Torperley
Huxlell
Teerton
Pefton cast
Harthill chap
Chowley
Buckley
Dunkin

Farnworth
Cuerdley
Thepele
Appleton
Penketh
Runkhorn
Ouer Ruckhorn
Hulton cast
Morton
Norton
Messe flu
Stockhm
Aston gran
More
Ketewink
Dareshu
Preston
Aston gran
The caft
Weber flu
Newton
Kyngsley
Croton

Bewsey
WAR
Sankye
Aston gran

M

FIG. 61

EBORACENSIS PARS

TRIÆ

DAR
BIÆ
PARS

ORIENS

Myddlehurst
Tame flu.
Ashton under lyne   Stalay hall   Eynsell
Dunkenfeld   Hollingworth
Watley
Denton chap: Godley   Mottram   Glossep
Chalsworth
Redysshe
Harden   Mellor chap:
Portwoodhall   Bothumsall
Flixton Vrmston Stretford chap: Goyte hall
Chowerton chap: Diddesbury   Marpull chap: Goyte flu.
Carinton   Ashton on mersee bank   Barlow   Owlerset
Partinton   Sale   Northen   Bredhall
Warburton ch.   Redinges   Withinshaw   Chedle   STOKPORT
Timperley   Baggeley   als Stopford.   Torrinton
ALTRINCHAM.   Brandon sup mont   Norbury
Hollen flu.   Danhm   Poynton   Dysley deyne
Lymme   Ashley   Ryngey chap: Newhall   Erdley hall
High Leghe   Rousthorn Busly flu.   Pownell   Hanford   Wylly bridge
Mellington   Mere   Tatton   Wymslow   Wodford   Taxhall Shawcrosse
Ouer Tabley   Mabberley   Adlyngton   Shrigley
Knottesforth   Chorley   Newton chap: Pot chap: Ouerton
Chapel in the stretz   Butley   MACLES
Pichmere   Bouthes   Monterum   Presthbury   FELD
Budworth   Nether tabley   Marthall Alderley   Alderley becon   Bollinton   FOREST.
Holford   Toft flu.   Ollerton   Ranoo
Peuer flu.   Chelford chap: MACLESFELDE.   The Chamber
THWICHE   Nether peuer   Ouer peuer   in the forest
Shurlache Shebrok   Holme   Ilosток   Honburye   Sutton   Shutlyngeslau
Whatcroft   Siddington   Ridge   hill
Warton   Goulstre   Gosworth   Wharnford
Croxton   The armitage Carrinchm
Kinderton   Cranage   Twamlow   Marton chap: North Rode
Middlewich   Holmes chap: Suithamley grange
Darnall grange   Cotton   Dane flu.
Sproston   Dauensport   Bosley
Mynshull   Bradwall   Eaton
Warmyncham   Sandbach   CONGLETON
Erdesurick   Smethwick   als Congerton.   Astbury
Chorlton   Whelok   Bydulph
Copnall   Haslyngton   Moreton   Whelok flu.   Molecot hill
Acton   Oslinston   Haslyngton hall   Rode hall
Weston   Barthumley   Churchlawton
NANTWICHE.   Hough   Talke chap:
Slapeley   Widdenbury   Betley   Audley
Barderton   Duddinton   Wrynehill
Hatherton   Madeley eaft
Hankelow   Madeley
Aldelem   Anneley chap:
Ombermere   Ourre
Burladam   Titley   Bearston   Knighton

STAF
FOR
DIÆ
PARS.

Christophorus · Saxton · deseripsit ·

Scala Miliarium

Franciscus Scatterus sculpsit
Anno Dni 1577.

PIÆ PARS.

WESTMOR
LANDIÆ
PARS

DVNELMENSIS · EPISCO:
PATVS · PARS

BARNARD CAST:

Applegarth forest

Swaledale forest

T H E   N O R T H   R I D I N G

RICHMON

Wensedale

Bishopdale chase

THE WEST RIDING

KIRKBY LVNSDALE

SETTLE

Bowland forest

Gisborn

Cledre
Mytton

COLNE

BRIGGOW CAST:

Wharfdale

RIPLEY

Knaresburgh forest

KNARESBVRGH

WETHERBY

BRADFORTHE

LANCASTRIÆ

PARS

CEST
STOPPFORTH PARS

DERBIÆ
PARS

OCCIDENS

FIG. 62

EBORACENSIS
Comitatus (cuius Incolæ olim
Brigantes appellabantur) Lon-
gitudine Latitudine hominúq;
numero reliquis illuſtrior.
Anᵒ Dñi 1577

OCEANVS

LINCOL-
NIÆ PARS

NOTTIN-
GAMIÆ
PARS

Blakay morr

the foreſt of pickering

Pickering

Yorke would

RIDING

WIGHTON

SCARBROVGH

BRIDLINGTON

BEVERLEY

HVLL

Humber

BARTON

Marſhe lands
Diche marſhe

Axholme
inſul:

BVRTON

DONCASTER

BLVTHE

WORKSOP

Chriſtopher Saxton deſcripſit

Scala Miliarium

Auguſtinus Ryther Anglus ſculpſit : Anᵒ Dñi 1577

ORIENS

137

CVMBERLAN
DIÆ
RAVENGLAS
War burthwai
PARS St. John chap:
Seaton
Whidbeck
Wethinn
Mullun Cast

Langdale qua
Wrenosse hill
Eskdale
Blakha

Brathey
Lonsfol
Hawkeshead
Coniston
Satterhoms tenenberg
Sowthon
Graythwat
Nibthwai
Staveley
Sowberthwat
Blawith
Wodland chap
Broughton
Crfonure
Kirkby
Drigg ford
Coulton

Clorgergate
Ambleside
Camgaeth
FVRNISH
FELLS
Carpmanfell

Wenandermere
KENDALL
Wynsler chap
Crossbute
New bridge

Louick chap
Hamsfeldhall
Lyndell
Haw chap
Curlandes
Hawker

WESTN
di
pa
pa

Duckon castle
St. arth
Hay cote
Newbton
Leee
Arelash
Glaymoncke
Uldogham

Leuen sand
Winder
Sand

Walney chap
Beger
Newbton
Ramside
Fowney Jusell
the pyle of fowdray
S. En

Sunderland point

LANCASTER

Cokesandabbey

Shirsshead

Hackinfal
hall
Reff
hall
Pillin hall
St. John chap
Nateby hall
Pylling mosse
GARSTANG
the Grange
Hambleton
Nether
Rowchf
Essham
in Felt
Thornton hall
Stavnnall

OCEANVS

INDVSTRIA NATVRAM ORNAT

Scala Miliarium.

Christopherus Saxton descripsit

1 2 3 4 5 6 7 8 9 10

Remigius hogenbergius sculpsit

OCCIDENS

Marton mere
Westbyhall
Dymns
KIRKHM

Marton meer
Skelbrick hall
Harlwich hall
Raffall
Barton
ORMISKIRK
Aushton
Fermby
Altmouth
Fasce
Sefton
Crosby
Hello
Kirkbye
Letherland
Walton
Bank hall
Derbye
Ewton
LIVERPOOL
Wallasee
Hellbre
fusell

Liepole pole
the blackrock

CES

FIG. 63

25

EBORA

LANCASTRIÆ
Comitatus palatin vera
et absoluta descriptio
Anno Dñi 1577

CEN
SIS
PARS
DER
BIÆ
PARS

TRIÆ PARS

ORIENS

Ingleboro hill

Clapham

Crosse of grete

GISBORN

Brasewell

Gillirk

Rimington

Barnside

COLNE

New church

Whaley

Burnley

Widdophead

Seyperden

Mansfeld

BLACKBORN

Bacup

Rossendale

Tedmerden

The batenges

Darwen chap

Littleborugh

Newhall

ROCHEDALE

Taune

Saddleworth

BURY

Shaw chap

Chaterton

Myddleton

Oldom

Foxdenton

Blakeley chap

Mytchurst

the Werdhead

MANCHESTER

Stalay hall

Dunkenfeld

Harden

Mottram

WIGAN

Meller chap

Goythall

STOPFORD

Chedle

WARRINGTON

Norton

NORTHVMBRI

DVNELMENSIS
Episcopatus (Qui comitatus
est palatinus) vera et
accurata descriptio.
Anº Dñi. 1576

PARS

OCCIDENS

CVMBER
LAN
DIÆ
PARS

WEST

MORE

LANDIÆ

PARS

EBORAC

Hoddon

Houghton
Thorkley

Ovingum
Wlam
Ryton

Ouiston
Eltringe
Prudho cast
Crawcroke

Bradl cast
Myndley
Tyne flu

Hedley

Aperley
Darwencote Derwen

Newlande
Byarside
Ebchest
Matfenley

Whittenstall

Shotley
Shotley bridge

Aspersheales
Barkinside

Pensheley
Isforth

Blak hedley
Benfeldside

Cronkley
Acton

Coufide hall
Newbigin
Blanchlande
Edmondbyers

Rullamhope
Ramshon
Pontaysak
Rowley

Newbigin
Derwen flu
Hunsterworth

Siltonsholes
Knichley

Est halon flu.
Withhill

Coorgy
Satley chap

West alon flu
Wiscrop

Blaly laties
Rolley

Wiyate
Stanhope pk.
Weredale

Burdop flu
S.t Johns chap
Were flu
Est Yate

Stanhope
Frosterley

Vnthank
Woodcroft hall
Bradl

Teesdale
Bishopley
Mylbouses
Landew
Walsingm

Harperl

forest
Rollyop

Brotherp
Hanset

Durtpit chap

Mayland

Holwick
Grodigm

Myddleton

Gaunlefie flu
Helwick crag

Argul beke
Lonton
Flotwith

Lune forest
Argill house
Lathekirk
Eggleton
Langley
Shotle

Lune flu
Mickleton

Rombaldkirk
STAYN

Cuddeston
Shetley
Harwood hogg

Banderskarth hills
Baudr flu
Harwood
Streatlam
Snotterton
Clet

Notra
BARNARD CAST

Crogg
Stratforde
Woffwick

Reare croste
Eggleston
Rokeby

The Spittle on stainmore
Thorp
Wielsfo

M

26

OCEANVS

E R

INDUSTRIA NATURAM ORNAT

· PESTIS PATRIÆ PIGRICIES ·

HARTLEPOOLE

OLD CAST NEW CAST

DVRESME

DARLYNGTON

YARƐM

PARS

ORIENS

Christophorus Saxton

Scala Miliarium

· AVGVSTINVS RYTHER SCVLPSIT AN· DNI 1576 ·

WESTMORLANDIÆ
et Cumberlandiæ Comit
noua vera et Elaborata
descriptio. An° Dni 1576

CHRISTOPHORVS SAXTON DESCRIPSIT

AVGVSTINVS RYTHER ANGLVS
SCVLPSIT AN DNI 1576

FIG. 65

NORTH · VM

BRIE

M

PARS

Elizabeth D.G. Anglia Regina

DIEV · ET · MON · DROYT

DVNELMEN

SIS · EPISCO

PATVS

PARS

EBORA

CEN

INDVSTRIA · NATVRAM · ORNAT

SIS

PARS

ORIENS

Cristenbury cragg
The gele cragg
The House Stedls
The Spy cragg
C V M
made adam
Haltwhistle
Wall towne
Thirlwall east:
Bellister cast:
Our deaton
Nether denton
Denton hall
east
Staverside
Blenkensop
Lethrestonhaughe
Haltwesle
Ashborne
The terne house
Whitesm
Knaresdale
Slaggeford
Thornhope
Williamston
Kirk haugh
Aline flu:
Whitwater
Gowbyr
Anstermore
Croplin churche
Emissle
Garaih
The hoofel
Elsgill
Alsenfell
Knock
Newbiggin
Melmerbye
Ousbye
Skrewthe
Langwrbye
Culgaith
Kirkland
Blencorn
Skelborne
Broughton east:
Temple Sowerby
Kirby thure
Brampton
Crakenthorp
Newbiggin
Langton
Morton
Bolton
Morton pyke
Trout beck flu:
Barton Kelbrt
Warcop
Burgh cast:
Murtraw magna
Ormefide mag:
Ownefide pua
Blaterne
Sowerby
Nateby
Winton
Sandbury
Ketton
Crosby east:
Crosby rauenfwathe
Asby mag:
Asby pua
KIRKBY STEVEN
Hartley cast:
Smardal
Soulby
Wharton hall
Nateby
Waitby
Wharton hall
Mallersstange forest
Howgill
Hufeat morvell hill
Sedbergh
Garsdall
Rillinston
MIDDLETON
Dent
Kendall cast:
KENDALL
Holstton
Wutland
Crosseake
Prestton chap
westorn chap
the county ssttons
Leuens bridge
Myshoorpe
Ferleton
KIRKBY LAVNSDALE
Whitterton
Berton
Foreton knott hill
Burton
Arnside toure
Watton
Thurland cast:
Burton
Barwick hall
Hoenbye east:

Holwick
Middleton
Laith kirk
Aregill house
Barnard cast:
The spittle on stainmore

K
L
W
E
MORE
LA
RS
ES

SCOT
IAE
PARS.

OCCIDENS

REDESDALE

TYNE DALE

CVMBERLAN
DIAE
PARS.

Carlisle

FIG. 66

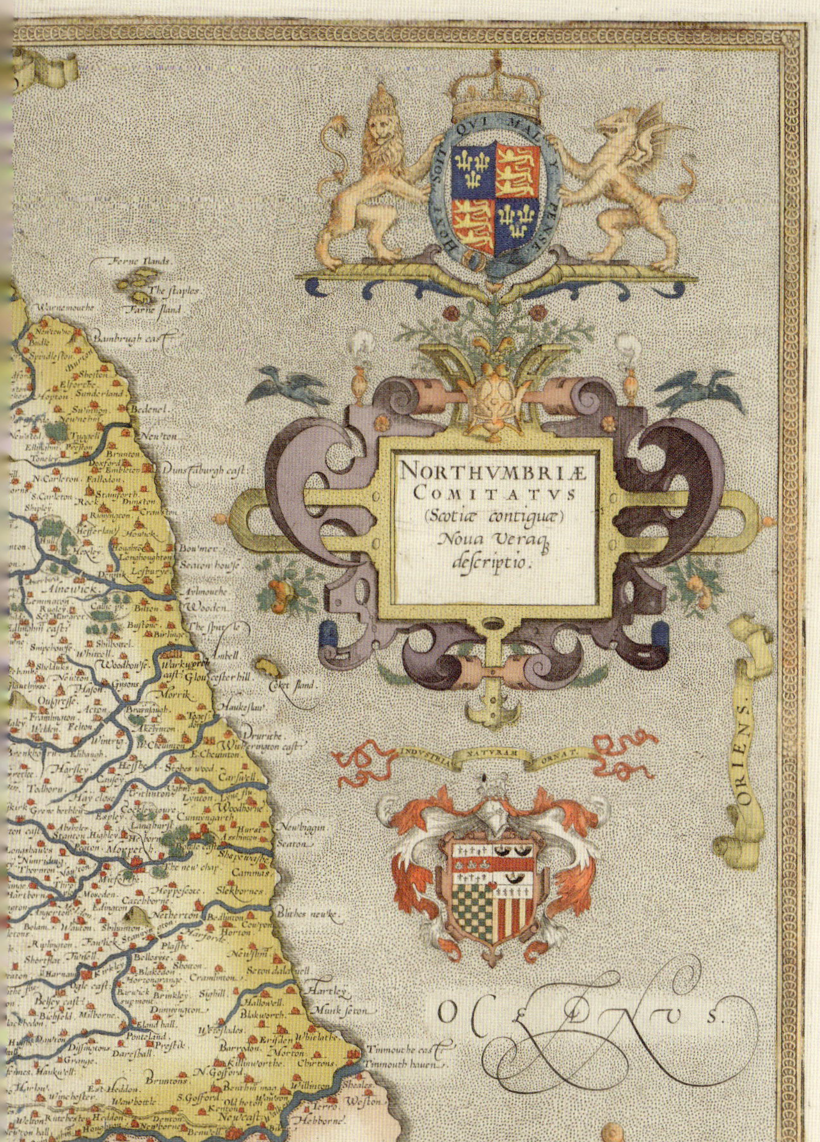

HONI SOIT QVI MAL Y PENSE
NORTHVMBRIÆ
COMITATVS
(Scotiæ contiguæ)
Noua Veraq;
descriptio.
INDVSTRIA NATVRAM ORNAT.
ORIENS.
OCEANVS.
DVNELMENSIS EPISCOPATVS PARS.
CHRISTOPHORVS SAXTON DESCRIPSIT
Scala Miliarium
1. 2. 3. 4. 5. 6. 7. 8. 9. 10.

Coat of arms and royal crest with the inscription:

MONVMETHENSIS
Comitatus Regis
Henrici quinti
natalitijs celeberrima
An° Dm 1577

BRECKNOK
PARS

GLAMORGAN

PARS

INDVSTRIA·NATVRAM·ORNAT

·Christophorus Saxton descripsit·

Scala Miliarium

OCCIDENS

FIG. 67

29

REFORDIÆ PARS

Keynechurche
Treuergaen
Gorwy
Gethridge east
Llamoyth
Huntshil
Skenfrith east.
MONVME
TENSIS
PARS
Norten
Whitchurch
Wolfenbicknor
Lawernhall
Wolfhetoune
Gennaren
St. Maughan
Penrysseney
Llangwaner chap:
Perthier
St. Michaell
Dixton
Phont awel
Rochefeldt
Stanton
Llanyhangel
MONMOUTH
Graceliu
Tyan
Wonaftow
Newland
Penrose
Dingeston
Mickelroy
Pennalt
Treaegabe
Comarvan
Penclawithe
St. Breuels
Denchfe
Trylegh
Llandewy
Langouen
Llamyffen
Trlleghgrange
Brockeres
Llandfere
Llanyhangel
terrornwyth
Gwerneffowre
Chapehil
Llangeure
VSKE
Wolfmewton
Parcoith
Pontery chap:
Langomer
Kilgoruck
Chepfton
The graunge
Llanllowel
Newchurch
Mounton
Strigle east.
CHEPSTOW
Shurenewton
Mounton
chap:
Marthllwecheth
Runston
Matharne
Druhm
Cerke
Brittsley
St. Pier
Llanuairr
Aust
Kemis
Llemughes
Perofkewet
St. Triacle chap
Caerwent
Sudbrec
Llanbed
Denston
Llamel
Brdle
Reogat
Trein-tu chap
Pinnegrd
Llambewang
Coldyreet
Llanmecheniell
Woudys
Langton
Chay.tm rock
Bryfheton east
Nagor
Chefol mill
Llanwarn
MORE
Redwick
Wryfton
Seburn flu
Goldclyffe
Goldeclyffe poynt
The dommy Hand
Kingas rode
Perfhutpoynt
Avon flu
BRISTOL

GLOCESTRIE PARS

ORIENS

SOMERSETENSIS PARS

GLAMORGĀ
Comitatus, australis
Cambriæ pars descriptio.
Anᵒ Dñi 1572

E R

CARMAR DEN PARS

OCCIDENS

Llaneddye

Bettus

Llanguge

Ystradgunles

Capel br...

Kehbelath

Llandilo valabont

Llansamled

Cadoxtowne

Llanylte

Llangenarche

Llanfamled

Neath ab NEATH

Capel gunllo

Llangoywelach

LLANELTHYE

Thiy flu:

Forste Coidfrank

Hoghor cast

S. Foline

Brion ferye

Mich

Burra flu.

Bachhannis frisul

SWANSEY

Bagland

Whitford poynt

ABERA

Llannyemwere

S. kenets chapell

Webly

Bishopston

Oystermouth cast

The holme

Llanmadok

Cheritton

Llanridien

Pengwerne

Ilston

Pennarth

Mumbles poynt

Llangenyth

Rinolston

Parkevelly Pennmayne

Pennarth cast

Bockinston

WEST GOWRE

Knolston

Pennarth poynt

Rossilye

Llanddewye cast

Penrise

Nicholastowne

Ocwiche

Wormeshead poynt

Porthynon

Ocwich poynt

INDVSTRIA NATVRAM ORNAT

Scala Miliarium.
1 2 3 4 5 6 7 8

Christopherus Saxton descripsit

ME

S

FIG. 68

30

Map

RECNOC

Melthe flu.

bradwelthye

D A R S

Wattriuechan flu.

Capel nantye

Cumag flu.

Penderyn

Taphachan flu.

Vaynor

Morlaffhe caft:

Marter tidull

Aberdarr

Cap: brathtat

Bedwelthye

Capel glodis

Terreftent

Kethligayer

Taratgh flu.

Faldray

Llanwunnyo

Axon flu.

Ogmore flu.

Llanuabor

Bedwes

ncorug.

Eftryduodok

Therwan

Naugher

Caerfily caft:

Rumney flu.

Englyffyltan

Arthora buttes

hill

Kruenmable

Llangynewart

Ewenny flu.

Taf flu.

Llanyltidyandrox

Bettus chap.

Llandouodok

Egge flu.

Lhfuanne

Llanedarn

nguniwid.

Peterfton

fup mone:

Llancryffent

melmes

op

Sct: Brides fup ogmore

Llanhayrne

Pencerche

Caf: coche

Llanyffen

Rumney

Whitchurch

Lloyngraf

Cothye caft

Prior caft:

Caft meneche

The vader.

Cotymer chan

Tilcot.

Lyftnalshone

Rothe

pue

Coytcherche

Llanlydd

Iftradowen

yke

Sct: bryde

LLANDAF

The peple

Haloston

Nalch

Sct marjas hill

Sct: Pagans

ARDIF

caft

New caft

Tallauant caft

Pendoyloyme

Llanbeder

yuro

Llandydock

BRIDGE

END

Longan Kethlgarne

caft:

Llanfanor

Welfhe Sct donetes

Sct: George

Marchermaure

Wenny e

Welfhe newton

Leckwith

Newton notage.

Coulston

Penton mil

Llanmaes

Ogmore caft:

Llmquian caft:

Bolston Sct: Nicholas

Sct Lethans

Llandoung

Llyfworney

Hanbl: thin

Llancrythed

Gwennow

Wonfionet

Coampin

Pennarth

Clemens towne

Sct Hillorye

Bonffhows

Pebarth

Pennarth hay.

Nashe pua

Landogh

Bewpere

Brucgyffe

Curalloyde

Walterftowne

Sct Andros caft:

Cogan

Culmercock

poynt

Sct: Brides maior

Landow

Llambangle

iupta cowbridge.

Sct: mary church

Llancarnan

Eghholold

Moulton

Culoyston

Cog

Wyke

Llanheithery

Merthirdouan.

Dunrauen

Nashe magna

Eglosbruez

Gilfton

Penmark

Barrye

Sylver

Marcroes.

Llanmaies.

ancully

Fluunin caft:

Dredruckan

Rougy

Barry

Sct: Donetes caft

Llanuwyr

Funtgare

Purckevy caft

Nashe poynt.

Bouertion

W. Aberthin

Sct Athan

St: Aberthin

Barrye

Fatul.

Sylve inful.

Sylve infula:

ORIENS

NO

NVME

THEN

SIS

PARS

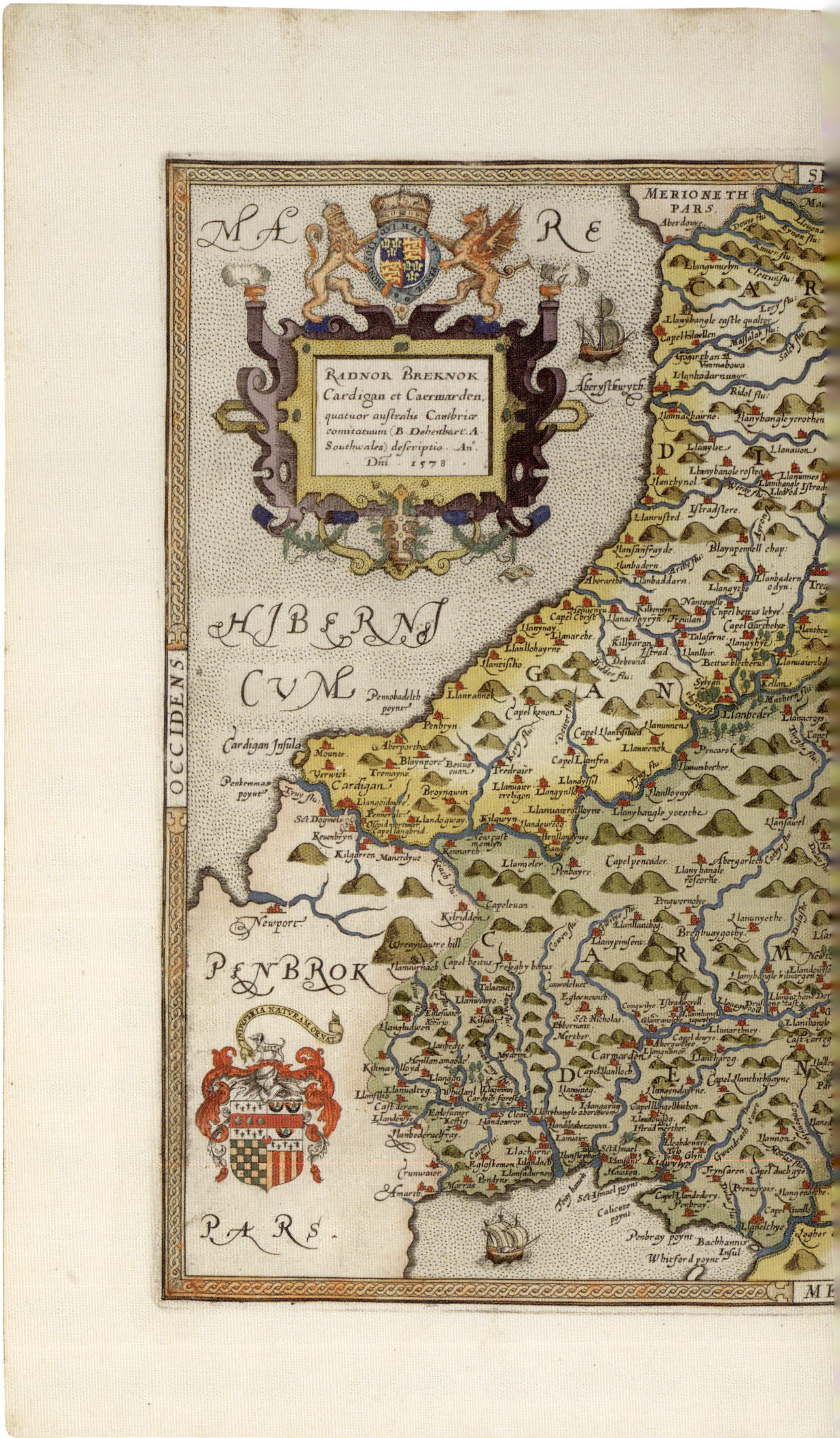
RADNOR BREKNOK
Cardigan et Caermarden,
quatuor australis Cambriæ
comitatuum (B. Deheubart. A.
Southwales) descriptio. An°.
Dni. 1578.
MARE
HIBERNICUM
PENBROK
PARS.
OCCIDENS
MERIONETH PARS.
Aberystwyth
Cardigan
Cardigan Insula
Newport
Carmarden
Kidwely

FIG. 69

31

ONTGOMER PARS

SALLO- PIÆ PARS

HERE FOR DIÆ

ORIENS

RADNOR

BREKNOKE

GLA MORGAN.

MONVME THENSIS PARS.

PARS.

Scala Miliarium

Chrystoferus descripsit Saxton.

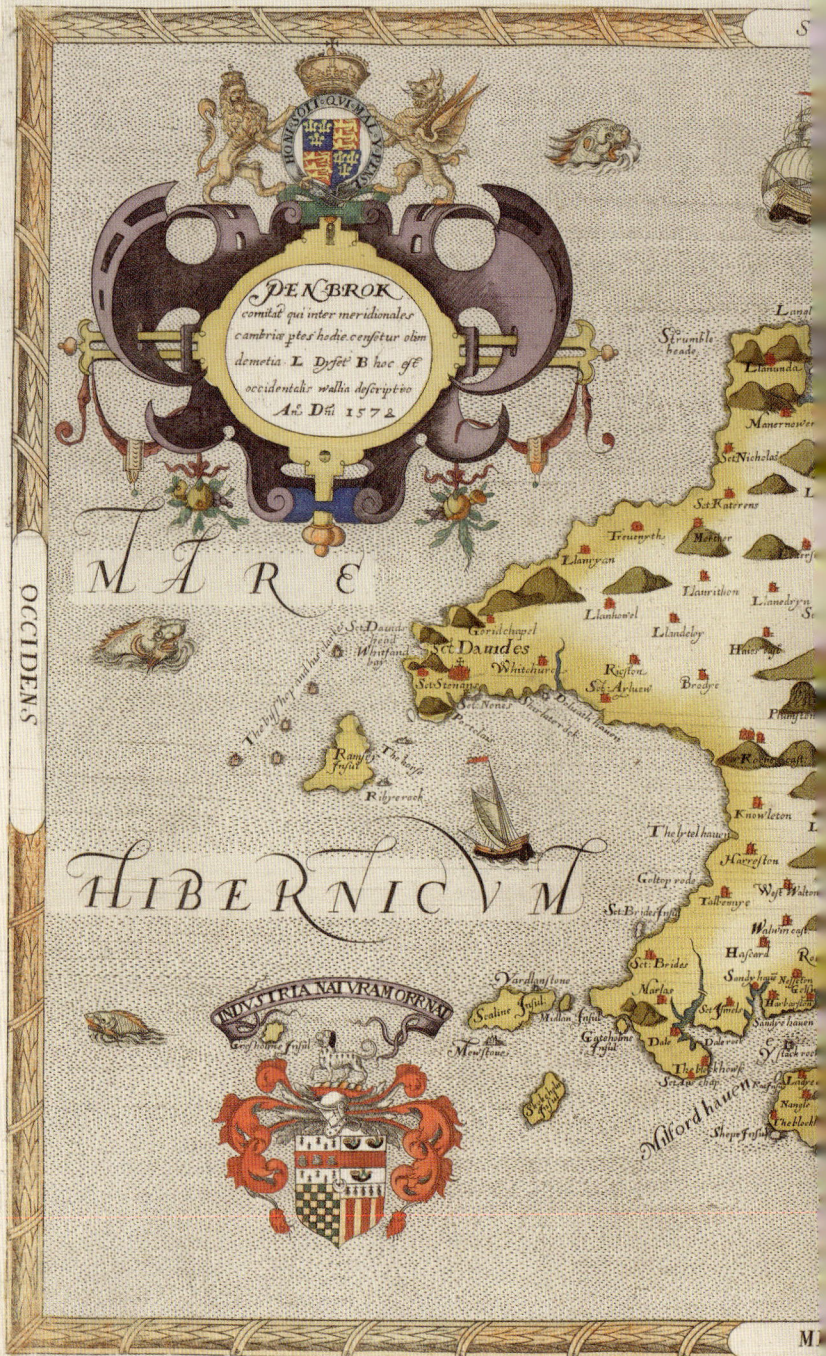

MARE

OCCIDENS

HIBERNICVM

PEMBROK
comitat qui inter meridionales
cambriæ ptes hodie censetur olim
demetia. L. Dyfet. B hoc est
occidentalis wallia descriptio
An̄ Dn̄i 1572

INDVSTRIA NATVRAM ORRNA

FIG. 70

32

CARDIGAN PARS

CAR MAR THEN PARS

ORIENS

Penhemarpoynt

Tuy flu
Cardigan
Llangordmore
Sct: Dogmels
Eglesfwicher
tyrn
Offewidmortimer
Capel Laughrid
Treuethel
Kilgarrencaste
Manerdne
Kenarth
Llantwood
Capel Kilvaure
Reach
Bayud
Brydelthe
Llanyhangel penbeder
Capel colman
Cap: enan
Neverne
Egleffervow
Nontgwin Dewith
Kilsy deo
Molenay
Newport
Nevern
Whitchurch Cap: kestellan
Chegre
Kilgwin
Wrenn vaur
hil
Llanne allyrdeg
Cap: bretus
Pentuains
Moeuil
Perech: hil
Clahy
Llansuirnach
Moel
Castel honyre
Mokaghlogdee
Llanglydwen
Llandlo
Castlebighe
Llandelman
The mote
Maneloghay
Kilymanelloyd
Ambleston
Llysurayne
Llamkeven
Llanelilo
Walton
Clachaston
Blethreston
Egremond
Cast: deram
Llandewyre
Llandredr uelfroy
Leonardar chap:
Wyston
Llaughaddon
Crone
Slebech
Robeston
Nerberth east
Camaston
Sefterhowses
Kiluan
Reach
Nerberth west
Cast: nwhery
hill
Picston caft:
Mynware
Newton
Mugleton
Templeton
Crunmefer
Vwchurch
Ofmaston
Dyrnaston
chap:
Marey
Brulton
Martheltrey
Renalston
Cold: rain: west
Larwar
Risecaft
Yearhaston
Begyly
Codkenlee
Lawrenny
Crefsel Jeffreyston
Sa: Tsffel
Llangum
Benton
Willamston pke
Wethamston chap:
Burton
Redbart
Upton
Manheston rock
Carew caft:
Coston
Teubye
Penbroke
Naster
Gunfreston
Sct: Katerens
Palmey
Llantay court
Sct: Florence
Prulay
Kilherpoynt
Lanffoy
Muneton
Jamestow Northard
Caldey Isfoll
Orielton
Trewent
Hoggeston
Marberbury Ludfoy
Kerixmahren
Freshwater
Ludfoy poynt
Sct: Pattriark
Sct: Twinels
Louston Stackpol
Stackpoole orde
South Carew Bofshesten
Brode haven
Kerikmalo
Sct: Gouens poynt
Sct: Gouen

Chrifoforus Saxton deferibit
Scala Miliarium
1 2 3 4 5 6 7 8 9 10

FIG. 71

33

MONTGOMERI ac
Merionidh, duorum borialis
cambriæ comitatuum. B.
Gwinedhia A. Northwales
nuntupar descriptio
Anᵒ Dñi 1578.

INDVSTRIA NATVRAM ORNAT

VIRGIVIVM SIVE HIBERNICVM

MARE

OCCIDENS

Talackrey
Gronant
Prestatin
Meliden
Gulgraue
Gwenusker
Llanasaphe
Treer cast.
Diart
Relugnevide
Potruthan
Whitford
Rudlland east
Combe
Llandrighlo
Ormeshad poins
Llandidno
Penem
Egles reste
Llangusteuiyn
Llanddlas
Hendray
Abergele
Dylart
Llansansherr
Sct Asaph
Cairens
Llansanfraid
Llanchan
Maystnynan
Abergele
Demyrchion
Maghegreg
Pentuary
ABERCONWY
Bettas
Capel Eunhown maien EN CLVYD
CAR
Eluy flu.
Caierteane
Llowenye
Henllau
Llandurn
Eglos uagh
Frcholes
Whichurch
DENBIGH
Llanytda
Llanbeter kenayn
Mamanah
Llanuaier
Stead flu
Llatunm
Llanrugt flu
Llansennan
Llanyayder
Tretteu
Bachnbid
Gwide
Gwethryn
Darrog
Nansslyn
Llanrugbwen
Plase
Llyngerieneth
Clawedek flu
Capel kysylhyeck
NAR
VAN
Llynydulyn
Llynraulwid
Llynaled
Clocaude
Llegoye flu.
Capel brettus
yrien ychan
Capel garmon
Dera
Llankerigedredion
Llanyhangle
PARS
Nsag flu
Capel pentreuidog
Bettu
Holyn
Llanpetimaghog
Therson
Pity euan
Llangum
Cenay flu
Llyn Coway
Llansderuel gade
MERIONETH
BALA
Dée flu
Scala Miliarum
PARS

Christoferus Saxton
describsit.

Remigius begenbergius sculpsi.

MARE
HIBERNICVM
SIVE
VERGIVIVM

MONA
INSVLA

Scala Miliarium
1 2 3 4 5 6 7 8 9 10

Christophorus Saxton descripsit

FIG. 73

10

CESTRI
Æ
PARS

Dee fla

FLYNT

PARS

Ormeshead point Penryn Llandrighli

Llandidne

Salne fufel:
Set Sivian chap:
he found meothe

ABER
CONWY

DENBYGH

NON NOBI QVI MALE PENS

PARS

Capel pentre ndog

NARVAN

MERIONETH

MONE INSVLÆ
mo de Anglefey, et Caernaruan;
duorumborialis cambriæ comitatuu
olim uene do cia. L. Gwynedhia
B. Northwalee. A deſcriptio
Añ Dñi: 1578

HARLECH

Bermouth

PARS

159

PARS

Teme flu:
Bettus
Begildye
Llanbadernuenythe
Llanuarewaterden
West
Cast Dynbod
The forest of Knukles
Skibborray   S.Tou.
Llannano
Knukles
& Hyop
Monaghtree
Knighton
Stand
Llanbister
Llangunllo
Westonhall
Pillethe
Whitton   Norton   Lly
Llaubister
Llanddwye
Blethuagh
The forest of Blethuagh
Cascop
Lhiton   Herefordia   Sto
pars:
Fuldibrok
Combey stoythe
Llansanfraid
Llanyhangle redithon
Ednall   New cast
Discoyde   Presta
RADNOR
Eland flu:
Rayader gowy   Nantmel
Comaron flu: Radnor forest
Kinerton   Angop   HI
Somergil flu:
Knull
Sct: Harmon   Combehire   Clowedok flu:
Garthuagh   Llanbadern
Llandegluy   Cast Ceueilles
New Radnor
Harton   Old Radnor
Llyngwyn   Llanyhangle religan
Kyneton
Hargast
Clarwen flu: Llanner   Llanhangel   Llanhangle nantmelan
Llanuthel   Wye flu: ychor flu: Llanadrindod
Hunt cast
Llestinan   Kethtalgarch   Hawye flu: Bettus chap:
Capel llamhangle prinpabon   Dyssart   Llansanfraid
Colwin cast   Cregrend
Glostre   Gwithel flu:
Colwey chap   Arro flu:
Glascomb
Llanyhangle abergweffen   Llanauon uawre   Llanelway   Rulen   New church
Llanthewye aber gweffen   Bryngwyn   Llanuhangle arro
Bry
Whi
Llanuareth   Llanbadern
Llanganten   Bealt   Abcredway
Llynboghlen   Cast Payne   Machaway flu:
Maysmynis   Wye flu: Llanbedder   Bettus
Llanyrtyd   Llanynis   Llanthewye comb   Landilo   Landewey chap   Clero
Llanquan   Portheroyes   Altemawre   Clyffor
Llanllouenuel   Capel Cunok   Hay   Kewsop
Yruon flu: Gwendor   Llanstephan   Dulas flu:
Llangamarche   Capel defrune honthye   Crecaderne   Llowas
Honthy flu: Llangoyd   Glaiesbury   Boughrud   Llanygon   Capelbrengo
Capel pylyn   BREKNO   Llyswen   Wye flu:
Istrodefyne   Merterkynok   Llandeuathley   Aberllleuenye
Isker flu: Llanyhangle uachan   Pipton
Capel newith   Llanyhangle nantbrane   Porthamble   Capel a fyne
Llanbrayne   Llandiloruayne   Broynclys cast
Istradwalter   Talachdye   Llanuyllo   Talgarth.
BREKE   Llywel   Trecast   Garthbrengye   Llangouilog   Cast Dynas
Llanuaterarbryn   Henrid pt   Battel cha   Llanthew cast   Llanyhagle   The fot
Llanymthefry   Trallong   Aberyster   Breknoke   tallyn   Llangors   Herefor
Capel ridbrue   Aberbrayne   Llansythfed   Newton   Llanwarnne   Llangtislye   pa
Llanyhangle muthuey   Uske flu: Capelbeitus   Aberkinuri   cast   Skethrog   Blaynilynue   Llanyhangle
Cledagh flu: Camlas flu: Touremaltwalbury   Cantreffe   Penketh   Llansanfrayd   comdye   Groueyflu:
Sawthey flu: Deumok   Capel ylldyt   Llanuranach   Gilston   Tretowre   Peterchurch
Llanthewyesant   Cray flu: Llanuygan   Llanddettye   Crecowell
Neath flu: Monuchdennye   Llangonider   Usk flu: Llangenye
The black   Trayuathe flu: hil   Llangattok   Llangro
mountayne   Capel Callwen   Melta flu: Llanelye
Herfey flu:
Capel senny   Taue uachan flu:
Istradwelthye   Capel nantye
Capel taue echan

FIVE

SAXTON'S CARTOGRAPHIC ACHIEVEMENT

ALTHOUGH SAXTON'S *Atlas* is an impressive and original achievement, it was not without some faults and shortcomings. It is hard to judge Saxton's cartographic accomplishment when in the present day we expect uniformity and consistency across a product range, an expectation only intensified by the advent of digital cartography which can produce absolutely consistent outputs without the imperfections of the human hand. Saxton emphatically did not work in such a world.

For a technical appraisal of Saxton's *Atlas*, a good starting point is the nature of the product itself: was it a county atlas? Some map historians have suggested that the idea of county mapping was not fully formed in his day, and, as we know, some of the counties are grouped together.[1] Nevertheless, the county was Saxton's unit of mapping whether the counties were combined or not. Their boundaries are given prominence, enhanced further by the addition of wide colour bands on coloured editions, the usual finished form. The single county went on to be the unit of mapping, and indeed for topographic history, from Saxton's time onwards, as we will see in the next chapter. This was an important legacy of Saxton's endeavour.

Whether Saxton's was the first national atlas is also an important benchmark. Though it drew to a certain extent on secondary sources, Saxton's was certainly the first such published atlas of the Kingdom of England. We have seen from European comparators discussed earlier that Saxton's was arguably the first published national atlas at such a scale. This point, though, is contentious as the political status of other territories such as Bavaria was not always comparable to that of England and some surveys remained in manuscript to protect national security.

A degree of internal consistency is also important for such a project. The maps are printed on royal paper size, about 51 × 64 centimetres – quite generous dimensions but not enormous for an atlas.[2] The common format of any atlas's page size itself ensures a consistent look to the maps, the sole exception being the largest county of Yorkshire, which appears in a fold-out map, which when folded is the same size as the others. The grouping of about half of the counties, though perhaps odd to the modern mind, does not detract from the uniform appearance of the *Atlas* significantly, and the depiction of county divisions on just a few of the maps does not really diminish the integrity of Saxton's work as a national atlas. In any case, the tabulated summary of statistical information on all the counties in versions published from 1590 seems to pull together all this disparate detail and give the *Atlas* a consistent character.

A national atlas also needs to be reasonably consistent in recording topographic details. The relatively small scale of Saxton's county maps allows only selected information to be shown; an editing process known as map generalization. In depicting cities, towns, villages and some hamlets, Saxton succeeded in providing a full graphic array of significant settlements in each county. Insets showing plans of towns had to wait for Saxton's successors, like Speed, but such additions can create clutter, detracting from the main purpose: a map of the whole county at uniform scale. Basic landscape features like field boundaries or individual

scattered farm buildings could not be shown; even the Ordnance Survey today does not map the former below 1:25,000, a scale around ten times larger than the average Saxton map. We know that Saxton did not show roads: this may seem like a major omission. However, while a few principal highways existed, often based on their Roman precursors, the tangled and dense array of tracks, lanes, paths, ways and other assorted routes which traversed the landscape made depiction of all impossible and choice between them probably invidious on these relatively small-scale maps. Much neater to omit them all.

Map accuracy is a further standard by which they may be judged, and several researchers have evaluated the accuracy of Saxton's county maps. For instance, the *Viae Regiae* project, at the time of writing, is using a range of historical gazetteers to 'tag' Saxton's place names and other mapped features on a modern base map.[3] Most studies conclude that Saxton's mapping is of tolerable accuracy and quite impressive for its time. There are few significant errors, the depiction of Land's End being one rare case; the peninsula is shown pointing west, rather than towards its true south-western orientation. An indicator of positional accuracy is latitude and longitude; Saxton does not show these on his county maps, not unusual in his day, but his *Anglia* map does show these parameters at 10 minute intervals along the margins. Saxton's maps are very 'modern' in showing north at the top, a convention which had not yet been universally adopted. As was common though not universal practice, there is no key to symbols or colours, but most representation is intuitively obvious.

Saxton's maps may have proved inadequate for some purposes. We have seen that the grouping of Kent and other counties on one map made it rather crowded. This probably explains why Kent on its own was mapped again in more detail over a decade later. Symonson's map of Kent appeared in 1596 and its larger scale permitted greater topographic detail. The strategic importance of this county, nearest to the European continent, revealed a contemporary need for an improvement on Saxton in this instance, whilst also reflecting the enduring priority of coastal mapping.

HOW SAXTON'S CONTEMPORARIES USED HIS *ATLAS*

It became apparent to his contemporaries very quickly that Saxton's *Atlas* had utility far beyond that which the government-commissioned project may have originally envisaged. That value was practical, and also symbolic. The intended function of the maps as a tool of government was amply met: a states-man could see the kingdom at a glance and at his chosen level of detail. We have seen that Burghley annotated his proof maps and saw the value of collating them into a book of maps himself. The potential to customize a base map by adding detail was only becoming recognized in Saxton's day. An example in The National Archives in London is Saxton's 1576 map of Nottinghamshire and Lincolnshire, annotated

with gold and red to highlight the manors and places belonging to the Duchy of Lancaster and Honour of Bolingbroke.[4] Whatever purpose a map may be drawn for, it can be augmented with selected detail to serve another, in this case recording Crown property, an important source of state revenue, a few decades after Saxton's base map was printed.

It seems very likely too that Elizabeth's spymaster, Sir Francis Walsingham, used Saxton's maps to conduct his espionage, or 'spiery' as it was then known, on behalf of the regime. Burghley annotated his draft county maps with security-related information and we have every reason to suppose that Walsingham did the same. The State Papers confirm his keenness on maps; he had wall maps on display in his gallery in the Savoy, between London and Westminster.[5] We know that Walsingham owned a copy of the atlas, now in the Library of Congress in America, the only known copy printed on vellum, and with Walsingham's coat of arms on the front and back of the contemporary binding. It is not known how the spymaster may have used it, but then again Walsingham, as befitting his role, was known for never leaving a trail of evidence.

Saxton's maps could also be used for local administration, a use probably envisaged by Lord Burghley. County officials, such as Lord Lieutenants and their deputies, high constables, and sheriffs, could see the layout of their juris-dictions at a glance, as well as neighbouring ones, enabling them to maintain law and order in their localities and provide a militia in times of need. Some areas in Elizabethan times were still beyond the neatly managed confines of the state and needed special attention. The border counties of northern England were overseen from York by the Council of the North, whilst from Ludlow the Council of the Marches kept tabs on Wales and the English counties abutting it. These courts would have found Saxton's maps an asset in their oversight of lands beyond the Privy Council's gaze. At a still more local level, manors and parishes maintained legal and spiritual discipline through local clergy, gentry and nobles. Here again, a map of the county might be useful in managing a locality; for example, if a pauper entered a parish seeking poor relief, it might be useful to know where they came from. In particular, the appearance of the maps was timely in relation to the 1572 Vagabonds Act.[6] This legislation ordered that the justices locate the needy poor within their geographical division of the county and appoint an individual to gather funds for their relief. County maps could aid the allocation of JPs as well as locating those in need.

More subjectively, Saxton's *Atlas* symbolized national unity: the image of the queen followed by a map of the kingdom and then all its constituent parts make an immediate impact on the mind. We know that Elizabeth's England was far from serene below the surface, but Saxton's array of national and local maps provided an image of a calm and seamless surface; a well-ordered kingdom and its neat array of internal divisions, each with uniform

status, binding the realm together in the mind. However, the symbolic potential of maps could be subverted. Centrally gathered sources of information are usually the tool of the politically powerful, yet as power balances changed within the kingdom so could the cartographic upper hand. We will see this in relation to the Civil War in the 1640s when derivatives of Saxton's maps were used by Parliamentarians as well as Royalists. The political and military potential of the maps could not be contained once they were published.

Decoration on Saxton's maps also had political and social importance for what it symbolized; an important use of maps recognized in contemporary accounts. Frederick of Wurttemberg visited Lord Burghley at Theobalds in 1592. On seeing what was probably an embellished copy of Saxton's 1583 wall map and all the other beautiful decorations, he was moved to say that 'no king need be ashamed to dwell there'.[7] This reaction illustrates the great status ownership and display of maps could confirm and especially one so close to a monarch as Burghley.

BRINGING THE TUDOR LANDSCAPE BACK TO LIFE

Saxton's maps tell a story of mid-Elizabethan England in vivid detail; of an overwhelmingly rural land where many medieval vestiges lingered. Castles were still more than ornamental reminders of a vanished past; woods and forests, important for building and timber, occupied far larger areas than today; and much more of the land was still thinly settled and uncultivated. Extending our gaze into particular counties is illuminating. A study of a selection of Saxton's maps gives us an intimate look at every county in the Elizabethan period, bringing both map and Tudor locality back to life and evoking elements of continuity and change. Therein lies their main historical value.

The map of Kent, Sussex, Middlesex and Surrey is a good starting point, portraying the home of the court and the centre of political power in and around London. This was the only map to show a comparatively large city, for in Elizabethan times London was around sixteen times larger than its next rival, Norwich. An up-to-date image is given of St Paul's Cathedral without the spire lost in a lightning strike in 1561. London Bridge is also shown and the metropolis is indicated as a large huddle of churches and other buildings. The numerous places which now constitute Greater London, such as Acton, Camberwell and Plumstead, appear as small places far removed from the metropolis. Just over the border into Berkshire, Windsor is marked with greater prominence than the size of the town may warrant, unless its royal associations are considered. Important timber resources such as the Ashdown Forest are shown, as is the royal forest of Windsor at the edges of Surrey and extending into neighbouring Berkshire.

Yorkshire, the largest English county, appears as a fold-out map, double the size of the other *Atlas* pages. The county was Saxton's home, and 'Dunnyngley' is shown in spite

of it never amounting to more than a small hamlet or group of farm buildings; it seems that Saxton was content to be partial and give Dunningley undue prominence. This depiction was perpetuated by many later derivatives. Although one county, the three divisions known as ridings are presented almost as separate counties, each divided off with broad distinct coloured bands. It is a large and diverse county: the map depicts the more thinly settled Pennine edge, in contrast to the array of villages and churches in the plains to the east. Empty areas of marshland still existed, as exemplified to the south of Howden. The eye is drawn to York, at the junction of the ridings, the chief city of the county and the seat of the second highest prelate. Saxton's map shows how much has since changed; later industrial centres like Leeds, Sheffield and Bradford dominate the cartographic image of Yorkshire today.

Moving to a very different county, the map of Suffolk depicts Seckford's home just west of Woodbridge. Only the largest and grandest mansions are usually indicated by Saxton, but for his patron he makes an exception. 'Sekford' is depicted ambiguously; is it a house or a settlement? It never was the latter, in fact, but was a hall, and any other similar-sized manor house would not usually be shown. As with Dunningley, later derivatives of Saxton's maps perpetuate the undue prominence of the location. In contrast to Yorkshire, Suffolk is a medium-sized county fitting comfortably on one sheet. Like its northern neighbour

Norfolk, there is a very high density of fairly evenly spaced parish churches, giving the appearance of a neat and orderly landscape. The settlement hierarchy is dominated by Ipswich, shown with its several churches. A three-masted ship is shown in Orwell Haven, reflecting the local importance of nautical navigation.

Lancashire, rather larger than Suffolk, which had around 500 parish churches, had only just over 70. Notable on Saxton's map are the many chapels, subordinate to these few parish churches. Such chapels commonly had greater significance to local people than the often-distant church. Had Saxton restricted himself to depicting parish churches, his map of Lancashire would have seemed rather empty and the county appear little populated. A striking change from the present is that on Saxton's map Manchester and Liverpool are depicted as ordinary towns, in contrast with their vastly expanded status today as cities, separated off as metropolitan counties from Lancashire.

The midland county of Warwickshire is shown together with its north-eastern neighbour, Leicestershire. The cities of Warwick and Coventry stand out in Warwickshire. In a small spur of territory near the north-western margins of the county is 'BROMYCHM' with just a three-spired church symbol indicating an ordinary town. Nowadays, of course, England's second city of Birmingham would dominate any local map, and it too has been hived off to be part of the metropolitan West Midlands

county. Warwickshire appears well settled, with rolling countryside overlain with some areas of woodland. Shakespeare's birthplace of 'STRETFORD' is shown on the River Avon as a small town. Its famous neighbour of Shottery, home of the bard's wife, is not depicted, having not then entered the popular imagination.

We may still think of Shropshire as predominantly rural, as it was in Saxton's time. However, the tranquil depiction of the county on Saxton's 1577 map belies its status as the cradle of the Industrial Revolution less than a couple of centuries later. Saxton's 1577 map shows a marcher county far from the court. It is hilly country, mountainous near its western edge, the border with Wales. Many tall hills are shown, such as Brow Clee Hill, and many woodlands are evident. Settlements are fairly evenly distributed, though sparser towards Wales. Little detail is shown across the Welsh border, probably because Saxton had yet to complete his mapping of the principality. The towns and villages around Madeley and Broseley, later including Ironbridge, were to be transformed. The new town of Telford stands there today.

Saxton's maps give us a detailed impression of the Tudor landscape but are also valuable for specific kinds of historical study. His maps are a unique contemporary graphic record of place names and other landscape features of significance to him and his contemporary society. Far more place names are included than on any previous maps of the whole country; Saxton's maps are a fairly complete record of settlements in late Tudor England and Wales. Although there are some small variations in spelling, one is struck by the overall continuity of settlement names in the four centuries since, and most place names today existed in Saxton's time.

As well as changes in the relative importance of settlements, which we have observed, some places have sprung up since these late Tudor surveys. Tunbridge Wells in Kent was an entirely new town in the early seventeenth century, catering for the fashionable appeal of spas at the time. Milton Keynes, though shown by Saxton as an ordinary Buckinghamshire village of 'Middleton Keynes', is now a large late-twentieth-century new city covering the ground of many former villages in the vicinity.

The colour-coded delineation of county boundaries lets us see the now lost territorial organization of the kingdom in Elizabeth's reign at a glance. Many of the detached parts of counties were rationalized in Victorian times by merger with neighbouring ones. The Gloucestershire map, among others, reveals this amply, containing two isolated patches of Wiltshire within its bounds and an outlier of Berkshire on its border. There are four fragments of Worcestershire towards the north, and outside the county four detached parts of Gloucestershire. This county is far from alone in having a complex array of territory. The depiction of these enclaves and exclaves reveals not only the complex county geographies of the time, but also tells of a very different mentality; one searching not for rationality and tidiness in spatial arrangements, but honouring a centuries' old legacy of complex landholding and administrative arrangements.

We have seen that there are, of course, some notable changes in the geography of the country since the 1570s, and Saxton's maps help us learn of these. His maps can be used by historical geographers, archaeologists and others to study changing settlement geography, such as contrasting the settlement hierarchy in Saxton's maps with today's. Although Saxton does not use a key, we can readily infer a hierarchy of settlements. Studies of environmental change are also facilitated. Dunwich in Suffolk appears as a fairly prominent town on the Suffolk coast on Saxton's 1575 map. With coastal erosion, what was once a medieval city and even a Saxon bishop's see is today reduced to a hamlet on the shore. Likewise, at least one church on the coast of Kent has disappeared under the waves: Warden on the Isle of Sheppey. Saxton's maps can give us some idea of the scale of coastal erosion over several centuries. One study uses Saxton's Yorkshire map as evidence that the present-day principal hydrographic features of the River Humber existed in the 1570s, though it seems that Saxton straightened the bend of the river to fit within the map frame.[8]

CONTEMPORARY SPIN-OFFS FROM SAXTON'S *ATLAS*

Saxton did not let the cartographic grass grow under his feet. Within a short time of completing his county atlas he made his first

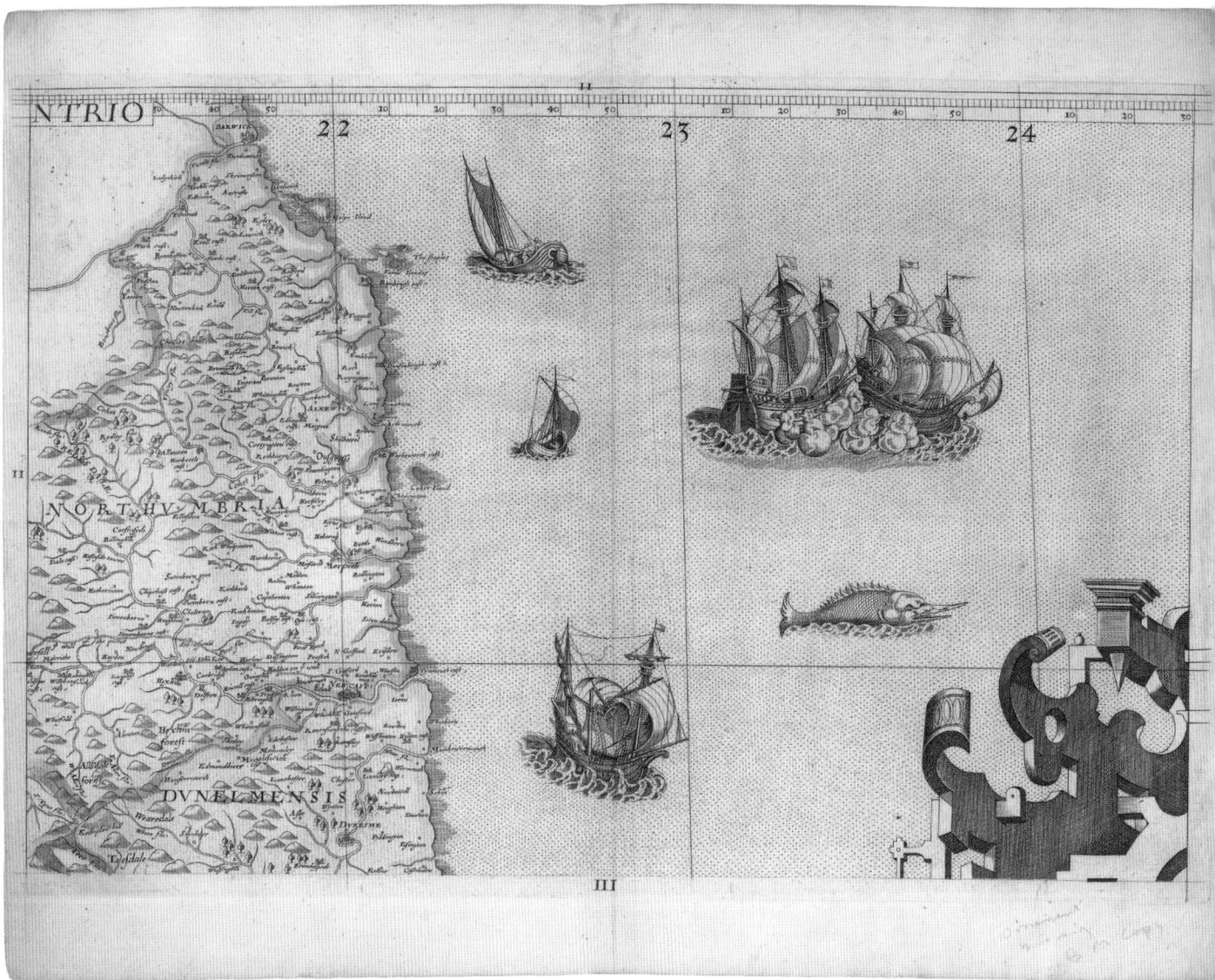

FIG. 74 Part of north-east England on Saxton's 1583 wall map, *Britannia Insularum In Oceano Maxima,* probably engraved by Augustine Ryther. In twenty sheets and at over 150 × 120 centimetres, it is a large and impressive cartographic précis of Saxton's county maps and a powerful symbol of the geographical manifestation of the realm.

significant derivative map. The 1579 *Atlas* maps were superb for a detailed view of any county in the kingdom and the map of Anglia provided a useful overview. The new product was a wall map, a different format (FIG. 74). The idea was not new; Gerard Mercator had engraved one in 1564; but Saxton's surveys meant that a completely new one could be made. Saxton's wall map was published in 1583, just four years after his atlas, and was entitled *Britannia Insularum In Oceano Maxima*. It is generally agreed that Augustine Ryther engraved this, as he did a number of the county maps.

The wall map shows an impressive amount of detail, though necessarily less than the county maps of which it was a by-product, since at near to 1:500,000 it is around half the average scale of those more detailed maps. The wall map is very large, measuring nearly 122 by 152 centimetres, composed of twenty sheets. Saxton's wall map was a distinct improvement on Mercator's. The accuracy of the coastline is much better, and the Isle of Wight, absent from the county maps, now appears. It is intricately engraved and, like Saxton's 1579 *Atlas* maps, nicely decorated with ships in the seas and oceans around coastal counties. It carries a large royal coat of arms and a potted history of England since Roman times; features enhancing the potential of the wall map as a bolster to patriotism and vulnerable royal power.

Only two copies of the wall map are known to survive today. Wall maps are easily damaged by varnish and light exposure and are soon discarded upon redecoration, especially as tastes and values change. One copy is at the British Library in London, with the separate sheets bound in a book. The other is in wall-map form, held by Birmingham Public Libraries, and has a decorated border with arms of English nobles. Many more copies must once have existed; we have evidence that it adorned the walls of the Queen's Gallery at her Whitehall Palace and probably Burghley's seat at Theobalds in Hertfordshire, judging from visitors' accounts.[9] It seems that monarch and lord treasurer surrounded themselves with cartographic reminders of the territory that was both their power base and burden. The wall map was to reappear in various guises in successive decades, as will be seen in the next chapter. The creation of this open display format gave Saxton's cartography greater visibility, literally.

Further product diversification followed, serving to make Saxton's maps the classic late Tudor view of England and Wales, to be perpetuated for many years. Probably the most impressive evolution of the wall-map idea was the stunning Sheldon Tapestry maps of the 1580s, derived from Saxton's county maps (FIG. 75). Many of these came to the Bodleian Library from the antiquarian Richard Gough, with more bought at auction in 2007, while other parts are scattered around, including significant sections now owned by the Victoria and Albert Museum in London. Maps as tapestry wall hangings are rare in this period in England, and even more fragile than wall maps.

FIG. 75 OVERLEAF A part of the Sheldon Tapestry map, based on Christopher Saxton's county maps. This extract shows part of Worcestershire, recently conserved by its owner, the Bodleian Library. The tapestries were commissioned by Robert Sheldon in the 1580s to grace his Warwickshire home. Assembled, they cover a vast area of 21 × 4 metres.

KINTON
TRIPLETON WITTON
DOWNTON
LUDFORD
BRINGEWOOD CHAS
ASHFORD KIRKENEL
CRETECHA
COMAM
NASHECHA
WHITTON
KNIGHTON
LINRVCH
PENSOX
ABERLEY
ASTLEY
H ER ESTHAM
ROCHFORD PARS
ORLETON
STOCTON
WHITLEYMA
SHREVLEY

ASTON
HEREFORDPARV
BURFORD
TENBVRY
NETHERHANDLEY
STANFORD
ABERLEY HILL
WHITLEY PAR

THE GRANGE
ATFORTON
RYCHARDS CAS
WOOFERTON
BRIMPELO
KYRRE
OVERHANDLEY
SHELSLEY BECHAM
WOODBERY HILL

WYGMOR
NETHERLEE
YETON
MORTON
BIRCHAL
COMBERTOU ASHTON
BURRINTON
STOKEBLIS
OVERSAPY
SHELSLEY WELSH
MARTLEY

OVERLEE
LUG FLVD
CROFT CAST
ELTON
LAYSTAS CHAP

SHIRLEY
AYLMISTER
LUCKSTON
YARPULL
LUSTON
KIMMALTON
NETHERSAPIE
CLIFTON
WICHENFEC VERN FLVD

CONVE
SVBDEL ONEY
ASTON
EYTON CHA
STOCKTON
LEMSTER
BICKLETON
NETHWOOD
WOLVER LAWE
TEDSTON DELAMOR
COLINGTON
RENGWICK
COTHRIDGE

STANBACH
STAVNTON
WHEYLEY
EATON
STOKE
BROCKMANTON
PIDLESTON
THORNEVRY
EDWINLOCE
WACKTON
TEDSTON WAFERS
WHITBORNE
TODENHAM
BRODWARE

DOCKLEY
CHALOWINRAFF
KNIGHT WEKE
UVLSAY
LYE
AVENICA

PEMBRIDGE
MARSTON
DELVMMA
NEWTON
HOPE
HAMTON
HUMBER
RISBVRE
GRENDONEPI
GRENDONWAREN
BROMYARD
AVENBVRY STANFORD EPI
NEWTON
STVCKLEY
COWLEY
MAL

WESTON
BROXWOOD
WONTON
LOCVPLETATA
WIGORN COMI
RIC HYCKES
CANNONPEON
BODENHAM
COWARN PAR
STOKELACY
MONDERFIELD
ACTON BECHAM
CREDLEY
MATHORN

MORTON IEFFREYS
BYSFROM
EASBACHE
CASTLEFROM
BOSBVRY
COLWALL
VERN

MERDEN
OGVLE PITCHERSOCVL
CAMFROM
ESTNOR

W HYDE
YARLEY
STRETTON
ASPERTON
MVNSLEY
LEDBVRIE
BRVM

SCALA MILIARIVM
1 2 3 4 5 6 7 8
BEGGERS WESTON
TADDINGTON
STOKEEDYB
THE WORLDESEND
VALTON

DORMINGTON
SVSTON
WHICHWASDRVVEN DOWNE BY THE REMOVYNG OF THE GROVND
MARDEPAR
BRANSBOROV

BREDWCRDYNE CHA
MON
HAMTON
BRXITON
HEREFORD
WYE FLVD
ROTHERAS CHA
DINEDER
MODERFORD
KINASTON CHA
MARDEMAG
WOLLHOPE
DYMOCK
KEMBLE

THE BACHE
THE GILDEN VALE
DORSTON CAS
EATON
CLAYHONGER
OVERBOLINGHAM
LOWER BOLINGHAM
HAMLACYD
FAWNSHOPE
PVTLEYCHA
SALERSHOPE
YATTON

HERE FORD

DORDAL · HADSAR · FECKNAM PARKE · FECKNAM · SPARNOLL · WVLVARDINGTON · NORTON
DROITWICH · SPETERS · BRADEY · COVGHTON · AWELODGE · WOTTON · EDSON · BEARLEY · SNITTERFIELD · SHERE
SALOP · AWNE · BEACHAMS COVRT · KINERTON · AVLCESTER · ASTON CANTLEY · BISH HAMP · WASEVR
HINDLIP · ODINGLEY · HIMBLETON · INCKBARROW · ARROW · HASELER · BLESLEY · BISHOPTON · CLOPTON · ASTON
MARTEN · HUDDINGTON · CRAFTON · BINTON · MORTON · RAGLEY · EXAL · WIGSFORD · GRAFTON · DRAITON · BINTON · LVDDINGTON · STRETFORD · LOXI
WARINGTON · TIBBERTON · CROWLE · VPTON SNADSBVRY · FLYFORD · WETHLEY · MORHALL · BIDFORD
CLAYNS · BREDICON · NORTH · BEVINGTON · BROME · MILCOT · CLIFFORD

HAKETS BRAVGHTON · ROWLENCH · ABBERTON · ABBOTS MORTON · SAWFORD · WELFORD · ATHERSTONI
STECHLEY · NAVNTON · BISHAMPTON CHURCH LENCH · HARVINGTON · DOSSINGTON · PRESTON · ALDE
WHITTENTON · WHITELADY ASTON · MPPLETON · CLEVE · MORTON SICKWEY · QVEINTON · WHITCHVRCH
WORCESTER · BATNOL NORTON · WOLFERTON · NORTON · NORTHLITTLETON · FEBWORTH · BRODMARSON · ADMINGTON
KERSEY · STOWTON · PARSHORE · LENCHWICK · VENAM LITTLETON · SOVTH MIDDLE LITTLETON · A
PIRTONE · BESFORDE · WIKE · CRAPTHORN · EVSHAM · CAWHONIBORN · THE VALE OF EVESHOLIE · MICKLETON · STOKE
STOKE · BIRLINGAM · CHARLTON · BRICKLANTON · BADSEY · BRADFORTON · CHURCHHONIBORN · ASTON · HITCOT · LVINGTON
EVELOD · YOVNGES · DEFFORD · COMBERTON PARVA · OVERTON · BENGEWORTH · HAMPTON · EBRIGHTON · COMPTON SCORFIN
HANLEY · EARLSCROME · EKKINTON COMBERTON MAGNA · ELMLEY CASTLE · HINTON · CHILDES WICKAM · VELOSAY · SENBVRY · CHARINGWORTH · STRETI
VPTON · STRENSHAM · HILGROVE · ELMLEY · WOLLERS HIL · ASTON VNDERHYL · SEDGEBARROW · SOMERVILS ASTON · CAMPDEN
WELLAND · QVEENEHIL · TWINING · NORTON CANDERTON · OVERBVRY · WORMINGTON · BVCKLAND · BRODWAY · PAXFORD · HANCINGE · ASTON · DORNE
ORTON · RIPPLE · BREDON · KEMERTON · BECKFORD · WASHBORNE MAGNA · DVMBLETON · STAVNTON · STANWEY · SNOWSHILL · NORTHWICK · BLOCKLE · BATSFORD · LEMMINGTON
LONGDON · HITTON · ASHC · ASTON · WASHBORN PARVA · ALDERTON · TVDDINGTON · TODDINGTON · BVRTON ONTHEHILL · MORTON HENMARSH · SHER STOVRE
CROWE · BVSHLEY · TEDDINGTON · AVLSTON · DICKSON · DIDBROKE · HAYLES · LOVTSDEN · LONGBOROW · EVENLOD
PENDICKE · FORTHHAMPTON · DIPHURST · STANLEY · GRITTON · FARMCOT · TEMPLE GITINGE · CONDICOT · REDWELL · S
ALDERSPIELDE · CHASLEY · LEY · WINCHCOMB · SVDLEY CASTLE · OVERSWELL · STOWE ONTHE OLDE
STANTON · TVRLEY · SOVTHAM · POSTLIP · NETHER GITINGE · ODDING

RVDA · FECKNAM FOREST · AVON FLVD

MERIDIES

THIS · SOWTHLY
PART · WHICH · HEAR
BELOW · TOWARDS
GLOCESTER · FALL
OF · CORNE · AND
GRASSE · GREAT

Four maps were originally commissioned by Ralph Sheldon for his new mansion at Weston in south Warwickshire.[10] A member of the local gentry, an MP for Worcestershire and an office server in his county, Sheldon became enthusiastic about the new fashion for tapestries. They were becoming a common domestic accessory to elites, providing decoration, comfort and luxury, and conferring status. A cultured man, he was keen to sponsor learning, giving £50 in his will for the extension of the Bodleian Library. He persuaded his father to set up a tapestry works at Barcheston in his county. The Sheldon tapestry maps were to be its most famous output; others including more everyday items like cushion covers. The four maps covered his home county of Warwickshire, Worcestershire, Gloucestershire, and one map of Oxfordshire and Berkshire combined. Assembled together they are a vast 21 metres long and 4 metres high, providing a magnificent woven panorama across the English South Midlands, almost coast to coast. It has been suggested that this enormous size was because Sheldon told his tapestry designer, whose identity is still unknown, that he had 80 feet (or over 23 metres) of wall to cover in his new house at Weston. Saxton's wall map was a 'mere' 5 × 6 feet and would not have fitted the bill, or the wall.[11]

In style, the tapestries are rather more picturesque than Saxton's county maps, as befits their role as ornamentation, and so much more obviously exaggerate certain features to obtain striking visual effects. Important mansions are drawn in perspective, villages are shown as a cluster of buildings, and churches stand high above their surroundings. Trees are drawn very large and park palings and walls are enlarged for emphasis, while rivers are drawn far more sinuously than their true courses. Marginal decoration includes the Sheldon coat of arms, verses on the county's characteristics, and extracts from Camden's *Britannia*, a recent travelogue.

The tapestry maps are undoubted works of art. Woven in wool and silk, they deftly weave together the landscape and history of this swathe of Elizabethan England. Weston House, Sheldon's new seat, is at the centre of the four tapestries, but their geographical scope extends far beyond his landholdings. The maps highlight the various seats of his family and friends, most of whom, like him, were Catholics. It is quite possible that a subtle form of cartographic propaganda was behind the tapestries. The wealth and geographic spread of his network were displayed in the lavish form of tapestry maps: a powerful message to the Protestant establishment of their presence and status, though also perhaps a dangerous gambit.

The wall map and tapestries were rich sources of propaganda, and thus instruments of power for the Elizabethan regime. In this vein, another grand manifestation of Saxton's maps is the famous image of Elizabeth known as the Ditchley portrait of circa 1592, now in the National Gallery in London (FIG. 76). This oil painting by Marcus Gheeraerts the Younger was commissioned by Sir Henry Lee, until recently the queen's 'Champion'; effectively her master of ceremonies. Lee idolized his queen and was one of the chief proponents of her myth. The portrait shows Elizabeth standing on a globe of the Earth depicting the counties of England derived from Saxton's maps in vivid distinct colours. She stands roughly on Oxfordshire, Lee's home county, and looks towards the sun and away from the impending storm, appearing to have superhuman mastery of the meteorological elements. Elizabeth is represented as a woman of her age; itself an indicator of her strength and self-belief in not falling back on an insincere younger likeness.

This portrait was probably drawn to represent a highly symbolic entertainment enacted at Lee's home, Ditchley in Oxfordshire, in September 1592.[12] In its portrayal of the queen it is an allegory of the forgiveness he sought from Elizabeth for now living with his mistress, Anne Vavasour, and being in her thrall when he should have reserved all affection for his sovereign. The portrait is typical of Gheeraerts's style. He was one of the most sought-after painters in court circles, developing a fashion for symbolic and fantastic backdrops for his portraits rather than the traditional blank background. Interestingly, it seems he was acquainted with the Sheldon family, which may explain their common recourse to Saxton for the cartographic backdrop.

The Ditchley portrait is highly significant in the cartographic history of England. In showing the counties in distinct colours it

FIG. 76 The Ditchley portrait of Queen Elizabeth standing on a map of England, painted by Marcus Gheeraerts the Younger, circa 1592. The iconographic power of the cartographic image of England with the monarch astride it is powerful and unambiguous. Saxton's maps have entered the popular imagination as the image of the country.

draws closely on Saxton's county maps. As such, it evokes an instant familiarity with Saxton's work, assuming that it has entered the popular imagination as 'the' image of the country. At the same time, only a few counties near the south coast can be seen, the rest of the portrait being dominated by the figure of Elizabeth standing majestically above the map. Her dominion over the country is represented unambiguously. The imperative of flattering the queen trumped all other considerations.

At the other end of the size scale, and potentially reaching right across the social scale, are the sets of geographical playing cards using reduced versions of Saxton's county maps on the reverse (FIG. 77). Their maker was William Bowes and and one of Saxton's

FIG. 77 Saxton's maps make a cameo appearance in the form of playing cards. These examples show six of the Welsh counties, the mapping greatly simplified, from a pack of fifty-two cards, each showing one of the counties of England and Wales. Made by William Bowes, 1590. These cards, as well as being used for games, could aid geographical instruction.

engravers, Augustine Ryther. It just so happens that a conventional deck has fifty-two cards, in four suits of thirteen values (without the Joker), and that England had then forty counties and Wales twelve, making a total of fifty-two. As with tapestries, survival rates of the cards are not good, but one notable set is preserved in the British Museum, dated 1590. This set has sixty cards, the remaining eight being made up of further imagery supportive of the Elizabethan regime: a portrait of Elizabeth, maps and views of England and Wales and of London, and four textual accounts of the history, governance and character of the kingdom and a description of London. Within each suit, the ascending number of each card relates roughly to county size, giving the player a quick visual impression of card value and an incidental geographical education.

The playing cards are not in themselves of cartographic significance, although they are thought to be the earliest geographical cards by seventy years and came eighty-five years earlier than any others showing England's counties.[13] Their importance lies in their further diffusion of Saxton's maps, ensuring their familiarity with a still wider audience, probably well beyond the elite. The county depictions are crude and necessarily very simplified and small-scale, but, in showing the shape and brief contents of each county, they serve to create iconic county images in the mind. They must have had a didactic role as well as providing entertainment. Towns

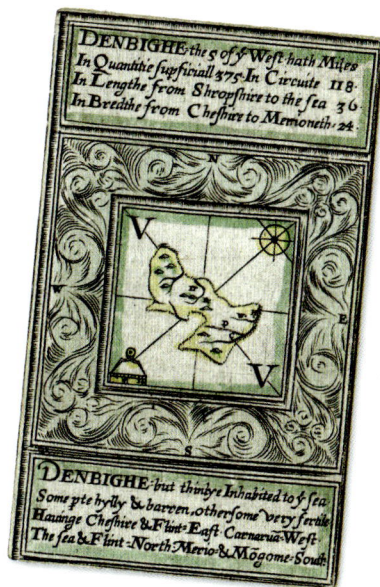

are indicated by their initial letters, a possible educational guessing-game; and summary information is given of the dimensions and acreage of the county. Each county is afforded a two-line descriptive summary; for instance, Monmouthshire is 'plentifull of corn, grass, wood and all other necessarye provision of victualls'.[14]

PUBLICATION AND DISSEMINATION OF THE *ATLAS*

There was a slowly developing English map trade by the mid-sixteenth century, lagging behind that in books, and it was nearly all based in London. Rare before Elizabeth's reign, maps in books and as separate sheets came to be published in greater numbers. Specialist London print sellers and publishers did not really develop until the end of the sixteenth century, with firms such as that established by John Sudbury and George Humble. Publishing in general was a precarious business in Saxton's time, with a few entrepreneurs doing well and others ending up as paupers when their publishing projects did not come to fruition. Map production, in particular, was a costly and still more risky business than books, and the case of Saxton's project shows that it probably required government support and subsidy in the sixteenth century. Government support for maps needed to be cost-effective for an administration like Elizabeth's with many calls on its limited resources. Her ability to issue licences, permits, passes and leases on lands meant maps were cheaply commissioned. This

may account for Saxton publishing his *Atlas* himself.

We know that Saxton's individual county maps could be acquired separately or the *Atlas* could be compiled on demand, and also that individual sheets were amassed at proof stage by Lord Burghley and assembled into an atlas. This might account for variations in the order of pages and content between exemplars. There is no title page, at least not in the modern sense with a date and other publication details. The atlas was not published as a uniform edition in 1579; internal evidence suggests that up to about 1581 the atlases were compiled on demand rather than as a standard volume. The price of sheets for the atlas was initially high, restricting its circulation to the wealthy. The expiration of Saxton's exclusive licence in 1587 may have made publication cheaper, though we have observed that early on there may have been a deliberate policy of keeping the price high to restrict circulation. This may explain why most surviving early copies of the atlas date from 1590 and after.[15]

We know little of how Saxton's maps were marketed and sold. They may have been sold directly by Saxton to those familiar with his project, although we do not know that he had actual retail premises. He may have sold them wholesale to other retailers as well as at annual fairs. Courtiers and statesmen were probably the first to place orders; we have seen there was a growing appetite among them in this period for maps as tools in statecraft. By the 1570s, demand for maps, though still lagging behind the technical ability to make them, was starting to seep beyond official circles. It is thought that a few antiquarians and other scholars may have been purchasers. Saxton's maps also gained currency with the gentry and aristocracy, who had an obvious interest in seeing a cartographic picture of the county from which their status and its material basis emanated.

The very publication of Saxton's *Atlas* to an audience wider than court circles or government agents may seem anomalous in a time of political censorship, and the close guarding of information in a time of heightened national security as under Elizabeth. The Stationers' Company gained a royal charter under Queen Mary in 1557. However, the royal privilege granted to Saxton in 1577 meant his *Atlas* did not need to be entered into the Register of the Company and he was therefore immune from any interference it may have tried to wield over his *Atlas* publication. This was just as well, as the Stationers' Company had powers to monitor all publications and impose severe penalties, including imprisonment without trial, on those deemed transgressors. The royal backing for Saxton's project gave Lord Burghley and his circle effective control of the project. They had to weigh competing national security considerations. On the one hand publishing maps could aid the enemy. On the other hand there was a propaganda dividend in setting out maps of an array of counties, evoking local pride, and all belonging to one kingdom, evoking state unity. It seems that with Saxton's *Atlas* the latter triumphed.

THE RECEPTION AND IMPACT OF SAXTON'S *ATLAS*

The series of by-products of his maps issued in the decade or so after the *Atlas* further entrenched Saxton's maps as the dominant visual image of the geography of Elizabeth's realm and showed their appeal in capturing the popular imagination. An impression was clearly made on contemporary topographers who used Saxton's maps while he was still making them. Raphael Holinshed in his 1577 *Chronicles* refers to them obliquely in his dedicatory preface to Lord Burghley, noting that the charts which Reyner Wolfe spent much of his time on were not as complete as might have been wished. In lieu of Wolfe's mapping, Holinshed noted the 'great charges and notable enterprice' of Thomas Seckford in procuring the 'chartes' of the several provinces (counties) of the realm. Holinshed says he hopes that 'in tyme he will delineate this whole lande so perfectly, as shal be comparable or beyonde any delineation heretofore made of any other region'.[16] Holinshed goes on to make direct reference to Saxton himself in his detailed topographic accounts when describing the River Darent as joining the Thames 2 miles from Erith on the Kent side and rising near Tandridge in Surrey. In the 1587 issue of the *Chronicles* William Harrison says he has been informed by 'Christopher Saxtons card [map] late made of the same'[17] and by consulting other men, which he immodestly claims makes his account perfect and exact. He hopes such work will continue for all shires of England at

Seckford's expense, urging, 'Would to God his plats were once finished for the rest!'[18] Clearly Christopher Saxton's efforts had attracted a growing number of devotees. Similarly, the noted chorographer William Camden, about whom more in the next chapter, though not including maps in his first edition of *Britannia* in 1586, did praise Saxton as a chorographer (one who maps small areas or localities), and presumably as his inspiration in emulating similar work.[19]

More commendation of Saxton's work came from other topographers and cartographers in the wake of the *Atlas's* publication. In 1596 John Norden acknowledged Saxton in his Preparative to *Speculum Britanniæ*.[20] In undertaking his description of England, Norden credits on the very first page the most painful and praiseworthy labours of Christopher Saxton. In his 1603 *Description of Pembrokeshire*, George Owen observes that the printed maps of Christopher Saxton were 'usuall with all noblemen and gentlemen, and dayly perused by them for their better instruction of the state of this realme'.[21]

The very excellence of the maps made them a potential double-edged sword. We have seen that Elizabeth's reign was characterized by a great sense of insecurity and impermanence. Who knew that she would rule for over forty-four years in great contrast to the short and tempestuous reigns of her two half-sibling predecessors? Correspondence now in the British Library reveals this sense of concern. A letter of late 1585, referred to earlier, probably from the queen's envoy in Paris to Sir Thomas Walsingham, claims that English Catholics in exile were trying to get hold of a book of maps of each county in England lately published from which they might better know where in each shire 'every Papiste' lived and how the country might thus be invaded.[22]

Some have even argued that, far from promoting the royal grip over the territory, over time, the representation of the kingdom on a map, however unwittingly, promotes the land itself at the expense of the monarch. Maps intended as a means of control cannot always be kept under control. With a map, people can visualize their country and its parts for the first time. This may help a regime manage its territory, but it can also help hostile forces to subvert it, as was feared in the letter to Walsingham referred to above. As we will see, later derivatives of Saxton's maps sometimes marginalized or omitted the royal image or other symbols of royal power. To be effective a map needs to maximize the topographic content at the expense of marginal features: the territory might seem more significant than the monarch ruling over it, and local and national identity might prevail over loyalty to a dynasty.[23]

Another unintended effect of Saxton's mapping came from the varying scales at which the counties were mapped. Larger in scale than some neighbours was the map of Pembrokeshire, though several English and Welsh counties were mapped at still larger scales. Milford Haven in Pembrokeshire was the landing place of Henry Tudor on his way to conquer the kingdom. This may have given the county a special resonance as the birthplace of the Tudor dynasty. For the same reason, it was a good place for future invasions and therefore needed to be mapped in detail on security grounds.[24] Pembrokeshire, then, had a map to itself and it was suggested by contemporaries that this may have made those unfamiliar with local geography think it was larger than it is, Owen saying 'Superficially, … Penbrokshire seemeth to be one of the biggest shires of Wales'.[25] Such an error might make the authorities in London think that Pembrokeshire should pay more tax, supply more soldiers and other resources than its true size would justify. At the same time, there were complaints that other Welsh counties were grouped together, necessitating the cramming of one town next to another.

Saxton's maps were clearly making an impact for good or ill. A further measure of their reach and influence is the number of *Atlases* printed and their ownership. There are no records of printing and publication, so totals cannot be enumerated precisely. One detailed study of Saxton's work, a few decades ago, lists 47 extant copies in the United Kingdom and United States, but has to omit several known to be lost and some held in private or institutional hands.[26] The total figure has been put elsewhere as at least 60 and perhaps nearly 100, figures which seem very plausible given the likely rate of loss and the probable existence of undisclosed copies.[27] Probably a good number of individual sheets were sold as well. Though fairly small in number, the maps would have reached many of the fairly small Elizabethan political elite. Interestingly,

this high double-figure number of probable copies is similar in magnitude to the size of the Elizabethan aristocracy whose coats of arms are represented in the *Atlas*.

This small elite who bought Saxton's *Atlas* was usually educated in the international tongue of the day: Latin is used throughout the marginal details and introductory pages as was commonplace for learned publications then. There was no real language barrier, however, because as self-explanatory partly pictorial images the maps themselves could be perused by anyone able to afford them or be shown them, and this would apply to derivatives like playing cards. Many Saxton *Atlases* are now held in publicly accessible libraries or archives. Quite a few of these were originally, or at an early stage, held privately, mainly by members of the aristocracy and gentry, and the repository catalogues are helpful in showing such provenance. Some copies now in the British Library originated from former royal collections; others in provincial libraries and archives in the UK and abroad have sometimes come from donations or purchases from aristocracy and gentry in years past. For instance, a Saxton *Atlas* now in Lichfield Cathedral Library probably once belonged to William Seymour, the second duke of Somerset. Seymour was not the original owner as he held the title only from 1660 and he may not have inherited the *Atlas*. A copy at the Morgan Library in New York has a book plate of Henry Somerset, the second Duke of Beaufort. He only held this title from 1699 and so likewise was not the first owner. It seems likely that many of the *Atlases* were in aristocratic hands from the start or from an early stage.[28]

REWARDS AND RECOGNITION FOR SAXTON

Saxton's work was clearly valued by contemporaries, though not without occasional criticism. He was certainly well regarded by his royal patron. We know he was given orders for assistance in 1575 and 1576, and in the following year received a ten-year publishing monopoly. It is not easy to disentangle these practical forms of assistance from signs of recognition and reward. Perhaps it is not necessary: the granting of privileges and royally sanctioned assistance are in themselves significant votes of confidence. Map-makers who followed Saxton, such as Norden, were not to gain such royal assistance or favour. Indeed, the 1577 licence served to praise Saxton, noting how he had already travelled through most of the realm and, for the great pleasure and utility of the queen's loving subjects, had drawn true and pleasant maps of the counties, their cities, towns, villages and rivers. He is commended on how very exactly and diligently his work has been done. This licence encourages him to continue with his survey, still under way, with the benefit of what today would be called intellectual property protection.[29]

We have seen that there is no evidence that Saxton was paid in cash for his labours, though he was clearly in a position to profit from them afterwards: his ownership was made plain in the granting of the publication licence. His main recompense was in kind. We know he was granted Grigston Manor in Suffolk in 1574 by the queen, right at the start of his project. He was soon offered further land grants or privileges; later in 1574 he was made bailiff of the ex-monastic land of the Priory of St John of Jerusalem near the City of London: a lucrative appointment allowing him to receive rents. In 1580, just after his *Atlas* came out, Saxton was granted a sixty-year lease of land in the parish of St Sepulchre without Newgate in the City of London, with permission to build, explicitly being exempted from a recent proclamation against doing so – a privilege indeed! Further remunerative opportunities came with the lease of the rectory and church at Scalby in his home county of Yorkshire in 1584, and his appointment as bailiff for Duchy of Lancaster lands in parts of Yorkshire, a senior appointment in the Duchy Court, and an office of profit.[30] Saxton was also granted the Freedom of the Liberty of the City of London in the Company of the Haberdashers in 1579, the year his *Atlas* was published: significant acknowledgement of his status and achievement by the capital's establishment.[31]

The ultimate symbolic recognition came when Saxton was granted armorial bearings in 1579, the year his *Atlas* was published. The original grant of arms does not survive, but a near contemporary record is found in the Bodleian Library (FIG. 78). The grant describes Saxton as a gentleman and confirms his worthiness for the honour for making, at the queen's command, a perfect geographical description of the counties of the realm, adding that this has been completed to his own everlasting remembrance and praise in view of time well spent on the task.[32] Though the granting of a coat of arms was no longer as exclusive an honour in Elizabeth's reign as in earlier times, it did still confer status on one who was too timid to put his name on the early county map drafts. With a coat of arms, Saxton had arrived.

As with many artistic and creative people, much of Saxton's recognition was posthumous; his name became more prominent on his maps and their derivatives after his death in around 1610. For nearly two centuries until the advent of the Ordnance Survey, his county maps were the basis for representations of England and Wales, as we will see in the next chapter.

FIG. 78 Christopher Saxton's grant of arms, from a book of pen-and-ink drawings of coats of arms of northern gentry families, sixteenth century. Saxton received armorial bearings in 1579 in recognition of work at the queen's command in making a perfect geographical description of the counties of the realm.

· OCCIDENS ·

· ORIENS ·

A Plat of the Manors of Bayford and
Godmanston in the parishe of Sittingborne
in the Countie of Kent. And made
by Christofer Saxton in the month
of September An̄ Dm̄i 1590

The content of the Manors
of Bayford and Godmanston

Soūi totalis   19_ _ _ _

SAXTON'S ESTATE MAPS

It is easy and perhaps tempting to romanticize historical figures, especially when, as with Christopher Saxton, little is known about their lives. The originality and nature of his achievement were great, but he could not rest on his laurels. Saxton was first and foremost a map-maker and needed to earn a living. Nevertheless, a number of years passed without any surviving evidence of work: at least from 1583, when his wall map appeared, until 1587 he seems to have been inactive. The period from 1579 may also have been less busy; the wall map is essentially an offshoot of earlier work. The perquisites and offices of profit he was granted, as well as engaging his time, may have given financially security for a while.

It may be no coincidence that his exclusive publication licence ran out in 1587, the very year he seems to have picked up surveying again. Perhaps as others began to plagiarize his work unhindered by the law, he started needing to earn money again. For the next phase of his career, Saxton turned to detailed, mainly rural, local mapping of two principal related kinds: estate mapping and mapping of land disputes. These were both much larger scale and more detailed kinds of cartography than his national and county mapping. His fame in producing his *Atlas* will not have harmed his reputation as a competent professional, invaluable in seeking commissions to map landed property disputes, which became more common as land changed hands more often.[33] Saxton made both kinds of map.

The large extent of Saxton's later work has only recently become apparent. Only a handful of his local manuscript maps were known in the early twentieth century, but now we know of around thirty-five, including some which survive as copies or not at all.[34] About twenty-four of these, especially the later ones, are maps of estates in Yorkshire, many within about 20 or so miles of Dunningley, but he did work elsewhere, including in Kent, Essex, Suffolk, Rutland and Lancashire. Saxton's detailed local maps were commissioned by a range of landowners, private and corporate, and for a variety of purposes.

Saxton probably established his reputation most firmly in London, where his county maps were engraved, printed and published. By word of mouth, he probably got his commission in 1588 from nearby St Thomas's Hospital to map its estates near Wye in Kent. He made several other maps for the same institution, including its manor of Aveley in nearby Essex in 1593. Unlike his county maps, these, and most of his local maps, were fairly spartan and restricted in content to details relevant to the maps' commission. The 1590 map of Bayford and Goodmanston in Kent is an exception, carrying a pair of dividers, elegant cartouches and showing estate boundaries in pink edging (FIG. 79). This map combines elegance with utility; one of the cartouches contains a tabulation of land parcel acreages in each manor. The attribution to Saxton is thought likely, but not certain; it was not his usual style. This, incidentally, may be further evidence that matters of ornamentation on the county maps, which did not much interest Saxton, were left to the individual engravers.

Maps illustrating property disputes were usually commissioned by the law courts rather than the

FIG. 79 An estate map of 1590 showing the manors of Bayford and Goodmanston in Sittingbourne parish, Kent. Although the cartouche describes it as made by Christopher Saxton, some have questioned this attribution as the map is more ornate than some of his other estate mapping.

landowners. One such job for Saxton was his map of Old Byland in the North Yorkshire Moors, commissioned in 1598 by the Court of Exchequer, which charged him with making a perfect plot of relevant places cited by the local, often elderly, witnesses in the dispute. The controversy was over ex-monastic land now divided between two owners and where, with increasing pressure on land, boundaries which once wended their ill-defined paths over barren land started to be significant and needed to be fixed. Protagonists had taken to placing 'bounder stones', and their opponents habitually removed them by dead of night. Saxton's expertise and objectivity as a scientific surveyor of land were much prized.[35]

As late as 1606 Saxton was employed by the Duchy of Lancaster to map a stretch of the Swinden Brook (now Water) in Lancashire in a dispute over water rights. His final map two years later, characteristically of a Yorkshire estate, seems now to be lost. From around 1601 Christopher Saxton started to make some maps with his son Robert, then aged sixteen, and the latter continued his father's tradition and made maps and surveys after Christopher's death, probably around 1610.

FIG. 80 A 1595 estate map of Maids Moreton, Buckinghamshire, made for All Souls College, Oxford, showing its property there. The map-maker is Thomas Langdon, a near contemporary of Saxton, and this is one of the elaborately decorated series of maps commissioned by Warden Robert Hovenden to clarify the college's landed property holdings.

...cote'

Potters hooke'

Parte' of Fol cote'

Parte' of

Fol

cote'

Parte' of Folcote'

Laklinsteade's Folcote meade'

Parte' of

Parte'

of Fol

cote'

Parte' of Folcotes'

Deepe' meade'

Potters hooke'

Radwell hill

Dripley furl

W E L L

Rishe waye furl

nedmore furl

Redmore furl

L D E

Mrs More'

More'

Close' hedg' furl

yalles' crosse' waye'

antell furl

spd

M E A   D   E

furlonge'

long surveing

long' fur

Brooke'

Shamley

F I E L D E

Meade' furlonge'

dle' meade'

Med

Colne Close'

Colne lane'

Burnt

Parte'   of

Bourton

Flaxland

Shoote'

Shorte' furl

Flaxlands

longe'

Bucklord

Buck hill

Buckford meade'

Parte'   of

Bourton

scala perticarum 18 §. pedis

H   O   L   L   O   W   A   Y   E

Elderne' furl

Holewaye' furl

F I E L D E

Water fur

Lowe'

halvery hill

helvey hill

Caud' waye' furl

Peg hill

Bourton

Parte'   of

Northe'

Easte'

Weste'

Southe'

ANGLIA

homĩu numero, rerũniᵹ ferè omniũ copijs abundans, sub mitissimo Elizabethæ, serenissimæ et doctissimæ Reginæ, imperio, placidissima pace annos iam viginti florentissima.

Anᵒ Dñi 1579

OCEANVS

GERMA...

SIX

SAXTON'S LEGACY

W E DO NOT know with certainty when Christopher Saxton died; no burial record has been found. He seems to have slipped out of life just as quietly as he came in. We know that he was still working in 1608, when he was in his mid-sixties, and in the same year his older brother Thomas remembers him in his will, which was proved in 1610.[1] Later documents, such as his son Robert's will, proved in 1626, no longer mention Christopher; so it seems likely he died some time before then.

Although his son Robert had a career as a surveyor, first working with his father and then alone until 1619, there is no evidence of a Saxton mapping 'dynasty' beyond this. Robert's work was restricted to local maps of areas of Yorkshire and it is unlikely he would have been remembered without this paternal link. It was Christopher Saxton whose name lived on through the many copies and derivatives of his

maps after his death and, if anything, became more prominent posthumously as it came to be included on title pages.

An epitaph by Dr John Favour captures this idea of enduring fame. Favour was a fellow of New College, Oxford, and in 1594, until he died in 1624, had the Crown living of Halifax, Yorkshire. He was quite possibly acquainted with Saxton at nearby Dunningley. A noted moderate, but active Puritan, Favour held great influence in the area. The epitaph survives in a manuscript now in the Bodleian Library (FIG. 81).[2] Favour says that though Saxton's mortal existence has ended, his fame lives on:

> His body cladd in earth in land & skye
>   his name
> Breaks forth, thoughe dead, he lyves
>   to cuntryes fame.

Writing this at some point before his death in 1624, Favour would be aware of Saxton's

FIG. 81 An epitaph for Christopher Saxton by Dr John Favour, fellow of New College, Oxford, early seventeenth century. This elegant tribute to Saxton's legacy soon after his death recognizes that his maps were already being copied or used as a source for new mapping and that his monument would be his work.

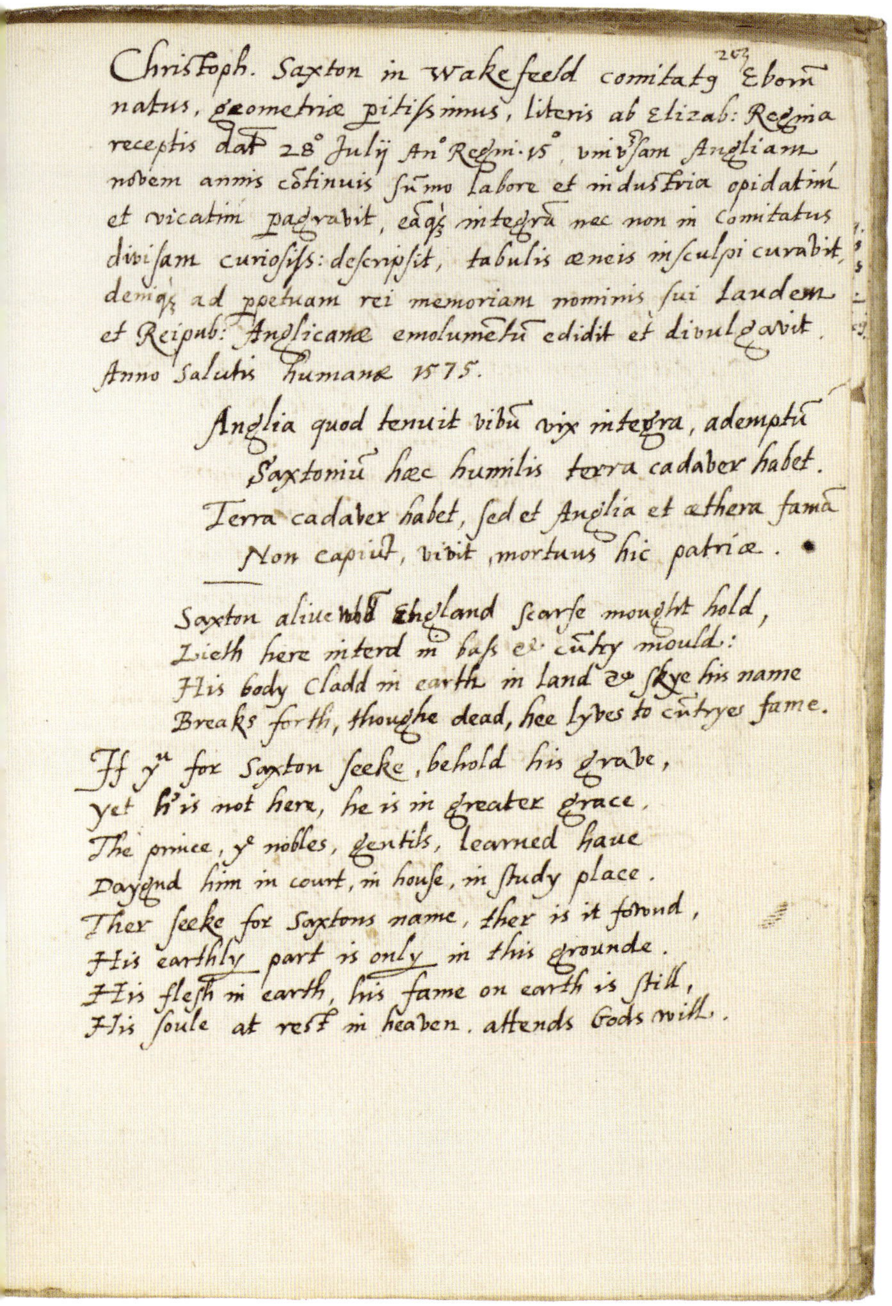

enduring fame already becoming evident in many contemporary and posthumous uses, copies and derivatives of Saxton's maps. The afterlife of Saxton's 1570s' mapping reveals complex interconnections of map-makers, engravers, patrons and publishers continuing long after his demise.[3]

The cartographic image Saxton created was perpetuated for the next two centuries, until almost the time of the Ordnance Survey, which superseded Saxton's *Atlas* as a byword for a national map. Almost all printed maps of England and Wales derived from his until late in the eighteenth century. Of course, the iconography was adapted with changes of monarch and dynasty, but the underlying impression of a stable polity created by a set of geographical images was a constant. Hence, Christopher Saxton created the image of England and Wales that was to endure for the rest of the pre-industrial era. Maps allowed subjects of the realm and the monarch to picture their country as a whole for the first time, and this enduring picture was Saxton's.

Christoph. Saxton in wakefeeld comitat[us] Ebor[um]
natus, geometriæ pitissimus, literis ab Elizab: Regina
receptis dat[um] 28° Julij An° Regni 15°, vniv[er]sam Angliam
novem annis c[on]tinuis su[m]mo labore et industria opidatim
et vicatim pagrabit, ea[que] integra nec non in Comitatus
divisam curiosiss: descripsit, tabulis æneis insculpi curabit,
dem[um] ad p[er]petuam rei memoriam nominis sui laudem
et Reipub: Anglicanæ emolumetu edidit et divulgavit.
Anno salutis humanæ 1575.

Anglia quod tenuit vibu vix integra, ademptu
Saxtoniu hæc humilis terra cadaver habet.
Terra cadaver habet, sed et Anglia et æthera fama
Non capiut, vivit, mortuus hic patriæ.

Saxton aliue wold Ehgland scarse mought hold,
Lieth here interd in bass et cutry mould:
His body cladd in earth in land & skye his name
Breaks forth, thoughe dead, hee lyves to cutryes fame.

If yu for Saxton seeke, behold his graue,
yet h'is not here, he is in greater grace,
The prince, ye nobles, gentils, learned haue
Daygnd him in court, in house, in study place.
Ther seeke for Saxtons name, ther is it found,
His earthly part is only in this grounde.
His flesh in earth, his fame on earth is still,
His soule at rest in heaven, attends Gods will.

WILLIAM CAMDEN'S *BRITANNIA*: SAXTON REAPPEARS

A significant early tribute to Saxton's maps was their inclusion by William Camden in the 1607 edition of his magnificent *Britannia*. Camden was a historian, herald and antiquary, and became headmaster of Westminster School in 1593.[4] A highly distinguished figure, he went on to found a chair in History at Oxford. Though not a map-maker himself, he travelled widely around the country collecting topographic and antiquarian information, even learning Old English and Welsh, such was his dedication. *Britannia* was a major work of scholarship on the geography and history of the British Isles, constituting its first full topographical survey; its scope extending beyond Saxton's England and Wales. The volume was first published in 1586 in Latin, and later in English with numerous revisions until 1806; leading some to say that Camden was to topography what Saxton was to mapping.

In Camden's *Britannia* Saxton's maps are accompanied for the first time by text about the counties, the one enlivening the other. The 1610 edition, the first in English, gives descriptions of each county. Kent, for example, is described as more plain to the west and 'full of shady woods'.[5] It is 'full of meadowes, pastures, and cornfields, abounding wonderfully in apple-trees, and cherrie-trees'.[6] Warwickshire north of the Avon, we learn, is mostly thick set with woods, but also pastures, cornfields and sundry mines of iron. Bremicham (now Birmingham, England's second city) is full of inhabitants and resounds with hammers and anvils, as most of them are smiths.

Saxton's maps allow the reader to picture and place these splendid and vivid descriptions. Of the 57 maps in *Britannia*, 41 are signed by Christopher Saxton, 6 by John Norden and the one of Pembrokeshire by that county's historian George Owen. There are maps of Scotland, Ireland and offshore islands, areas unmapped by Saxton; for England and Wales, his maps form the great majority. The mapping remains largely as Saxton constructed it, though the format is changed so that counties are now shown separately, and new engravers are named on the maps: William Kip and William Hole. Seckford's and Elizabeth's arms have disappeared; Camden stresses his patriotism in a fulsome dedication to King James I in the opening pages, as was politic. Furthermore, in 1597 Lord Burghley chose Camden to write a history of Queen Elizabeth's reign; a distinction which, along with his appointment that same year as Clarenceux King of Arms, confirmed his eminence. The use of Saxton's maps by one so highly regarded confers honour on the map-maker by association. Camden's resting place is Westminster Abbey; on his white marble bust he is shown holding a copy of his *Britannia*. It is often said that Camden did as much to reshape the historical image of Britain as Saxton did its geography. It is a pity, then, that of the two only Camden ended up with a monument in Poets' Corner.

An important early derivative of Saxton's county maps lends a footnote to the publishing

Respicias nostri Epitaphium ut ores pro nobis &c. Antiq pars 49.
Et cælo lenct ab mox Antiq pars. pag. 329.
Du prior ex aio dicit deduella 800. 498.

for our coll register. Looke uppos. paris pag. 272. regere in Esse.

written Bosseubier earle of Ewe buryed at Lysle
looke forthe pag 89

KENT.

a Collady in pari to
St Thomas. Antiq pari pag. 195.

A

Gawen buryed
at dober looke
hollyshird first
volume pag 92
non Joyabus ethel
Antiq pari 53.9 542
god by billow pag 544.
non a young
Bishop. An. p. ani
pag 558.

Rumney Marsh.

Pli. li.15.ca.25.
Cheries were
brought over
into Britaine
about the
yeere of our
Lord. 48.
2 36.

Prowesse of Kentishmen.

Iulius Cæsar.

See Romans in Britaine. Page 35.

He Region which we call *Kent*, extendeth it selfe, in length from West to East fifty miles, & from South to North 26. For situation, it is not uniforme as being more plaine toward the West, and full of shady woods; but higher Eastward, by reason of hils, mounting up with easie ascents. The Inhabitants distinguish it as it lieth South-east-ward from the *Tamis*, into three plots or portions, they call them steps or degrees; the upper wherof, lying upon *Tamis*, they say is healthfull, but not so wealthy: the middle they account both healthfull, and plentifull: the lower they hold to be wealthy, but not healthy: as which for a great part thereof is verie moist, yet it bringeth forth ranke grasse in great plentie. Howbeit everie where almost it is full of meadowes, pastures, and cornfields: abounding wonderfully in apple-trees, and cherrie-trees also, which being brought out of *Pontus* into *Italie*, in the 608. yeere after the foundation of *Rome*, and in the 120. yeere after, translated from thence into Britaine, prosper heere exceeding well, and take up many plots of land: the trees being planted after a direct maner one against another by square, most pleasant to behold. It hath villages and townes standing exceeding thicke, and well peopled, safe rodes, and sure harbours for ships, with some veines of iron and marle: but the aire is somewhat thicke, and somewhere fogie, by reason of vapours arising out of the waters. At a word, the revenues of the Inhabitants are greater both by the fertilitie of the soile, and also by the neighbourhood of a great citie, of a great river, and the maine sea. The same commendation of civilitie and courtesie which *Cæsar* in old time gave the inhabitants, is of right due unto them: that I may not speake of their warlike prowesse, whereas a certaine Monke hath written, *How the Kentishmen so farre excelled, that when our armies are readie to ioyne battaile, they of all Englishmen, are worthily placed in the Front*, as being reputed the most valiant and resolute souldiours. Which, *Iohn of Salisburie*, verifieth also in his *Polycraticon. For good desert* (saith hee) *of that notable valour, which Kent shewed so puissantly, and patiently against the Danes, it retaineth still unto these daies in all batt.iles the honour of the first and fore-ward, yea, and of the first conflict with the enemie.* In praise of whom *William of Malmesbury* hath likewise written thus, *The country people and towne-dwellers of Kent, above all other Englishmen retaine still the resent of their ancient worthinesse. And as they are more forward, and readier to give honour, and entertainment to others, so they be more slow to take revenge upon others.*

Cæsar (to speake briefly by way of Preface, before I come to describe the particular places) when he first attempted the conquest of our Island; arrived at this countrey; but being by the Kentish Britans, kept from landing, obtained the shore not without a fierce encounter. When he made afterward his second voiage hither, here likewise hee landed his armie: and the Britans with their horsemen and wagons encountred them couragiously, but being soone by the *Romanes* repulsed, they withdrew themselves into the woods. After this they skirmished sharply with the Romane *Cavallery* in their march, yet so, as the Romans had every way the upper hand. Also, within a while after, they charged the Romans againe, and most resolutely brake through the mids of them, and having slaine *Laberius Durus*, Marshall of the field retired safe: and the morrow after set upon the Foragers, and victualers of the campe, &c. which I have briefly related before out of *Cæsars* owne Commentaries. At which time, *Cyngetorix, Carvilius, Taximagulus, & Segonax* were great commanders of Kent (whom he, bicause he would be thought to have vanquished Kings, termeth *Kings*) whereas indeed they were but Lords of the countrey, or Noble men of the better marke.

After the Romane Empire was heere established, it was counted under the jurisdiction of the President of *Britannia Prima*. But the Sea coast which they termed

story of Camden's *Britannia*. The notable Flemish engraver Pieter Van den Keere made a series of miniature county maps, reducing the size and detail from Saxton. These were published in Amsterdam between 1605 and 1610 and then reproduced by the noted Dutch cartographer Willem Blaeu in 1617 in his abridgement or epitome of William Camden's *Britannia*.

JOHN NORDEN'S COUNTY MAPPING SCHEME

John Norden was the first person after Saxton to envisage a new set of county maps. He is perhaps better remembered as a surveyor than a map-maker, producing mainly written inventories of Crown property based on extensive fieldwork in his post as Surveyor of Crown Woods in southern England from 1600.[7] He also published a notable polemic, the *Surveyor's Dialogue* of 1607, in which he defends the surveyor against the suspicions of the surveyed in an imaginary conversation between a map-maker and a farmer. His writing extended beyond surveying to encompass twenty-four devotional works. As a strong supporter of the Elizabethan church settlement, these were partly intended to gain favour and patronage, the latter singularly eluding him. Favour comes cheap; financial support is another matter for a cash-strapped government.

A near contemporary of Saxton, born in 1547, Norden conceived his *Speculum Britanniæ* project (the looking glass of Britain), as early as 1583 as a series of county topographical guides, with the maps intended to accompany the text. Unlike Camden, who was not a cartographer, Norden planned to use his own newly surveyed maps. Though the first map, of Northamptonshire in 1591, was closely based on Saxton's, his later eight county maps were original surveys. Norden pays appropriate homage to Saxton at the opening of the *Preparative* to his *Speculum Britanniæ*: 'I The most vnworthye, being imployed (after the most painful & praisworthie labours of M. Christopher Saxton) in the rediscription of England.'[8] Norden's Middlesex map of 1593 shows roads and has insets of the cities of London and of Westminster; in this he went well beyond Saxton (FIG. 84). Excepting Northamptonshire and Cornwall, his first and last maps, all were of counties in south-eastern England. Only some of the maps were published at the time of surveying in the

FIG. 82 A page of Camden's county description of Kent in his magnificent volume *Britannia*. This edition was translated from Latin to English by Philemon Holland, 1610. The inclusion by the highly regarded Camden of Saxton's maps is a tribute to the map-maker. The maps and text complement each other.

FIG. 83 OVERLEAF One of Saxton's maps in William Camden's 1610 edition of *Britannia*. This uncoloured map shows Norfolk by Christopher Saxton, re-engraved by William Kip. Taken together, Camden's text and map for each county provide a full topographic picture for the reader.

The names of the hundreds of
this mappe

1	Smithdon	17	Clacklowse
2	Gallowe	18	S. Grenehowe
3	Grenhawe	19	Laundiche
4	Holt Hu	20	Forehowe
5	N. Orpingham	21	Humilearde
6	Tunsted	22	Hensted
7	Happinge	23	Claueringe et Loddon
8	W. Fleag	24	Grimshoe
9	E. Fleag	25	Wayland
10	Frebridge extra li	26	Shereham
11	Brethercros	27	Depewade
12	Hayneforde	28	Gileros
13	S. Orpingham	29	Dis
14	Tauerham	30	Erisham
15	Blofelde	31	Mitforde
16	Frebridge in Mershe la:		

O C E A

BRANODVNVM

Sct Edmonde

Hunstanton

THE WASHE

Clenchwarton
Croskeys
Turrington
Wolpole
Old Linn
MERSHE
Tylney
Sct Maries
Estmeton
Walton
LANDE
Wignell petre
Walsoken
Wisbich 16
Elme
Emneth
Owtwell
The old podick
Saltern lode
Vpwell
Th new podick
Maden lode
PARTE
Criok lode
OF
Littleport
LACKFORD
CAMBRIDGE
HV
Ely
SHIRE
20

Tichwell
Thornham
Holme
Brancaster
Buruhm
debdale
Burnhm
uerten
Burnham oure
Welles
Holkhm
Suscay
Ringstad
Stanboo
Dockingen
Sutten
Burnham thery
Burnham market
2
N. Krake
Marham
Wighton
Old Walsingham
Blakney
Wyston
Glansford
Langham
Laurshe
Cokthory Marsham
Egmore
Felde Dawlinge
Houghton
Thisford
Hinderingham
Brunton
Gunthory Thurn
WALSINGHAM
Burny
Hicham
Scasforde
Fringe
Berwick
my brakes
S. Krake
Bermere
Sedisterne Waterden
Bagthory Gatesend
Snetsham
Ingles thorp
Bircham
E. Rudhm
N. Basham
W. Basham
E. Basham
Snoring m
Swanton
Burre
Burst
Wulterton
Dasingham
W. Radhm
Taterset
Taterforde
Dunton
Thorpland
Fulmerton
Sandringham
10
Newton
Houghton
Helloughton
E. Rancham
FAKENHAM
Skulthory
Ketleston
Sibborke
Woodi
Hilder
Flinham
Aunur
W. Ranchm
Cherforde
Poddingnorton
Riburgh m
Riburgh m
Gest
W. Wotton
W. Risingchase
Hillington
S. Rancham
Tostes
Colkirke
Gedwick
Testerton
Gateley
By
S. Wotton
Raydon
Congham
Wellingham
Westeham
Tetleshall
Wissingsed
N. Elmham
Brisley
Worthing
Betley
Gaywood
Bawsey
Esiat
Harpley
Ruffham
E. Lexham
Hornyngtost
Luchham
Stanfeld
E. Bilney
Linn
Myndm
Wikin
Gayton
W. Lexham
Meltham
Massingham p
W. Winch
Midleton
E. Winch
Gayton thorp
Massingham ma
19 Kempston
Longham
Gressenhall
N. Kunten
Bylucy
Castle Aker
Newton
Dunham m
Beston cu Bittering
Germans
Pentney
W. Aker
Dunham p
Fransham m
E. Dercha
Wormey
Walton
E. Aker
Fransham p
Stearnyng
Yoxham
Cottofhull
Shuldham
Sorle
W. Bradnam
Watteliugton
Holme
Garbisthorp
Nerboro
Neckton
E. Bradnam
Whinbo
Wallington
Marham
Nerford
Swafham
N. Picknham
Holmehale
Meudkn
Stradfet
12
Bicham well
S. Picknham
Shipdam Letton
Berrow
Stow
Berton
13
Cley
Holten sup
mont
Sahan Ovington
Carbrock
Cranwo
Crimpolsham
Bexwell
Kirsingham m
Ashell
Thraxten
Skoulton
Woodri
Downham
Rustou
W. Dereham
Wereham
Godderston
Hilboro
Kirsingham p
Watton
25
Denber
Bowton
Oxboro
Fouldon
Bedney
Morton
Easton
Rockland
Ellingham
Fordham
Wretten
Stoke
Didlington
Langforth
Coulston
Cranchowse
Tattington
Thurston
Stanforde
Tomson
Brockles
Stow
Helgey
Northolde
Igboro
W. Wretham
Shropham
Southrey
Metholde
Coulston
Munford
24
Tostes
E. Wretham
Hockham
Larlingforde
Feltwell
Wilton
Weting
Downham
Ellington
Rewdha
Ouse pva flu
Hockolde
Wangforde
Branden
Croxton
Bretenham
Bridgeham
Siluerton
Bidlesworth
Thetforde
SITOMAGVS
Rushforth
Lakenheath
Elden
Bernham
Knatshall
Estwell
Mildnell
PARTE OF S
Ewston

Ouse magna flu

NORFOLCIAE

comitatus, quem olī

ICENI Insederunt. Continens in Se opida
Mercatoria XXVI Pagos et villas DCXXV Vna
Cum singulis hundredis et fluminibus in eodem.
Auc'ore Christophoro Saxton.

William Kip Sculpsit

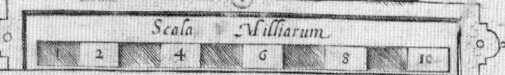

Shrimgham Gunton
Beston Cromere Sustrand Trimingham
E Beckham Elmerton
W. Beckham Felbridge Oxtrand Gunninghom 5 S. Reppes
Gresham Rowton N Reppes Thorpmerket Paston Brunholme
Bakensthorp Hanworth Sufted Mounsley Backton
Plumsted Metton Trunch Knapton Crimothory Walcate
Winterbermingham Thwate Bradfeld Swafeld Ridlington Hasboro Eckles
Berningham Albey Coulty Antingham Witton Rufton P Prufted Pawling Hemfted
Wickmere Erpingham Suffelc N walsham Henyuge Inghom Loshigham Waxham
Wulterton Calthep Bannigham 6 Stalham Horfee E Somerton
Mannton Ingworth Tuttingham Wurlted. Sutton Hayham Winterton nesse
Etteringham Skeyton Burre 13 Hickinge 7 W. Somerton
Hayden Bleckling Oxted Lamnes Dilom Smalboro Martham W. Somerton
Oldon Alesham Westwick Tunfted Vfted Catfelde Thurne Rolefbey Hemmesbey
Sall Caston Masham Branton Scotto Belowe Berton Hornig SctBenct Burtos Scrathey Sct Michiall
Heverland Heminghn Hobbes m: Slawley Ashmanhall Reppes Obey Ormesbey
Beton Hobbes Horfted Couhhill Basiwick Obey Filbey Mouldbey Ormesbey
Repcham Swanyngton Felthorp Haynsforth Freckenhamb:h Ludham Belokby Throgobey Runham Cafor
Wichingham Tauerham 14 Sct Fathes Crostwick Sallewes Heulington Rancworth Clipsby Stokesbey Hernebey Cafor 9
Lynne Atellbridge Horsforth Spikesworth Wodbaftwick Walsham Vpton Fishley Acle Hauegate Yermouth
Weston Morton sug nunt Rackey Witton Boyton Burgh Ca GARIENIS flu:
sing Ringeland Hellesden Spretton Plumfted burlinghm Wickhamton 15 Tunstall GARLANONVM Ostium
Humyham Bowthorp Catton Thorp Pafwick Brofton Blofelde Southwood Moulton Belton Gorleston
Colton Bayber Hayham Brundale Lingwood Lympenhew Redham Ashbye Hopton
Berford Marlingford NORWICH Trowse Strumpfall Hafingham Frethorp Fritton LOVINGLAND
Carleton Melton p. Erlham Lakenham Bucknamsery SctOla. Hernaftet Lounde
Bernhan Melton m: Colucy Cringleforde Keswick Hierus flu: Thorp Herwaftet Somerley Carton
Wramplingham Hethersei Swardston Intwood Armingak Rockland Carleton Hokingham Thurleton Blunston Gunton
Crounthorp Kettering Dunston Caftor Hellington Laurelev Ashbye Norton Wheatakerboro Shipton Oldon
Wimundham Hethell Braken Moherton VENTA ICENVM Chedgraue Holts Raninnham Winston Albye Leistoffe
Als Windham Ashwill Swenesthorp Shotesham Howe Thurston Loddon Toftemenachorum Wheataker Carleton Kirkley
Morleys Fundenhall Weninghm Newton Saxlingham Broke Sisland 23 Wernlingham Barnbey
Hopton Flardon Hemnall Kirsted Mundham Skotto Gillingham Beckles Gislain Rakefelde
Tacefton Therston Taibers Wotton Thwate Brome Ellingham Fugate Rushmere Kesland
Forncet Stretton Topcroft Dickingham Barsham Weston Gilford
Bunwell Moulton 27 Shelton Meurnyg thory Boddingham Erisham Shepemedow Henfted Benacre
Carleton Estington Wackton Hardwick Denton Bungay Kyngesfeld Alboro Willingham Saterlev Couehith
Tibenham Titshall market Pulham 30 Redgell Flicton S. Elmon Sct Johns Redsham p. S hanfeld Ellowe Wrentham
Tucknham Titshall mary Storton Sct Cros Redsham m: Sct Cove
Banham Gissinge Wilsferling Dickleb: ro Pulham mary Homersfeld Sct Margaret Sct C Michael Easton Sowewlde
Kenyngale Shelfhanger Burston 29 Thelton Brodfile Nedcham Mendham Southelnham Rumboro Bremton Henham
Garbulsham Ferfeld Billingforde Thorp Waybred Blliboro
Lopham p. Roydon Osmondfton Dis Selam Wingfelde Wethersdale Halefworth Wenhasten Walderswick
Lopham m: Brissingha Octe Hyoen Hevenngham Dunwiche
Redgraue Wartham Palgraue Sturton Brome Deuham Horhm Laxfelde Sibton
Aye

SVFFOLKE

Scala Milliarum
2 4 6 8 10

K 2

1590s; others appearing in Camden during the following decade, and some later used by John Speed.

The *Speculum* project failed to extend beyond a small number of counties essentially because government financial support was not forthcoming, not for want of trying. Financial support was a sore issue with Norden; he spent much of his career trying to gain it, with little success. We should remember, though, that Saxton was not paid directly in cash either, and so perhaps Norden should not have expected to be. Like Saxton, he received a series of passes from the Privy Council for several years from 1593, which authorized him to travel and make 'perfect' maps and charts and requiring JPs and local officials to assist him.[9] He was also ordered to be given access to all relevant ancient records – help beyond that given to Saxton.[10] Such passes were vital to map-makers venturing into unfamiliar areas as inquisitive outsiders.

In spite of this backing, it has long been thought that Norden had great financial struggles, an idea he did nothing to discourage. He signed off the *Preparative* to his *Speculum Britanniæ*: 'At my poore howse neere Fulham. 4. Nouember. 1596.'[11] In 1599 Norden was refused a new pass, a circumstance usually linked to his perceived political affiliations. He had dedicated a number of religious tracts, often of rather intemperate and Puritan tone, to the Earl of Essex, a rival of Robert Cecil. Astonishingly, Norden tried to suggest a case of mistaken identity; there were two John

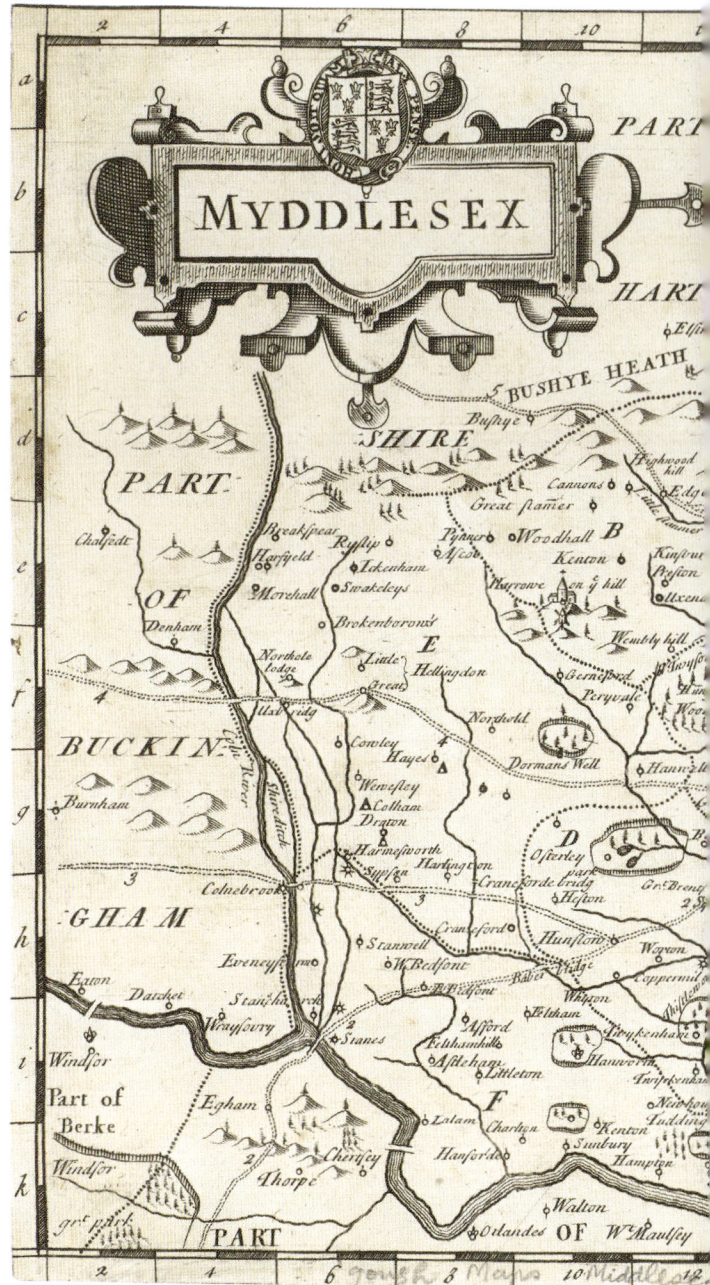

FIG. 84 John Norden's 1593 map of Middlesex. This map depicts the capital and its surrounding county in more detail than Saxton's map of the south-eastern counties while adding roads and inset maps of the cities of London and Westminster. However, Norden's mapping project was only to cover a few counties.

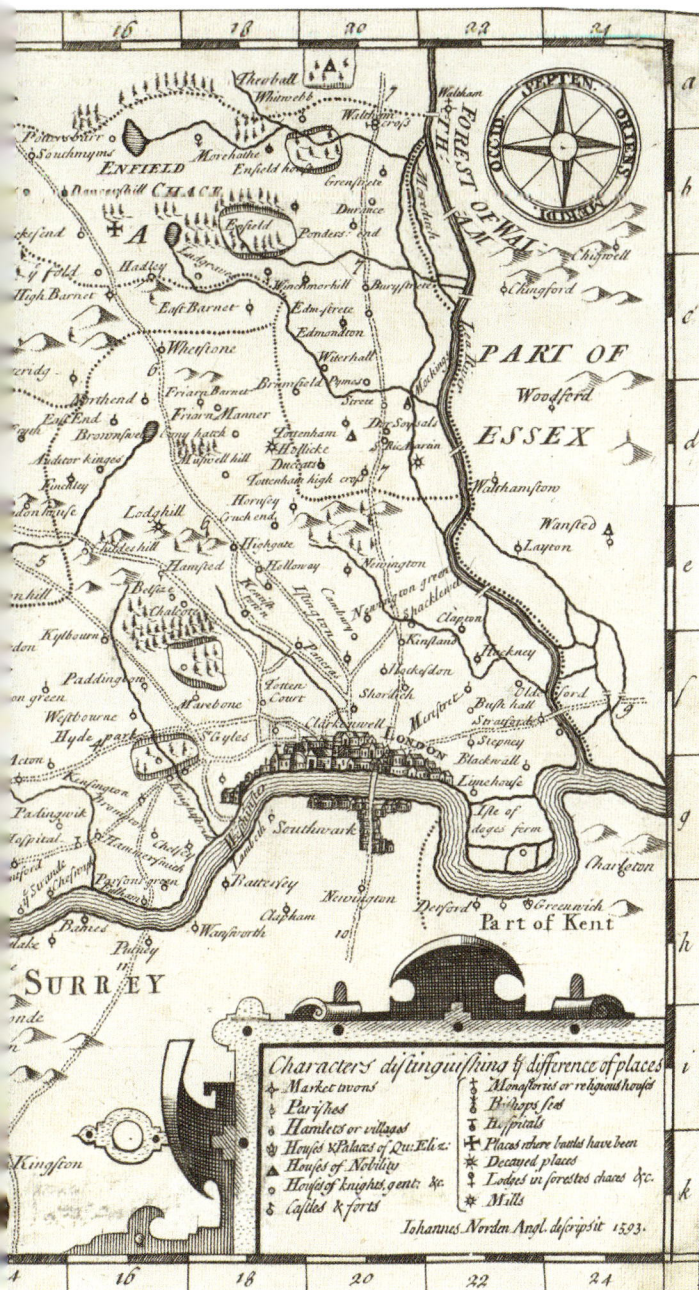

Nordens – a religious polemicist in Kent, and he, the innocent party, a surveyor in Somerset. This was clearly known to be nonsense by the Privy Council.[12] The episode cut short and ended his *Speculum* project. Saxton appears to have done nothing similarly foolish to disturb his reputation with the court.

In spite of his friction with the authorities, Norden's maps were well regarded by many. Camden included his half a dozen or so county maps rather than Saxton's in his *Britannia*. Indeed, most later maps of counties which Norden mapped were based on his rather than Saxton's for the next century and a half or so, probably because he had added useful internal county divisions to his maps, a grid reference system and a legend. Saxton, though, had got there first and Norden is very likely to have used his maps at least as a very substantial starting point.

WILLIAM SMITH, THE 'ANONYMOUS' MAP-MAKER

Another significant attempt to make a new set of county maps after Christopher Saxton was, strangely, an anonymous effort circa 1602–03, just at the very end of Elizabeth's reign. We do not know why these maps carry no name, but in the early twentieth century convincing evidence emerged that their maker was William Smith. Like Camden, Smith was a herald and topographer; furthermore he was a playwright. In 1597 he was appointed as Rouge Dragon pursuivant of the College of Arms, a

Map

Characters distinguishing the difference of places

Market towns
Parishes
Hamlets or villages
Houses & Palaces of Qu: Eliz:
Houses of Nobility
Houses of knights, gent: &c.
Castles & forts

Monasteries or religious houses
Bishops seet
Hospitals
Places where battles have been
Decayed places
Lodges in forrestes chaces &c.
Mills

Iohannes Norden Angl. descripsit 1593.

post confirming his favour with the Crown, important for any map-maker.[13]

Smith was interested in topography and had lived for around five years in Nuremberg in Germany, a flourishing centre of cartography where he would have deepened his knowledge of map-making considerably.[14] As early as 1568, and so before Saxton's county maps, he drew a town plan.[15] He attempted a national county survey in the last years of Elizabeth's reign, partly with a view to improving on Saxton, but his projected survey was never completed. He made just twelve county maps, ten based on Saxton, the remaining two on Norden. Smith did add some information of his own, such as a key to map signs, hundred (or county division) boundaries and more place names, whilst increasing the scale of some maps. It is likely that Smith did not take his project further because John Speed was starting a county mapping project of his own and the market would not bear two concurrent projects.

A SEVENTEENTH-CENTURY MAPPING SENSATION? JOHN SPEED'S *THEATRE*

A major new lease of life for Saxton's maps was John Speed's *Theatre of the Empire of Great Britain* of 1611. For some, Speed's name might be better known than Saxton's, but in terms of cartographic achievement this is unjust. He was more a historian than a map-maker. Speed was born in Cheshire in 1551/2 to quite a wealthy merchant tailor family, and like Norden had theological interests, though did not push them to the point of controversy. He published a wall

map of Canaan in biblical times in 1595, and in 1598 presented a series of maps to Elizabeth, thus establishing a cartographic track record early on.[16] Though from a fairly comfortable background, Speed still needed patronage and official introductions. These came through Sir Fulke Greville, a statesman and administrator, who served both Elizabeth and James I and rose by 1614 to become Chancellor of the Exchequer. Recognizing his skill and potential, Greville gave Speed an allowance to free him from the need to continue his manual work as a tailor, and so concentrate on his historical and topographical researches. Greville also effected introductions to famous antiquaries of the time such as Camden and Robert Cotton, and Speed joined the then Society of Antiquaries, a predecessor of the current one, alongside them. He also gained the sinecure post of 'customs waiter' with a room in Custom House, providing material support alongside establishment recognition.[17]

Speed had conceived and worked on his *Theatre* for some years, the maps being made between circa 1602 and 1607; publication was in 1611/12 (FIG. 85). Its subtitle reveals its aim: *presenting an exact geography of the kingdomes of England, Scotland, Ireland, and the iles adioyning.*[18] Speed's work brought maps together with textual descriptions of the history and antiquities of each county. In these respects, Speed's *Theatre* was modelled in its title and conception on Ortelius's *Theatrum Orbis Terrarum* of 1570. Speed's was the first published atlas of the whole of the British Isles. It was to be a collaborative publishing venture; at first, he had considered going it alone, but for commercial reasons was forced to pass his copperplates to the booksellers George Humble and John Sudbury, who gained a twenty-one-year licence to publish the *Theatre* from 1608.[19] Humble and Sudbury, the major publishers and print-sellers in London at the time, were indispensable in marketing Speed's work. Every map carries the notice that it is to be sold in Popes Head Alley against the Exchange by John Sudbury and George Humble.

Importantly, on 17 June 1607 Speed gained a pass to be presented to local officials.[20] It reveals his aim to go beyond Saxton in mapping the towns, and recording arms of local nobility and important antiquities in each county, where he was to be aided without let or hindrance. Always vital, such passes became especially necessary to gain cooperation and remove obstacles to a survey, and when the plague was virulent and many places closed their gates to outsiders. The *Theatre* contains sixty-seven maps, mostly of counties, all now on separate pages, as well as some introductory general maps. Unlike Saxton's, Speed's maps have text on the back, describing the geography, history and antiquities of each county, making the present and the past seem to merge into one. Many of the maps were derived from Saxton, a few from Norden and one or two of islands off the British coast from others, though augmented to varying degrees by Speed. It is possible that Speed chose maps other than Saxton's where he thought there had been

a later improvement. For instance, the Kent map is based on Symonson and that of Sussex based on Norden. Both of these counties were grouped together also with Surrey and Middlesex in Saxton's *Atlas* and so Speed may have wanted more detailed maps with a less congested appearance. The description on each map 'performed by John Speed' seems to confirm it as a derivative work as far as the county maps are concerned. Speed added hundred boundaries to the maps, thus aiding local administrators, and included significant antiquarian information such as pictures of Roman objects and text on local battles.

Speed's main innovation was the addition of town plans to the margins of the county maps. The *Theatre* includes seventy-three of these, many being the first known plan of that place. It is thought that Speed made about fifty of these himself. The towns and cities are drawn in plan, and churches and notable buildings are indicated by numbers and letters and cross-referenced in an adjacent table, significantly adding to their utility. It might be said, however, that these insets and other antiquarian information in edges of the maps meant that Saxton's were cleaner and less cluttered images.

FIG. 85 OVERLEAF John Speed's map of the county of 'Glamorgan Shyre' from his *The Theatre of the Empire of Great Britain*, 1611. Speed's maps include insets of cities, in this case Cardiff and Llandaff. The maps also have text about the antiquities, history and geography of each county on the reverse side.

CARDYFE.

Shire hall

Castell

Black fryers

West Gate.

East Gate

Cokarton stret

The Spith

The Key

Mayer

THE SCALE OF PASES

GLAMO
With the sittuat
and an

PART O

PART OF

CARMAR

DEN SHEYRE

GEVELACH

WEST

OCCIDENS

Bettus

LLAN

Towy flud

Capel

Llaneddye

Llanuher

Kelibebilth

Llandilo
Talabont

Cadoxtown

Llangenarth

Llansamlet

Neath Abbey

Neath

HUN.

Llangoyuelach

Coidfrank
Forest

HUND

Llanelthye

Logher Castle

This flud

S. Iohns

Briton Ferye

Baglan

Bachhannis Islad

Burra stu

SWANZEY HUND

Swansey

A

Whiford poynt

Hannycawere

S. Kenetes Chep

Wobly

Pengwerne

Osternouth cast.

The Holme

Llanmadok

Llanriblien

Ilston

Mumbles poynt

Llangouyth

Cheriton

Park Browis

Pennarth

Bisshopston

Roslhye

Rosilhye

Penmayne

Pennarth
Cast.

Rockston

WEST GOWRE

Llanddeurye
cast

Knolston

Nicholas
Towne

Pennarth point

Paresse

Oxwiche

Wornelhead poyt

Perthynon

Oxwich poynt

The scale of English miles Anno Dom. 1610

1 2 3 4 5 6 7 8 9 10

Jodocus Hondius Cælavit

LANDAFFE

Tave flu:

...SHYRE
...eife towne CARDYFF
...FE described.

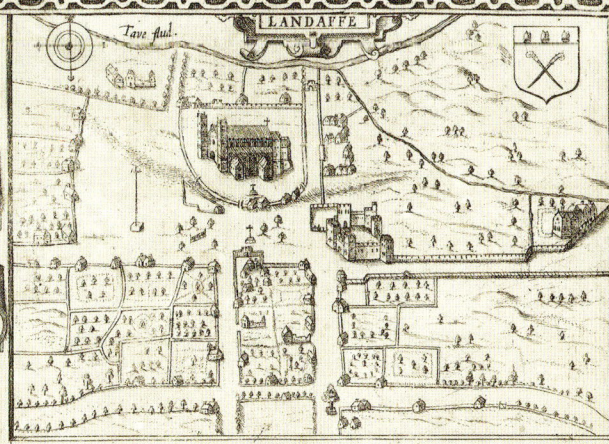

NOKE SHEIRE

Part of Rumny flud

EAST.

ORIENS

Mounmoth

Penderyn

Heath Vaelan fl.

Marlais cast
Marteridinl

Capel Brashteare

Custom flud

Abordare

Aron flud

LAN:

Capel Glodis

Kethiggayer

Faldray

CAERFILY

Chatugh flud

Glyncorng

Estry diuodah

Llanwunny

Ilauaber

Beckwes

NEWCASTLE

TRISSENT

Thevan

HUND

HUND HUND

Caerfily cast

Langynewart

Llanyttiduandray

Eglysflylian

Bettus Chaple

Llandouodok

OGMOR

Llantrisent

Krwenmable

Llanedarn

Llsfuahe

anggunwill

Peterston on y mount

Arthurs Bottn Hill

Penterche

Cast. Meneche

Castle Coche

Llanysken

S.Melins

S. Brydes upon ogmore

Llanhayrne

Whitchurch

CARDIF

Rompney

Llhaysfylyd

Treer cast.

DENIS.

The Rader

shire

Cothye cast

Llanryd

Llanharye

Coedmerchan park

Tileer

Llymgrar

Rocht

Llalefton

COWBRIDGE

Estradowen

S.Bryde

Llanfihangle

S.Fagans

Ely

Llysfelabont

Llandaf

The Spitle

Coytchurch

Nolton

S.Maries hill

Tollaunte cast

Pendoylonye

S. George.

Elay

CARDIF

The Pile

Kenfegge Cast

New castle

Llanbedervuro

Kayrey

Meck. with

HUN

Bridgende

Wefinye

Kethigarne cast

Penllyn cast

Llangan

Coulfton

Lanfanner

Welfh Newton

Bolfton

POWYS

S.Lethons

Llanyhangle cast

Caganpil

Llandydock

Mathermaure

Newton Nottage

owbridge

Llysworney

S.Hillery

Llanblethian

Landogh

Bewpar

Drewryffe

Llantrythod

S. Nicholas

Worlcton

Walterftowne

Wonfton cast

Eghheldid

Gwenonon

Llanmyhangle cast

daugh

Penfhyo wis cast

Cogan

Penarth poynt

Pennarth

Pennarth Baye

Great S.Brides

HUNDRED.

Blandow

HUND.

S. Mary church

Llanorervan

Llanbethery

Carallgyd

Moulton

S. Andros

HUN

Cadoxton

Cofta

Lanuerock poynt

Wyke

Llanhangle iuxta Cowbridge

Great Naffe

Eglos brues

Lancad

Funmun

Pennark

Merthrdouan

Barrye

Syly

Danraun

Llaumaics

Gilfton

Fantgare

Porkery cast

Marcroes

Llantwyt

S.Athan

Weft Aberthawe

Rowfe

Barry Island

Sylye Island

S.Donets caft

Beverston

Eaft Aberthawe

Barry Island

Nafhe poynt

Performed by Iohn Speede. And are to be folde in Popes head alley against the Exchange by Iohn Sudbury and George Humbell   Cum Priuigis.

Just as Saxton's was the first national county atlas of England and Wales, many regard Speed's as the major British mapping project of the seventeenth century, and indeed beyond, being reissued fourteen times until 1770. Perhaps so, but it was on the coat-tails of his predecessor. Speed drew on Saxton for style as well as cartographic substance; his maps were embellishments with some revisions and added features. Although mentioning his own extensive travel and field work, Speed admits in the opening pages of his *Theatre* that 'it may be obiected that I haue put my sickle into other mens corne, and haue laid my building vpon other mens foundations.'[21] Copying or borrowing from another was not construed as negatively in Speed's day as it is now: we can regard him as a fortunate beneficiary of Saxton's earlier efforts.

THE REVIVAL OF SAXTON: THE 'QUARTERMASTER'S MAP' OF 1644

Speed had derived most of his county cartographic detail from Christopher Saxton, whilst Norden, Smith and others had only succeeded in making new maps of a few counties, many of these owing at least something to their sixteenth-century predecessor. The curiously nicknamed

FIG. 86 Sheet Two of the 'Quartermaster's Map' of 1644 titled 'The Bishop-ricke of Durram and Cumberland, Westmoreland, Yorke-shire, Lancast-shire and Parte of Lincolnshire'. This six-sheet publication by the London print seller Thomas Jenner was engraved by Wenceslaus Hollar. Nearly all the topographical information is taken from Saxton's maps.

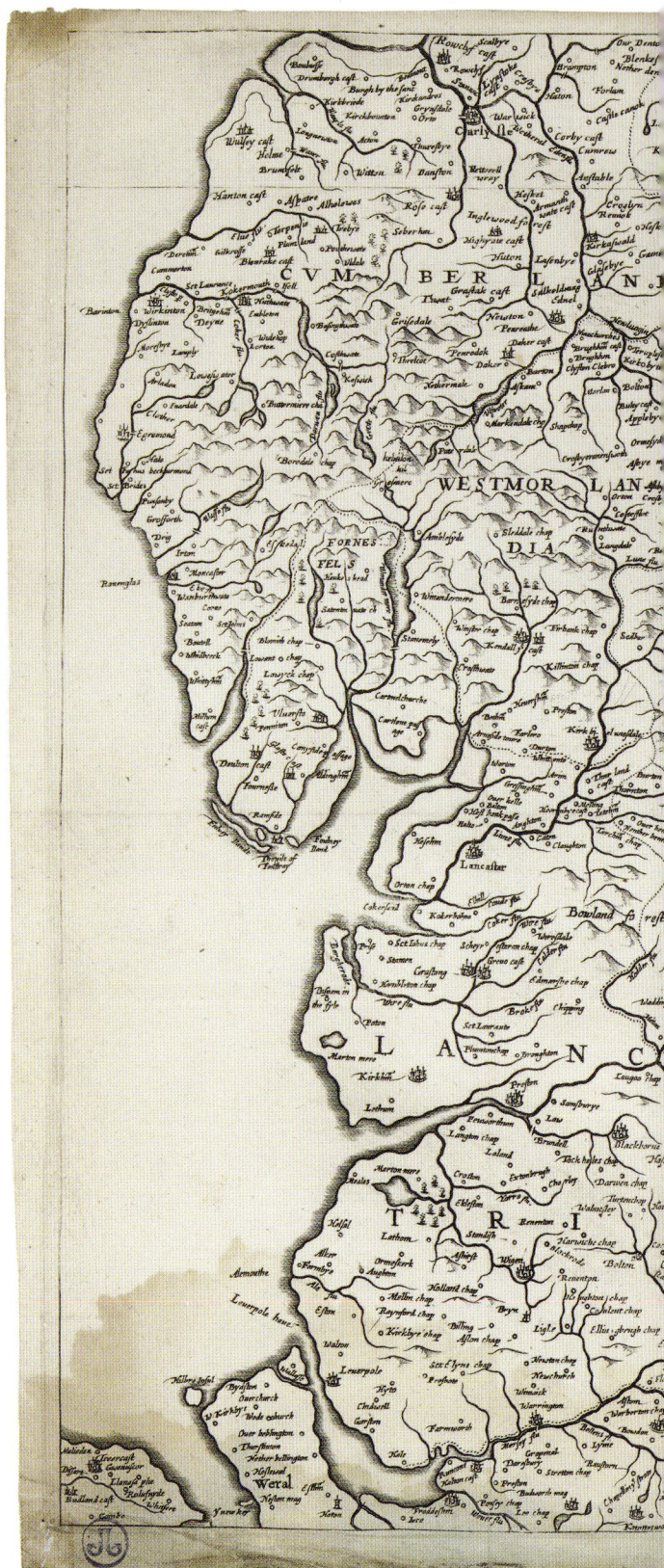

THE BISHOP=RICKE OF DVRRAM
AND CVMBERLAND, WESTMORELAND,
YORKE=SHIRE, LANCAST=SHIRE, AND
PARTE OF LINCONSHIRE

The Scale of Myles

'Quartermaster's Map' of 1644 is testimony to the longevity of Saxton's maps and also to how, as power balances changed, they could be commandeered by those in the ascendent (FIG. 86). This six-sheet publication, engraved by Wenceslaus Hollar, the eminent Bohemian etcher and draughtsman, derives practically all its topographic detail from Saxton's 1583 wall map – that, in turn, being derived, as we know, from his 1570s' county maps.

The so-called 'Quartermaster's Map' has long been associated with the Parliamentary cause in the Civil War, then fiercely under way. It was published by the major London print seller Thomas Jenner, based at the south entrance of the Royal Exchange. Jenner was a Puritan and many of his prints were commissioned by those on the Parliamentary side in the conflict.[22] By association, then, it has been assumed that the 1644 map may have been inspired by Jenner's religious and political loyalties. The map's title, however, is more ambiguous as to any political affiliation:

> The Kingdome of England & Principality of Wales, exactly described whith euery Sheere & the small townes in euery one of them, in six mappes, portable for every mans pocket … Vseful for all Comanders for quarteringe of Souldiers, & all sorts of persons, that would be informed, where the Armies be; never so commodiously drawne before this, 1644. Described by one that trauailed throughout the whole Kingdome for its purpose.[23]

Commodious (or convenient) the map may have been; original it was not. The text claims a general utility, especially for military purposes, but indicates no favour for either military side. As the topographic detail is taken from Saxton, we must deduce that it is he who travelled throughout the kingdom, and that his maps were still found useful nearly seven decades later. The map shows no roads and would therefore have had limited value for any army commander. But, as we know, Saxton did not map roads; nor had anyone else in the meantime.

In any case, the map had wider utility. Its maker and seller never called it the 'Quartermaster's Map', and it seems likely that it was essentially a commercial undertaking by Thomas Jenner, who instructed Wenceslaus Hollar, its engraver, to use available materials – that is, Saxton's – as speedily as possible to get a product out.[24] Obviously, no new survey was possible at this time of great danger and dislocation. Whilst the topographic detail is taken from Saxton, in the comfort and safety of a study or engraver's workshop it was possible to repackage the map in a new format; to sell an old cartographic sauce in a new bottle.

SAXTON REPUBLISHED: WILLIAM WEBB

As well as derivatives, there were to be republications of Saxton's maps in the seventeenth century and late into the eighteenth, with varying degrees of revision. The endurance of Saxton's maps demonstrates a continuing high regard for their currency and usefulness, but also reflects inertia created by the enormous

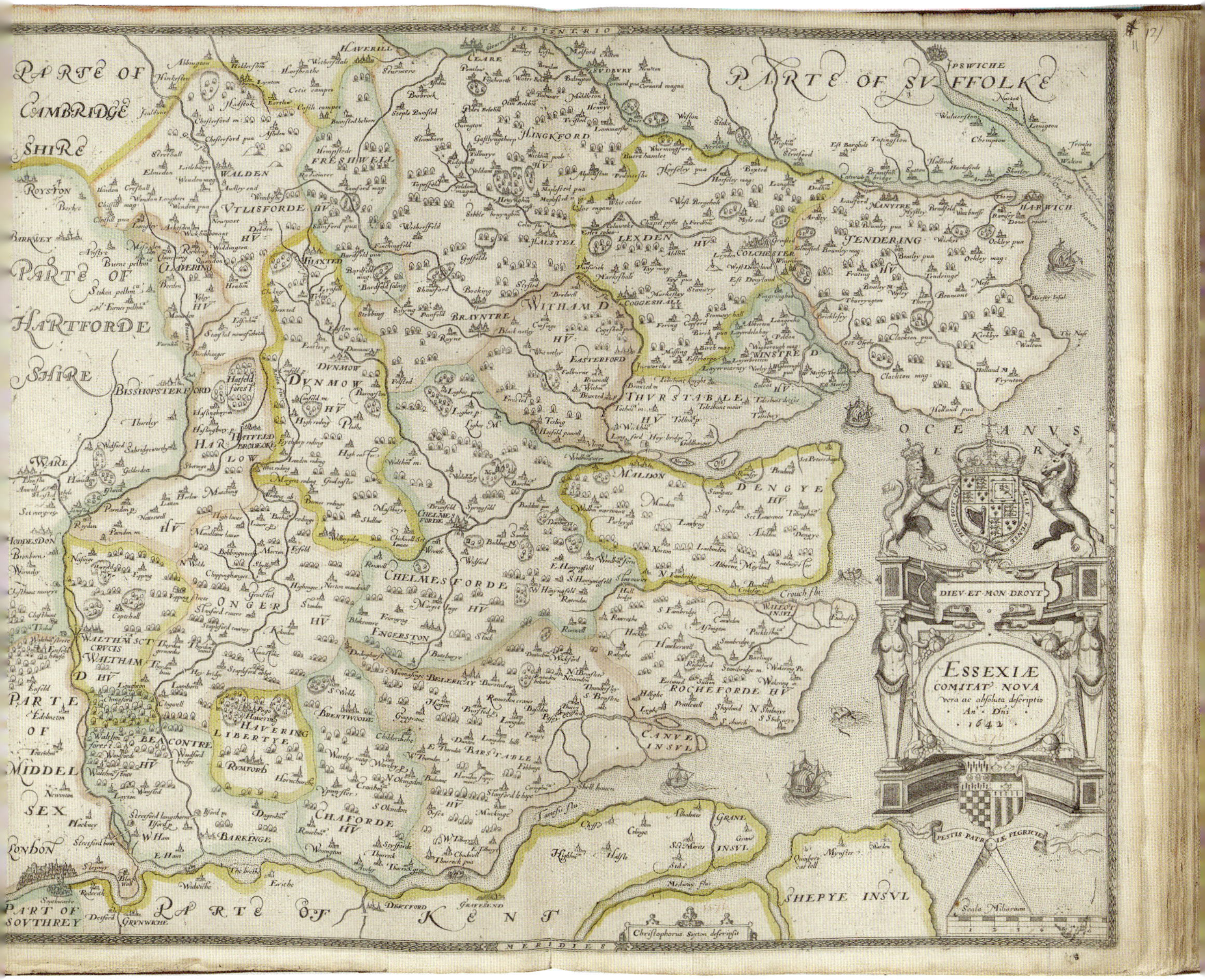

FIG. 87 Map of The county of Essex, 1642, in William Webb's edition of Saxton titled *The Maps of All the Shires in England and Wales*, published in 1645. Webb's maps are virtually facsimiles of Saxton's, with merely superficial modifications to make them appear new.

initial cost of engraving a copperplate. In the sixteenth and seventeenth centuries the owner of a plate was effectively its publisher. Being able to control printing by owning the plate – the physical means of reproduction – probably gave greater protection against copying than registering at it Stationers' Hall. Once a plate was produced, its owner would aim to maximize the number of subsequent restrikes to prolong its commercial life as long as possible. The successive owners of Saxton's *Atlas* plates were to perpetuate and enhance his work for nearly two centuries.

The first to breathe new life into Saxton's *Atlas* was William Webb (or Web) in 1645, who acquired the plates probably in the early 1640s (FIG. 87). Webb was a print seller and publisher who only came to maps later in his career, his main business being in portraits, such as a likeness in 1628 of Henrietta Maria, the consort of Charles I. He was one of many print sellers then operating in the City of London, his address on the 1645 Saxton maps given as 'the Globe in Cornhill'.[25] Webb's map boasted the title 'The maps of all the shires in England and Wales. Exactly taken and truly described by Christopher Saxton. And graven at the Charges of a private Gentleman for the publicke good. Now newly Revised, Amended and Reprinted.'[26] We can assume that Seckford was the private gentleman, even though his armorial bearings have now been removed and, as we have seen, Saxton's name came to greater prominence after his death. Webb's edition of 1645 was the first version of Saxton's

Atlas to carry a title page, and on this the name of Christopher Saxton stands out.

Despite Webb's claims about novelty, his maps are little more than a cosmetic retouching of Saxton's. He includes a few innovations, like a map of Ireland and just two town map insets across the whole volume. The maps are all redated 1642; titles are altered and duly updated, some being changed from Latin to English. The royal arms are now those of Charles I, although in a couple of cases Elizabeth's initials 'E.R.' have carelessly been left. We should remember that Webb's map, like Hollar's of the previous year, came out in the thick of the Civil War when fresh surveys, though in high demand, were all but impossible. Further evidence of this demand is the reissue, a year later, of Speed's atlas by William Humble. The carelessness and inconsistency of Webb's edition may reflect a rush to publish to compete with the 'Quartermaster's Map'.

PHILIP LEA: A NEW EDITION OF SAXTON?

From around 1689 Philip Lea republished editions of Saxton's *Atlas*, bringing together many revisions and new sources (FIG. 88).[27]

FIG. 88 Part of the map of Northamptonshire and neighbouring counties from Philip Lea's *The Shires of England and Wales. Described by Christopher Saxton*, 1689. Lea was a leading figure in the print trade of London in his era and had acquired Saxton's map plates a little earlier.

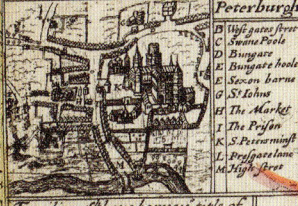

Lea was a globe maker, map seller and mathematical instrument maker, and one of London's leading figures in the print trade in the last quarter of the seventeenth century.[28] His shop sign on Cheapside in London, 'The Atlas and Hercules', nicely symbolized his occupation. He also had a stall selling maps at Westminster Hall, allowing peers and Members of Parliament readily to purchase his wares. For most of his output Lea seems to have been much more of a map specialist than Webb. He was apprenticed to Robert Morden in 1675, an engraver and very successful commercial map-maker, and the two collaborated in making prospects (views) of London. Lea is even reputed to have advised Samuel Pepys on cartographic matters; seemingly he was well-connected. After Lea's death in 1700 his widow Anne retained the stock and carried on the map business; one of the few women involved in the map trade in this era.

It is thought that Philip Lea acquired Saxton's map plates from a now unknown owner at some point between 1665 and 1680 and that this anonymous owner planned a new edition of Saxton, since some changes and this earlier date appear on Saxton's plates by the time Lea acquired them. However, as 1665 was a major plague year, followed the next year by the Great Fire of London, we can easily imagine why such a scheme was abandoned. By the 1680s, quieter times had arrived and the seamless Glorious Revolution of 1688–89 did little to disturb them.

In his first edition of the *Atlas* published circa 1689, just like Webb his predecessor, Lea made few material alterations to the plates. However, just a few years later in around 1693 he published an altogether more earnest revision entitled 'The Shires of England and Wales, Described by Christopher Saxton. Being the Best and Original Mapps…'. Lea's title goes on to state that there are many additions and corrections, and in this case his claims were valid. The great majority of the maps are Saxton's, with a few by other map-makers taken from other plates Lea owned. For instance, the map of Essex is a reissue of the 1678 map by John Ogilby and William Morgan, with Lea's name substituted and the date changed. However, Lea's atlas is a curious mixture; he also includes Saxton's map of Essex, adding his own refinements. So, for this and some other counties, the atlas presents more than one map; showing how ownership of plates influenced publishing content. That the great majority of the maps are still Saxton's shows not only that Lea wanted to get more years out of the plates, but also that he could plausibly publish them alongside more recent surveys.

Lea re-engraved the titles of all the maps, giving the work a uniform appearance, and in-corporated many improvements and additions. Hundred names and boundaries were added to all maps, together with town plans and coats of arms of local nobility and gentry; these appeal-ing to the vanity of potential likely customers. Lea added distinct symbols and a key for features like market towns, parliamentary boroughs and bishoprics. A major advance was his addition of roads, probably taken from John Ogilby's *Britannia* of 1675. Ogilby's maps were 'strip maps' showing only the route of the road and immediate detail along its course, not the landscape beyond. Lea's new edition of Saxton was thus the first comprehensive county road atlas of England and Wales to show roads in their wider geographical context. There was even an edition in French in 1693, suggesting a wider international appeal and respect for the work.

For all that was new in Lea's editions of Saxton's *Atlas*, he was still rather more a reviser than an originator. The geographical content is fundamentally as Saxton left it, and even the marginal detail such as coats of arms and town plans, not present in Saxton's 1579 work, are taken from John Speed, who himself borrowed map information heavily from Saxton. More than a century after Christopher Saxton had completed his surveys, its results were still taken seriously and considered worthy of publication.

SAXTON INTO THE EIGHTEENTH CENTURY: THE LAST EDITIONS

Well into the eighteenth century, various new printings of Lea's Saxton *Atlas* came on the market. By 1720 the print seller George Willdey seems to have acquired the plates, and in 1730 he published an edition in which the only novelty was the substitution of his own imprint for that of Lea.[29] Still called *The Shires of England and Wales…*, the maps are enticing if only for the notice each one bears: 'Sold by Geo. Willdey at the Great Toy, Spectacle, China-ware, and Print Shop the corner of Ludgate Street near St Pauls'.[30] Willdey's edition of Lea's version of Saxton was issued in around 1749 by Thomas Jeffreys, a hundred and seventy years after the Tudor map-maker's original county atlas: the maps really were hand-me-downs now! Jeffreys was geographer to the Prince of Wales, subsequently King George III. For this leading engraver, map-maker and map publisher of the day to link his reputation with these now vintage maps was an important vote of confidence in them, even though he later went bankrupt![31]

The very final run of Saxton's plates seem to be an edition circa 1770 published by Cluer Dicey, the last known owner of the now very worn remaining Saxton plates. He was a printer and publisher of cheap texts and prints, sometimes known as chapbooks, working from the sign of the Maiden-Head in Bow Church Yard in London.[32] The family firm also sold pectoral drops and 'Daffy's Elixir', and his father may have been portrayed among others as an alleged seller of quack medicines in a contemporary satirical print.[33] The republishers of Saxton after Lea made no changes whatsoever to the maps, except to the date and the title to reflect their own imprint. It was rather an unspectacular finale for the maps to end up as cheap prints. This concluded nearly two hundred years of Saxton's as the pre-eminent cartographic image of the country.

THE PASSING OF SAXTON AND A NEW GENERATION OF COUNTY MAPS

We have seen that most seventeenth-century English county maps were reissues of Saxton, Speed and others from the late Tudor and early Stuart era. There are many reasons for this lack of innovation. Royal patronage was never again as generous as that afforded to Saxton. The instabilities of the Civil War put paid to any surveying schemes. The great socio-economic changes to come in the following century were very little in evidence, so landscape changes were not sufficient to make new mapping seem essential. Nevertheless, from Saxton's time, the English map-buying public had gained an appetite for county atlases, sometimes more for ornament than use. Maps did not necessarily have to be completely up to date to serve the requirements and tastes of the map-buying public in this context. Maps were prized as forms of instruction drawing on map-customers' affinity with their home county.[34] Indeed, map sellers often promoted their wares as cheap, instructive and useful ornaments suitable for decorating domestic walls. They were seeking commercial opportunities to publish county atlases, whilst avoiding the great financial risks new surveys brought. Republishing Saxton, while merely updating the map's title, was a safe, if unexciting, option.

The format of the county atlas first inspired by Saxton continued for a while longer. *The Large English Atlas* of 1760 was, as its title

suggests, the largest atlas to date, measuring about 69 × 51 centimetres, compared with Saxton's circa 48 × 43 cm (or 19 × 12 inches, known as folio size). This venture was undertaken by the noted map-maker and engraver Emanuel Bowen and his son-in-law Thomas Kitchin. Bowen made a wide-ranging and significant contribution to British and world cartography in the eighteenth century, and from about 1747 was appointed geographer to King George II.[35] Although *The Large English Atlas* was generally on scales larger than Saxton's, this difference was not great enough to allow much more topographic detail to be shown. The main addition was roads, absent from Saxton's originals, and only some being shown on revisions such as Lea's. Taking the example of the 'Improved Map of the County of Stafford', its title goes on to claim it is 'Collected from the best materials, and Illustrated with various additional Improvements; with Historical Extracts, relating to its Natural Produce, Trade, Manufactures &c.'[36] Most of the 'improvements' are political rather than geographical in character, the map being dedicated to the county Lord Lieutenant, Earl Gower; and the seats of local gentry and nobility being listed. There are descriptions of towns and distinctive areas in the county, like the 'Moorlands'. Symbols are explained in a key for parliamentary towns, ancient forts, abbeys, new charity schools and post stages. These claimed improvements are presumably set against its most important predecessor, Saxton. The 1760 atlas does show items additional to those Saxton represented, but they are political, administrative and commercial rather than new strictly geographical elements.

Only by the mid eighteenth century were appreciably larger-scale, genuinely new, surveys of English and Welsh counties published in significant numbers. Progress was slow; by 1750 only fourteen English and two Welsh counties had been fully remapped as separate sheets at scales rather larger than Saxton's – that is, approaching 1 inch to 1 mile or larger, though the Welsh counties of Denbigh and Flint appeared on one sheet.[37] As the century drew on, it became clear that the 1 inch scale would become a minimum standard for the county map; a scale about four times larger than the median of Saxton's. The Ordnance Survey adopted the 1 inch scale at the turn of the next century and used it until the 1970s. This larger scale did not lend itself to atlas publication as many of the maps would have been enormous, making it impossible for all atlas plates to fit easily in a volume.

The critical break from Saxton was probably ushered in by, and reflected in, a cash inducement from a learned society. From 1759 the Society of Arts offered prizes for good new county maps at the 1 inch scale or larger and using the best modern surveying methods and instruments.[38] The prize reflected a desire among the Society's lobbyists for correct and current maps to a uniform standard and fostered by nationally organized support, in some ways harking back to the Crown's support for Saxton's enterprise a couple of centuries before. At scales around or greater than 1 inch to 1 mile it is obvious that a wider range of topographical information may be shown and in more detail than on Saxton's maps, which were cartographic inventories of places, usually shown by churches with some landscape features shown in between. The 1730–31 map of Huntingdonshire surveyed by William Gordon illustrates the greater detail possible (FIG. 89). At the large scale of 1½ inches to 1 mile it contains splendid kinds and degrees of detail, but takes up six sheets. The title claims it is 'actually survey'd after a new method'; the method not being explained but inspection of the map makes the claim convincing. The layouts of village settlements and isolated houses are shown. Local gentry are named and their coats of arms shown alongside their properties on the map detail itself. Similarly, the 'New map of Surrey' of 1729 is 'laid down from an actual survey by John Senex' and not derived from older sources. It shows a much more detailed network of roads than had been common before; smaller-scale settlements are depicted and even farms are named. Such maps represented a step change from the level of topographic depiction by Saxton and those in his tradition: a firm break from the past.

The Society's specification of the 1 inch scale as a minimum standard meant the final relegation of the smaller scales used by Saxton and his many copiers as the best maps available. Although its exacting standards were not always met, the Society's premium raised the bar of expectation for the scale, quality and technical finesse of county maps from now on. It was a spur to mapping activity, and once and for all made Saxton and his derivatives redundant; or, rather, take on a new roles as antiquarian curiosities.

FIG. 89 Part of *An Accurate Map of the County of Huntingdon* by William Gordon, 1731. In six sheets, this map of this small county at the very large scale of 1:39,000 (over 1½ inches to 1 mile) allowed considerably more detail than Saxton's or any other earlier maps.

Hamerton

Weston

His Grace the
Duke of Mountague

Upton

Hamerton
Grove

Sam. Smith Esqr

Alconbury
Wood

N — S T O N E

Salom
Wood

Anth: Duncombe Esq.

Buckworth

Weston

Leighton
Bromesvold

Alconbury

Barham

Leighton-
Stone

Wooley

Wabrige

Joseph Peacock Gent.

N D R E D

Little   Catworth

Spaldwick

Ellington

ton

Easton

Thorpe

Grafham

John Bigg Esqr

Limage

Brampton Wood

Brampton

Hinchingbro

Earl of Sandwich

St John Bernard
Bart

Perry

OXFORDSHIRE

REFERENCE TO THE HUNDREDS

1. Bampton
2. Banbury
3. Binfield
4. Bloxham
5. Bullington
6. Chadlington
7. Dorchester
8. Ewelme
9. Langtree
10. Lewknor
11. Pirton
12. Ploughley
13. Thame
14. Wootton

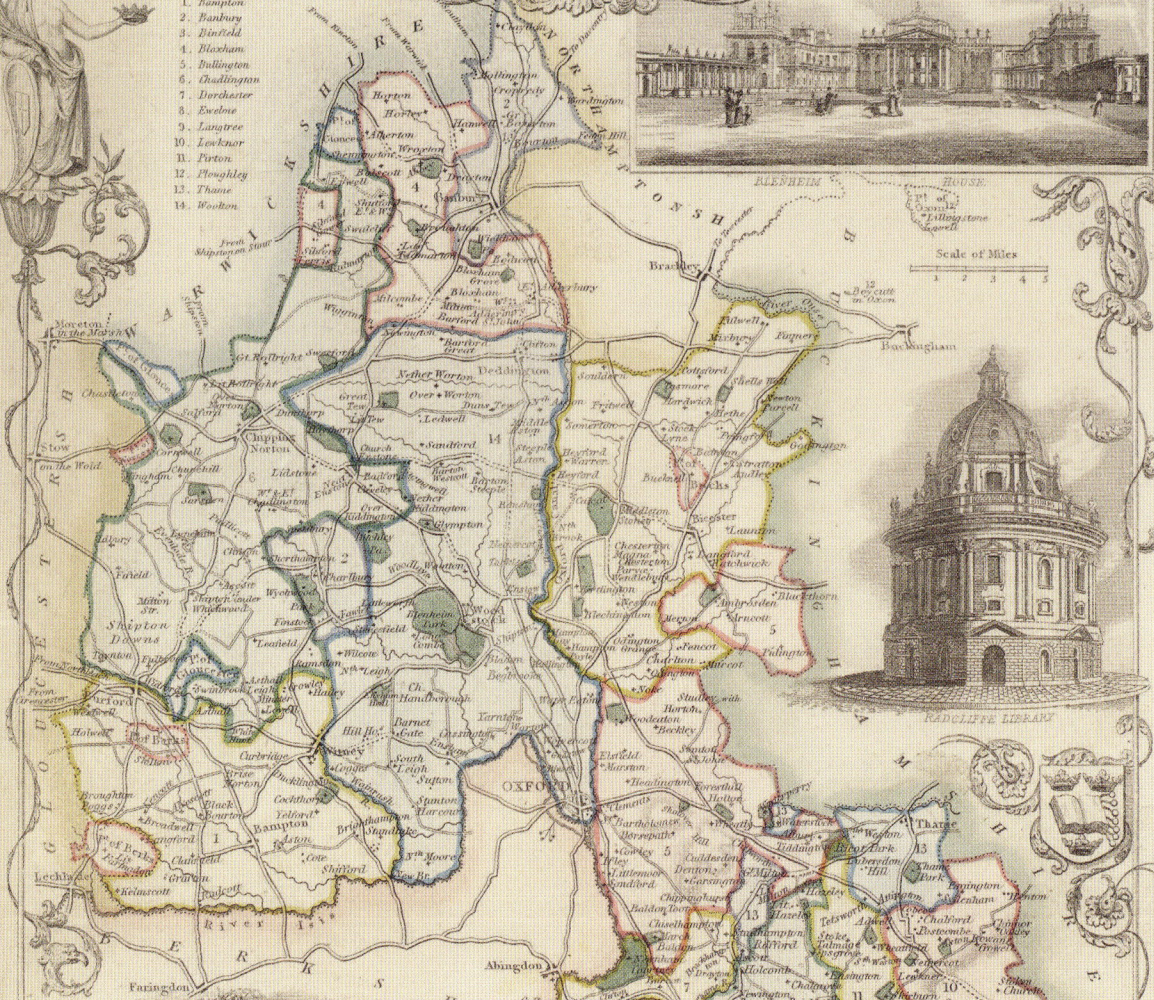

BLENHEIM HOUSE

RADCLIFFE LIBRARY

Scale of Miles
1 2 3 4 5

WARWICKSHIRE

NORTHAMPTONSHIRE

BUCKINGHAMSHIRE

GLOUCESTERSHIRE

BERKSHIRE

OXFORD

River Thames

Reading

Great Marlow

Engraved by JAMES BINGLEY, 37, Charles St., City Road.

London, G. Virtue, 26, Ivy Lane, Aug.t 1, 1830.

SAXTON BECOMES A COLLECTIBLE

H AVING FINALLY OUTLIVED their practical usefulness, Saxton's atlases were to become very desirable collectible items from the end of the eighteenth century and particularly into the present day. A compelling part of their allure is that as highly decorated and ornate objects they appeal to the art collector as well as those interested in historical geography and antique maps. The individual maps make attractive wall displays; and taken together a nicely bound atlas in calf leather with gold-tooled lettering would grace any library shelf. A visit to a long-established aristocratic or gentry library reveals shelves full of local historical and topographic works, including county histories and genealogies.

FIG. 90 The map of Oxfordshire in *The English Counties Delineated*, published by Thomas Moule in 1836. This two-volume set of maps is reminiscent of the county mapping of Saxton's day and can be regarded as its nineteenth-century successor, perhaps drawing on contemporary sentiment for a disappearing landscape.

Atlases feature among these, and a Saxton 'original' has long been highly prized in a 'gentleman's' library. It also appealed to local sentiment, the county, as we have seen, offering a sense of belonging and being the focus of local gentry and aristocratic society, whilst the combination of all the counties in one book crystallized national pride.

Indeed, this sentimental appeal of county mapping was captured by the publication in 1837 of Thomas Moule's atlas, *The English Counties Delineated*, in two volumes (FIG. 90). Moule was an antiquarian and a topographer who sold and published books. His county atlas harked back in many ways to Saxton's and can be seen as its Victorian successor. Moule's maps have elaborate borders, cartouches and sketches of country houses and local landscapes, and are engraved on steel, cutting production costs and making the atlas affordable beyond the gentry and nobility. Their success drew on nostalgia for a disappearing landscape and way of life heralded by industrialization and its spreading infrastructure.

Whilst the burgeoning nineteenth-century middle class could afford Moule's volume, original copies of Saxton's atlas tended to elude them. The provenance of many of the surviving Saxton *Atlases* reveals the social distinction of owning one. New College, Oxford, now has a copy which went through several hands before its donation to the college in 1940. It had originally belonged to Sir John Savile, mentioned earlier, a local dignitary in Saxton's county. Interestingly, a part of the Savile family tree is written on an end leaf, presumably by a family member, suggesting a connection in their mind between such a book of maps and genealogy.[1] As seen earlier, one of the Saxton atlases now in the Library of Congress in Washington DC was once the copy of Elizabeth's spymaster, Sir Francis Walsingham, showing the significance of Saxton's work to a major international map collection, but also originally to the Elizabethan statesman himself, whose coat of arms remains embossed in gold on the front and back of the binding. Not all copies were owned by noblemen, but many previous owners were important establishment figures with the resources or connections to acquire one. A good instance is the earlier provenance of one of the Bodleian Library copies.[2] According to a note on an endpaper, it was given in 1777 by the Reverend John Barnardiston, master of Corpus Christi College, Cambridge, to an antiquarian colleague and vicar, Michael Tyson.

The growing appeal of Saxton's *Atlas* is reflected, in part, in the accelerating market prices of copies, especially late-sixteenth-century originals. An 1839 reference book on printing observes that a Saxton *Atlas* was lately offered for £12 and 12 shillings (£12.60).[3] By 1884 a rare uncoloured copy on vellum was advertised for £80 by the London dealer Bernard Quaritch. Its quality meant that 'so fine and perfect a copy of the great desideratum of Topographical Collectors may never occur for sale again.'[4] By 1958 Quaritch was advertising a Saxton Atlas for £700. The big climb in prices seems to have occurred over the next decades. In 1989 an auction price of £49,500 was realized, and in the first two decades of the twenty-first century auction prices have exceeded £100,000 in some instances.[5] These price rises may reflect the fact that old maps, and in particular celebrated rarities like a Saxton original, are now a cherished and highly valued part of the wider art market. This is a great tribute to Christopher Saxton's achievement in mapping Elizabeth's realm in detail for the first time over four centuries ago.

NOTES

WHO WAS CHRISTOPHER SAXTON?

1. Note: From this point, 'England and Wales' is implied by England unless specifically stated. This was legal fact at the time, since from 1535 Wales was annexed to the Kingdom of England by statute.
2. The main source of biographical and genealogical detail on Christopher Saxton for this chapter is Ifor Evans and Heather Lawrence, *Christopher Saxton, Elizabethan Map Maker*, Wakefield Historical Publications, Wakefield; Holland Press, London, 1979. See also my article: David Fletcher, 'Saxton, Christopher (1542x4–1610/11)', *Oxford Dictionary of National Biography*, Oxford University Press, Oxford, 2004; online edition, current at the time of writing.
3. Evans and Lawrence, *Christopher Saxton*, p. 2.
4. Much useful information has been derived from David I. Bower, 'Further Light on the Lives of Christopher and Robert Saxton', *Imago Mundi*, vol. 67, no. 1, 2015, pp. 81–9.
5. I owe this information to David Bower, personal communication.
6. Extracts from the Lay Subsidies 1547–1621, from Evans and Lawrence, *Christopher Saxton*, Appendix 1.
7. Assessment details from Evans and Lawrence, *Christopher Saxton*.
8. Samuel Lewis (ed.), *A Topographical Dictionary of England*, S. Lewis, London, 1848. Various versions of this tale are told in Norrisson Scatcherd, *The History of Morley, in the West Riding of Yorkshire*, 2nd edn, S. Stead, Morley, 1874, p. 107.
9. Raphael Holinshed, Richard Stanyhurst and William Harrison, *The Firste [laste] Volume of the Chronicles of England, Scotlande, and Irelande: Conteyning the Description and Chronicles of England, from the first inhabiting vnto the conquest*, Imprinted for Iohn Harrison, London, 1577.
10. Evans and Lawrence, *Christopher Saxton*, p. 2.
11. Cited by Bower in 'Further Light on the Lives of Christopher and Robert Saxton', p. 86.
12. J.W. Walker, *Wakefield: Its History and People*, Privately printed, Wakefield, 1939.
13. D. Marcombe, 'Rudd, John (c. 1498–1579)', *Oxford Dictionary of National Biography*.
14. Quoted by David Marcombe, 'Saxton's Apprenticeship: John Rudd, a Yorkshire Cartographer', *Yorkshire Archaeological Journal* 50, 1978, p. 173.
15. Durham Chapter Records (prior's kitchen), register B, fol. 135, quoted by Marcombe, 'Rudd, John'.
16. Durham Chapter Records, Treasurers' Book no. 7 (1569–70), cited in Sarah Tyacke and John Huddy. *Christopher Saxton and Tudor Map-making*, British Library, London, 1980.
17. A vivid picture of late Tudor England is painted by Ian Mortimer, *The Time Traveller's Guide to Elizabethan England*, Vintage, London, 2013.
18. Paul E.J. Hammer, *Elizabeth's Wars: War, Government, and Society in Tudor England, 1544–1604*, Palgrave Macmillan, Basingstoke, 2003. p. 68.

THE ORIGINS OF SAXTON'S MAPPING SCHEME

1. London, British Library, Cotton MS Tiberius B V/1, f. 56v.
2. London, British Library, Additional MS 28681, f. 9.
3. Catherine Delano Smith et al., 'New Light on the Medieval Gough Map of Britain', *Imago Mundi*, vol. 69, no. 1, 2017, pp. 1–36.
4. Alfred Hiatt, 'The Map of Britain in British Library, MS Harley 1808', *Imago Mundi*, vol. 74, no. 2, 2022, pp. 173–88.
5. Rodney Thomson, 'Medieval Maps at Merton College, Oxford', *Imago Mundi*, vol. 61, no. 1, 2009, pp. 84–90.
6. R.A. Skelton and P.D.A. Harvey, *Local Maps and Plans from Medieval England*, Oxford University Press, Oxford, 1986.
7. I am grateful for the suggestions of the anonymous reader on this point.
8. Geoffrey Elton, *The Tudor Revolution In Government: Administrative Changes in the Reign of Henry VIII*, Cambridge University Press, Cambridge, 1962.
9. Peter Barber, *King Henry's Map of the British Isles*, Folio Society, London, 2009.
10. Ibid.
11. C. Delano-Smith and Roger J.P. Kain, *English Maps: A History*, British Library, London, 1999.

12. See Peter Barber 'The British Isles', in *The Mercator Atlas of Europe: Facsimile of the Maps by Gerardus Mercator Contained in the Atlas of Europe, circa 1570–1572*, ed. Marcel Watelet, Walking Tree Press, Tucson AZ, 1998.

13. See Peter Barber, 'Mapmaking in England, ca. 1470–1650', in David Woodward (ed.), *The History of Cartography*, Volume 3: *Cartography in the European Renaissance*, University of Chicago Press, Chicago IL, 2007, ch. 54.

14. 'Remembraunces' of Thomas Cromwell, February 1539, London, British Library, Cotton MS Titus B.i, fols 473–74; cited by Barber, 'Mapmaking in England', p. 1601.

15. Barber, 'Mapmaking in England', p. 1601.

16. *Sanctuaries Act 1540*, 32 Hen. 8. c. 12, 24 July 1540.

17. Peter Barber, 'England I: Pageantry, Defense, and Government: Maps at Court to 1550', in David Buisseret, *Monarchs, Ministers and Maps: The Emergence of Cartography as a Tool of Government in Early Modern Europe*, University of Chicago Press, Chicago IL, 1992.

18. See Peter Barber, 'Was Elizabeth I Interested in Maps – and Did It Matter?' *Transactions of the Royal Historical Society* 14, 2004, pp. 185–98.

19. See Robyn Adams, 'Sixteenth-Century Intelligencers and Their Maps', *Imago Mundi*, vol. 63, no. 2, 2011, pp. 201–21.

20. David Fletcher, *The Emergence of Estate Maps: Christ Church, Oxford 1600–1840*, Clarendon Press, Oxford, 1995.

21. Barber, 'Mapmaking in England'.

22. Ibid., p. 1624.

23. Nicholas Kratzer to Albrecht Dürer, 24 October 1524, in Albrecht Dürer, *Schriften und Briefe*, ed. Ernst Ullmann, 2nd edn, Reclam, Leipzig, 1973, pp. 142–3; cited in Barber, 'Mapmaking in England', p. 1598.

24. Marcus Merriman, 'Elder, John [Jhone Eldar], (fl. 1533–1565)', *Oxford Dictionary of National Biography*.

25. I owe this insight to a comment from the anonymous reader.

26. Retha M. Warnicke, 'Nowell, Laurence, (1530–c. 1570)', *Oxford Dictionary of National Biography*.

27. London, British Library, Additional MS. 62540.

28. R. Julian Roberts, 'Dee, John, (1527–1609)', *Oxford Dictionary of National Biography*.

29. 'Lloyd (Lhuyd), Humphrey', in P.W. Hasler (ed), *The History of Parliament: The House of Commons 1558–1603*, HMSO, London, 1981; online edition; current at the time of writing.

30. Evans and Lawrence, *Christopher Saxton*, p. 6.

MAKING THE COUNTY ATLAS

1. A.L. Rowse, *The Elizabethan Renaissance: The Life of the Society*, Macmillan, London, 1971.

2. Arthur Herbert Dodd, *Life in Elizabethan England*, new edn, John Jones, Ruthin, 1998.

3. Wallace T. MacCaffrey, 'Cecil, William, first Baron Burghley, (1520/21–1598)', *Oxford Dictionary of National Biography*.

4. See Stephen Alford, *Burghley: William Cecil at the Court of Elizabeth I*, Yale University Press, New Haven CT and London, 2008.

5. Janet Dickinson, *William Cecil and the Elizabethan World*, online talk, 2019, https://youtu.be/SeCL_wW7VK8 (accessed 16 March 2022).

6. J.H. Baker, 'Seckford, Thomas (1515/16–1587)', *Oxford Dictionary of National Biography*.

7. *A Cambridge Alumni Database*, entry for Thomas Seckford, https://venn.lib.cam.ac.uk (accessed 27 April 2023).

8. Charles Henry Cooper, *Athenae Cantabrigienses*, University of Cambridge, Cambridge, 1858.

9. Stephen Johnston, 'Mathematical Practitioners and Instruments in Elizabethan England', *Annals of Science*, vol. 48, no. 4, 1981, pp. 319–44.

10. London, British Library, Cotton MS Claudius D. vi, f. 12v.

11. Delano-Smith and Kain, *English Maps*.

12. Uta Lindgren, 'Land Surveys, Instruments, and Practitioners in the Renaissance', in David Woodward (ed.), *The History of Cartography*, Volume 3: *Cartography in the European Renaissance*, University of Chicago Press, Chicago IL, 2007, ch. 19.

13. Colin A. Ronan, 'Leonard and Thomas Digges: Inventors of the Telescope', *Endeavour*, vol. 16, no. 2, 1992, pp. 91–4.

14. Leonard Digges, *A boke named Tectonicon*, Thomas Gemini, London, 1562, Preface, unpaginated.

15. Silke Ackermann, 'Cole, Humfrey, d. 1591', *Oxford Dictionary of National Biography*; Humfrey Cole, British Museum website: www.britishmuseum.org/collection/term/BIOG67462 (accessed 2 May 2023).

16. John Dee, Preface to Euclid, *The Elements of Geometrie…*, trans. Sir Henry Billingsley, John Day, London, 1570.

17. Edward Worsop, *A Discouerie of Sundrie Errours…*, Printed by Henrie Middleton for Gregorie Seton, London, 1582.

18. Cited in Uta Lindgren, 'Land Surveys'.

19. William Ravenhill, 'Christopher Saxton's Surveying: An Enigma', in Sarah Tyacke (ed.), *English Map-making, 1500–1650: Historical Essays*, British Library, London, 1983.

20. I.M. Evans and H. Lawrence, *Christopher Saxton, Elizabethan Map-Maker*, Wakefield Historical Publications, Wakefield, 1979.

21. Lindgren, 'Land Surveys'. Apian's commission was princely, like Saxton's, coming from Albrecht, Duke of Bavaria.

22. Cited in Lindgren, 'Land Surveys'.

23. James P. Carley, 'Leland, John (c. 1503–1552)', *Oxford Dictionary of National Biography*.

24. Edward Lynam, 'English Maps and Map-Makers of the Sixteenth Century', *Geographical Journal*, vol. 116, no. 1/3, 1950, pp. 7–25.

25. See Evans and Lawrence, *Christopher Saxton*.

26. London, The National Archives, PC 2/10, vol. 2: *Privy Council: Register*, Printed in J.R. Dasent (ed.), *Acts of the Privy Council of England*, NS vol. IX, London, 1894. Quotations here are from an 1894 transcript.

27. London, The National Archives, Patent Roll. 16 Elizabeth, pt. 14 [no. 1121], m. 34. Reproduced in H. Fordham, *Christopher Saxton of Dunningley: His Life and Work*, Publications of the Thoresby Society, Leeds, vol. 28, 1928.

28. Original: London, The National Archives, PC 2/10, vol. 2: *Privy Council: Register*, 1575–6, p. 443. Source copied for transcription: *Acts of the Privy Council of England*, Volume 9: *1575–1577*, ed. John Roche Dasent, NS, HMSO, London, 1894, p. 94.

29. London, The National Archives, PC 2/11, vol. 3: *Privy Council: Register*, Printed in Dasent (ed.), *Acts of the Privy Council of England*, NS vol. IX. Quotations here are from an 1894 transcript.

30. Original: London, The National Archives, PC 2/11, vol. 3: *Privy Council: Register*, 1576, pp. 44–5. Source copied for transcription: *Acts of the Privy Council of England*, vol. 9, ed. Dasent, p. 159.

31. London, The National Archives, Patent Roll. 19 Elizabeth, pt. 9. [no. 1159], m. 21. Reproduced in Fordham, *Christopher Saxton of Dunningley*.

32. Bank of England Inflation Calculator, www. bankofengland.co.uk/monetary-policy/inflation/inflation-calculator (accessed 25 April 2024).

33. Arthur M. Hind, *Engraving in England in the Sixteenth & Seventeenth Centuries*, Part 1: *The Tudor Period*, Cambridge University Press, Cambridge, 1952.

34. Remigius Hogenberg, British Museum website: www.britishmuseum.org/collection/term/BIOG31790 (accessed 2 May 2023).

35. Elizabeth Baigent, 'Ryther, Augustine, (d. 1593)', *Oxford Dictionary of National Biography*.

36. Laurence Worms and Ashley Baynton-Williams, *British Map Engravers: A Dictionary of Engravers, Lithographers and Their Principal Employers to 1850*, Rare Book Society, London, 2011.

37. Lynam, 'English Maps and Map-Makers'.

38. This insight was provided by the anonymous reader.

39. See David Woodward (ed.), *Five Centuries of Map Printing*, University of Chicago Press, Chicago IL, 1975.

40. Ibid.

41. London, British Library, Royal MS. 18 D III, *The Burghley Atlas*, 1574–92.

42. William Shannon and Michael Winstanley, 'Lord Burghley's Map of Lancashire Revisited, c. 1576–1590', *Imago Mundi*, vol. 59, no. 1, 2007, pp. 24–42.

43. *The Burghley Atlas*, f. 51r.

44. *The Burghley Atlas*, f. 35r. British Library Catalogue Record.

45. 'Thomas Heneage', in Hasler, *The History of Parliament*.

46. *The Burghley Atlas*, f. 2v.

47. British Library Catalogue, Royal MS. 18 D III.

THE NEW PICTURE OF ENGLAND AND WALES

1. Laurence Worms, 'The London Map Trade to 1640', in David Woodward (ed.), *The History of Cartography*, Volume 3: *Cartography in the European Renaissance*, University of Chicago Press, Chicago IL and London, 2007, ch. 57.

2. R.A. Skelton, *County Atlases of the British Isles 1579–1703*, Carta Press, London, 1970.

3. London, British Library, Harley MS. 288 f. 163v; cited in Barber, 'Mapmaking in England', in Woodward (ed.), *The History of Cartography*, vol. 3: *Cartography in the European Renaissance*, p. 1630.

4. I am grateful to the external reader for this insight.

5. See, for example, Skelton, *County Atlases*. Note the starting date of 1579.

6. Ibid.

7. Bodleian Library, Map Res. 80. Former shelfmark: Fol. BS. 45. Christopher Saxton, *Atlas of the Counties of England and Wales*, [1579].

8. Although they were printed in monochrome, I describe here the colouring added to the majority of the atlases.

9. Scale data from Table 4 in I.M. Evans and H. Lawrence, *Christopher Saxton, Elizabethan Map-Maker*, Wakefield Historical Publications, Wakefield, 1979.

10. Barber, 'Mapmaking in England', p. 1626.

11. *Breed of Horses Act 1535*, 27 Hen. VIII, c. 6, and later legislation.

SAXTON'S CARTOGRAPHIC ACHIEVEMENT

1. See, for instance, Sarah Tyacke and John Huddy. *Christopher Saxton and Tudor Map-making*, British Library, London, 1980.

2. Christopher Saxton, *Christopher Saxton's 16th Century Maps: The Counties of England & Wales*, Introduction by William Ravenhill, Chatsworth Library, Shrewsbury, 1992.

3. https://viaeregiae.org/wiki/Saxton#Draft_Saxton_project_charter (accessed 21 November 2023).

4. London, The National Archives, MPC 1/212. Annotations c. 1608.

5. Cited by Peter Barber in 'England II: Monarchs, Ministers, and Maps, 1550–1625', in David Buisseret (ed.), *Monarchs, Ministers and Maps: The Emergence of Cartography as a Tool of Government in Early Modern Europe*, University of Chicago Press, Chicago IL, 1992.

6. *An Act for the Punishment of Vagabonds, and for Relief of the Poor and Impotent*, 1572, 14 Eliz I., c.5.

7. According to the diary of Frederick Duke of Württemberg, printed in William Brenchley Rye and I. Friedrich, *England as Seen by Foreigners in the Days of Elizabeth & James the First…*, J.R. Smith, London, 1865, p. 45; cited in Peter Barber, 'Mapmaking in England, ca. 1470–1650', in David Woodward (ed.), *The History of Cartography*, Volume 3: *Cartography in the European Renaissance*, University of Chicago Press, Chicago IL, 2007, p. 1607.

8. G. de Boer and A.P. Carr, 'Early Maps as Historical Evidence for Coastal Change', *Geographical Journal*, vol. 135, no. 1, 1969, pp. 17–39.

9. Rye and Friedrich, *England as Seen by Foreigners.*

10. Sheldon, Ralph (*c.*1537–1613), in P.W. Hasler (ed.), *The History of Parliament: The House of Commons 1558–1603*, HMSO, London, 1981.

11. Hilary L. Turner, 'The Sheldon Tapestry Maps: Their Content and Context', *Cartographic Journal*, vol. 40, no. 1, 2003, pp. 39–49.

12. Queen Elizabeth I ('The Ditchley portrait'), by Marcus Gheeraerts the Younger, NPG 2561. From www.npg.org.uk/collections/search/portrait/mw02079/Queen-Elizabeth-I-The-Ditchley-portrait (accessed 12 May 2023).

13. R.A. Skelton, *County Atlases of the British Isles 1579–1703*, Carta Press, London, 1970.

14. British Museum, *A complete pack of fifty-two playing-cards depicting the counties of England and Wales…*, Museum number 1938,0709.57.1–60.

15. See Barber, 'Mapmaking in England'.

16. The preceding quotations in this paragraph are all from Raphael Holinshed, *The Firste Volume of the Chronicles of England, Scotlande, and Irelande*, Imprinted by Henry Bynneman for Iohn Harrison, London, 1577, preface (Epistle Dedicatorie to Lord Burghley), unpaginated.

17. Raphael Holinshed, *The First and Second Volumes of Chronicles…*, Printed by Henry Denham, London, 1587, p. 51. The words 'chart', 'card' and 'plat' are among the many synonyms for 'map', past and present.

18. Holinshed, *The First and Second Volumes of Chronicles…*, p. 51.

19. Cited in Stephen Bowd, 'John Dee and Christopher Saxton's Survey of Manchester (1596)', *Northern History*, vol. 42, no. 2, 2005, pp. 275–92. I am grateful for Professor Stephen Bowd's information on this point; personal communication.

20. John Norden, *Nordens Preparatiue to His Speculum Britanniae*, Printed by John Windet, London, 1596.

21. *A History of Pembrokeshire,* from a manuscript of George Owen [with later additions and observations], *The Cambrian Register*, vol. 2, 1796, p. 55.

22. London, British Library, Harley MS. 288 f. 163v; cited in Barber, 'Mapmaking in England', p. 1630.

23. See Richard Helgerson, *Forms of Nationhood: Elizabethan Writing of England,* University of Chicago Press, Chicago IL, 1994.

24. I am grateful to Janet Phillips, my editor, for this insight. She further notes that Milford Haven is a location in Shakespeare's play *Cymbeline, c.*1610.

25. *A History of Pembrokeshire*, p. 55.

26. Ifor Evans and Heather Lawrence, *Christopher Saxton, Elizabethan Map Maker*, Wakefield Historical Publications, Wakefield; Holland Press, London, 1979, Appendix 10.

27. Skelton, *County Atlases*.

28. I am grateful to the staff of these repositories for helpfully supplying provenance details, and to the anonymous reader for extra information.

29. The Licence of 20 July 1577 appears as a transcript at Appendix 9 in Evans and Lawrence, *Christopher Saxton*.

30. Evans and Lawrence, *Christopher Saxton*, ch. 6.

31. London, London Archives, COL/CA/01/01/021/476/b, 23 July 21 Eliz. (1579).

32. See Oxford, Bodleian Library, MS. Ashmole 834 f.22v.

33. See Skelton and Harvey, *Local Maps and Plans*.

34. H. Fordham, *Christopher Saxton of Dunningley: His Life and Work*, Publications of the Thoresby Society, Leeds, vol. 28, 1928. For an up-to-date list of known Saxton local maps, see David I. Bower, 'Saxton Manuscript Maps and Surveys Not Described by Evans and Lawrence', *Imago Mundi*, vol. 62, no. 2, 2010, pp. 191–204.

35. For an interesting use of this map as a historical geographical case study, see M.W. Beresford, *History on the Ground: Six Studies in Maps and Landscapes.* Alan Sutton, Gloucester, 1984 (1957).

SAXTON'S LEGACY

1. Invaluable biographical and genealogical information on Christopher Saxton and his family is found in H. Fordham, *Christopher Saxton of Dunningley: His Life and Work*, Publications of the Thoresby Society, Leeds, vol. 28, 1928.

2. Oxford, Bodleian Library, MS. Wood D 13, p. 202. Extract of text transcription from Ifor Evans and Heather Lawrence, *Christopher Saxton, Elizabethan Map Maker*, Wakefield Historical Publications, Wakefield; Holland Press, London, 1979, pp. 6–7.

3. Readers wanting to follow the complex detail of

the many editions and derivatives of Saxton's maps should see Skelton, *County Atlases*.

4. Wyman H. Herendeen, 'Camden, William, (1551–1623)', *Oxford Dictionary of National Biography*.

5. William Camden, *Britain: or, A chorographicall description of the most flourishing Kingdomes, England, Scotland, and Ireland... Translated newly into English by Philémon Holland Doctour in Physick; finally, revised, amended, and enlarged with sundry additions by the said author,* George Bishop and John Norton, London, 1610, p. 324.

6. Ibid.

7. Frank Kitchen, 'Norden, John (*c.* 1547–1625)', *Oxford Dictionary of National Biography*.

8. John Norden, *Nordens Preparatiue to His Speculum Britanniæ*, Printed by John Windet, London, 1596.

9. Cited in Heather Lawrence, 'Permission to Survey', *The Map Collector* 19, 1982, pp. 16–20, which gives a very useful account of Norden's struggle to gain a pass.

10. For more on Norden's struggle for support, see R.A. Skelton and John Summerson, *A Description of Maps and Architectural Drawings: In the Collection Made by William Cecil, First Baron Burghley, Now at Hatfield House*, Printed for Presentation to the Members of the Roxburghe Club, Oxford, 1971.

11. Norden, *Nordens Preparatiue to His Speculum Britanniæ*, p. 31.

12. Skelton and Summerson, *A Description of Maps*.

13. Ian James Saunders, 'The Mapping of Lancashire by William Smith', *Imago Mundi*, vol. 67, no. 2, 2015, pp. 200–214.

14. David Kathman, 'Smith, William (*c.* 1550–1618)', *Oxford Dictionary of National Biography*.

15. Peter Barber, 'Mapmaking in England, ca. 1470–1650', in David Woodward (ed.), *The History of Cartography,* Volume 3: *Cartography in the European Renaissance,* University of Chicago Press, Chicago IL, 2007, ch. 54.

16. Sarah Bendall, 'Speed, John (1551/2–1629)', *Oxford Dictionary of National Biography*.

17. Ibid.

18. British Library Catalogue Maps C.7.c.5.

19. 'John Speed', British Museum website, www.britishmuseum.org/collection/term/BIOG141491 (accessed 19 May 2023).

20. See Lawrence, 'Permission to Survey', for the text of the pass.

21. John Speed, *The Theatre of the Empire of Great Britaine...*, solde by I. Sudbury and G. Humble, London, 1611, section headed 'To the well-affected and favovrable reader', page unnumbered.

22. John Horden, 'Jenner, Thomas (d. 1673)', *Oxford Dictionary of National Biography*.

23. British Library Catalogue record for Maps C.7.b.13.

24. George Fordham, 'A Note on the "Quartermaster's Map," 1644', *The Geographical Journal*, vol. 70, no. 1, 1927, pp. 50–52.

25. 'William Webb', British Museum website, www.britishmuseum.org/collection/term/BIOG151631 (accessed 19 May 2023).

26. Title taken from R.A. Skelton, *County Atlases of the British Isles 1579–1703*, Carta Press, London, 1970.

27. Harold Whitaker, 'The Later Editions of Saxton's County Maps', *Imago Mundi*, vol. 3, no. 1, 1939, pp. 72–86.

28. 'Philip Lea', British Museum website, www.britishmuseum.org/collection/term/BIOG156088 (accessed 23 May 2023); Skelton, *County Atlases*.

29. Skelton, *County Atlases*.

30. Catalogue record for 'The shires of England and Wales...', Bodleian Library, Map Res. 75.

31. J.B. Harley, 'The Bankruptcy of Thomas Jefferys: An Episode in the Economic History of Eighteenth Century Map-Making', *Imago Mundi*, vol. 20, no. 1, 1966, pp. 27–48.

32. 'Cluer Dicey', British Museum website, www.britishmuseum.org/collection/term/BIOG61419 (accessed 23 May 2023).

33. See British Museum, *Quackery Unmask'd, or, Empiricism display'd*. Museum number: 1849,1003.34.

34. An interesting study is Phillip Koyoumjian, 'Ownership and Use of Maps in England, 1660–1760', *Imago Mundi*, vol. 73, no. 1, 2021, pp. 32–45.

35. Iolo Roberts and Menai Roberts, 'Bowen, Emanuel (1693/4–1767)', *Oxford Dictionary of National Biography*.

36. Title from copy in the Bodleian Library, Allen 31. Map dated 1764.

37. David Smith, *Maps and Plans for the Local Historian and Collector*, Batsford, London, 1988.

38. J.B. Harley, 'The Society of Arts and the Survey of English Counties', *Journal of the Royal Society of Arts* 112, 1963–64.

SAXTON BECOMES A COLLECTIBLE

1. New College, Oxford, Library BT1.47.9. Copy-specific notes. I am also indebted to Alexandra Plane for valuable information on this copy.

2. Bodleian Library Map Res. 79, formerly Douce Prints b.27.

3. Charles Henry Timperley, *A Dictionary of Printers and Printing*, H. Johnson, London, 1839.

4. *Catalogue of English literature, poetic, dramatic, historic, miscellaneous; with works on the topographical and genealogical history of Great Britain and Ireland; ...,* Bernard Quaritch, London, 1884, unpaginated.

5. Gleaned from a variety of auction and media websites.

FURTHER READING

CHRISTOPHER SAXTON

Evans, I.M., and H. Lawrence, *Christopher Saxton, Elizabethan Map-Maker*, Wakefield Historical Publications, Wakefield, 1979.

Fordham, H., *Christopher Saxton of Dunningley: His Life and Work*, Publications of the Thoresby Society, vol. 28, Leeds, 1928.

Saxton, C., *An Atlas of England and Wales: The Maps of Christopher Saxton, Engraved 1574–1579*, Introduction by E. Lynam, British Museum, London, 1936.

Saxton, C., *Christopher Saxton's 16th Century Maps: The Counties of England and Wales*, Introduction by William Ravenhill, Chatsworth Library, Shrewsbury, 1992.

Tyacke, S., and J. Huddy, *Christopher Saxton and Tudor Map-making*, British Library, London, 1980.

WIDER CONTEXT

Buisseret, D., *Monarchs, Ministers and Maps: The Emergence of Cartography as a Tool of Government in Early Modern Europe*, University of Chicago Press, Chicago IL, 1992.

Cantor, L.M.,*The Changing English Countryside, 1400–1700*, Routledge, London, 2017.

Castor, H., *Elizabeth I: A Study in Insecurity*, Penguin Books, London, 2019.

Delano-Smith, C., and R.J.P. Kain, *English Maps: A History*, British Library, London, 1999.

Fletcher, D.H., *The Emergence of Estate Maps: Christ Church, Oxford, 1600 to 1840*, Clarendon Press, Oxford, 1995.

Harvey, P.D.A., *The History of Topographical Maps: Symbols, Pictures and Surveys*, Thames & Hudson, London, 1980.

Harvey, P.D.A., *Maps in Tudor England*, Public Record Office and British Library, London, 1993.

Helgerson, R., *The Land Speaks: Cartography, Chorography and Subversion in Renaissance England*, University of California, Berkeley CA, 1986.

Hind, A.M., M. Corbett and M.C. Norton, *Engraving in England in the Sixteenth & Seventeenth Centuries: A Descriptive Catalogue with Introductions*, Cambridge University Press, Cambridge, 1952; especially Part 1.

Hodgkiss, A.G., *Discovering Antique Maps*, Shire, Princes Risborough, 1996.

Mortimer, I., *The Time Traveller's Guide to Elizabethan England*, Vintage, London, 2013.

Pedley, M.S., *The Commerce of Cartography: Making and Marketing Maps in Eighteenth-century France and England*, University of Chicago Press, Chicago IL and London, 2005.

Skelton, R.A., *County Atlases of the British Isles 1579–1703*, Carta Press, London, 1970.

Skelton, R.A., and P.D.A. Harvey (eds), *Local Maps and Plans from Medieval England*, Clarendon Press, Oxford, 1986.

Smith, D., *Maps and Plans for the Local Historian and Collector*, Batsford, London, 1988.

Turner, G.L'E., *Elizabethan Instrument Makers: The Origins of the London Trade in Precision Instrument Making*, Oxford University Press, Oxford, 2000.

Tyacke, S., (ed.), *English Map Making 1500–1650: Historical Essays*, British Library, London, 1983.

Woodward, D., *Five Centuries of Map Printing*, University of Chicago Press, Chicago IL, 1975.

THE HISTORY OF CARTOGRAPHY

Woodward, D. (ed.), *The History of Cartography*, Volume 3: *Cartography in the European Renaissance*, University of Chicago Press, Chicago IL and London, 2007. (Available free online: https://press.uchicago.edu/books/HOC/index.html.

   The whole volume is of interest but especially ch. 19, Uta Lindgren, 'Land Surveys, Instruments, and Practitioners in the Renaissance'; ch. 21, Catherine Delano-Smith, 'Signs on Printed Topographical Maps, ca. 1470–ca. 1640'; ch. 22, David Woodward, 'Techniques of Map Engraving, Printing, and Coloring in the European Renaissance'; ch. 28, Roger J.P. Kain, 'Maps and Rural Land Management in Early Modern Europe'; ch. 54, Peter Barber, 'Mapmaking in England, ca. 1470–1650'; and ch. 57, Laurence Worms, 'The London Map Trade to 1640'.

PICTURE CREDITS

INDEX